Java
Algorithms

Scott Robert Ladd

McGraw-Hill

New York   San Francisco   Washington, D.C
Auckland   Bogotá   Caracas   Lisbon   London
Madrid   Mexico City   Milan   Montreal   New Delhi
San Juan   Singapore   Sydney   Tokyo   Toronto

Library of Congress Cataloging-in-Publication Data

Ladd, Scott Robert.
    Java algorithms : Scott Robert Ladd.
        p.   cm.
    Includes index.
    ISBN 0-07-913696-6
    1. Java (Computer program language) 2. Computer algorithms.
  I. Title.
  QA76.73.J38L33 1997
  005.13'3—dc21   97-46544
                                        CIP

McGraw-Hill

A Division of The McGraw·Hill Companies

1 2 3 4 5 6 7 8 9 0 DOC/DOC 9 0 2 1 0 9 8 7

P/N 047122-3
PART OF
ISBN 0-07-913696-6

The sponsoring editor for this book was Judy Brief. It was set in New Century Schoolbook by E. D. Euans, freelance designer for McGraw-Hill's Professional Book Group composition unit. The chapter opener art and icons were created by David Evans, freelance illustrator for McGraw-Hill's Professional Book Group composition unit.

Printed and bound by R. R. Donnelley & Sons Company.

McGraw-Hill books are available at special quantity discounts to use as premiums and sales promotions, or for use in corporate training programs. For more information, please write to the Director of Special Sales, McGraw-Hill, 11 West 19th Street, New York, NY 10011. Or contact your local bookstore.

This book is printed on recycled, acid-free paper containing a minimum of 50% recycled de-inked fiber.

To my lovely and talented daughters,
Elora, Rebecca, and Tessa.

I can never truly say "thank you" enough
for the all the "kid treasures" you've lavished on me —
the bird's nests and clay sculptures and crayon drawings
that show up on my desk, every day.

Keep 'em coming, kids.

TABLE OF CONTENTS

Introduction

Purpose and Objective

Java began as a tool for creating web-based applets. Some of us, though, saw a potential for greater things in Java; today, it is providing a powerful platform for mainstream applications. Here is a programming language with built-in support for networking, interprocess communications, and portable graphic interfaces. From the corporate Intranet to the desktop PC, Java is evolving into a power tool for 21st-Century software development.

Too many people still perceive of Java as nothing more than a toy for creating cute web applets. Certainly Java is well-suited to creating animated displays or fancy input forms, but to see that as the extent of Java's usefulness is a mistake. In writing this book, I wanted to dispel some of these limiting notions associated with Java. To that end, I've developed packages of interfaces and classes to implement some industrial strength algorithms. My goal was to show how Java works when applied to tough problems and complex concepts; in the end, Java has proven itself equal to the task.

Java does have one problem in its current state: it is an *interpreted* language, with a virtual machine turning compiled bytecodes into processor instructions. Applet performance can vary dramatically from platform to platform, and in no case is Java as fast as compiled C or C++. Of course, if you pay attention to Java evangelists, they'll tell you that performance isn't *really* all that important. And they're wrong. A slow program is a useless program; when people come to your web site, they will quickly follow a hyperlink elsewhere if they encounter a pokey applet. A beautiful user interface is useless if the underlying code is slow and clunky. The advent of native-code Java compilers will ease this concern somewhat, but even the best compiler can't make up for a poor program design.

I've written several books about algorithm implementation, and this book brings you my experience in the form of several Java packages. These classes are not simple ports of my older C++ libraries, Java is not C++, and I've developed the code herein accordingly. You *can* get good performance from Java; a well-written Java application will outperform the poorly-designed C++ equivalent.

One word of caution: Java is a young and dynamic (some would say chaotic) language. For the purposes of this book, I'm using the Java 1.1 language and class packages, as defined by Sun Microsystems in their JDK 1.1.3 release in July 1997. All of my code was developed using Sun's JDK and Microsoft's Visual J++; I've used Sun's *Java-PureCheck* application to verify that my classes are "100% Pure Java." All applets were tested with Netscape Navigator 3.01, Sun's HotJava, and Microsoft's Internet Explorer 3.01.

All that aside, variances in virtual machines can defeat the portability of even the most carefully crafted Java application. At the time of this writing, few virtual machines support the Java 1.1 standard — and a Java 1.2 standard is due to be delivered by Sun contemporaneously with the publication of this book. So keep in mind that Java is an immature technology, driven not by the needs of developers but by market forces and press releases.

As always, I wish you good fortune in your endeavors. Now let's begin by looking at polymorphism and sorting in Java.

Scott Robert Ladd
Silverton, Colorado
August, 1997

1

Sorting Things Out

Computer science seems to have a fascination with sorting algorithms — and for good reason, since almost any significant program needs to organize data. When dealing with a few items, sorting is a trivial task. But with more than a couple of items, sorting is no longer trivial. Algorithms abound for efficiently ordering data; the simplest techniques, Insertion and Selection Sort, can be implemented in a dozen lines of Java code. We'll also be looking at the two best techniques: *Shell Sort* and *QuickSort*. In the case of all four algorithms, We'll be developing code for sorting arrays of `Objects`.

A Framework for Sorting

To build generic tools in Java, we need to consider how the language treats objects. Where C++ uses templates and other mechanisms to implement a common object framework, Java adheres to a Smalltalk-like model where every class implicitly descends from `Object`. The `Object` class is abstract, meaning that all Java classes can be treated polymorphically within the context of `Object`.

In the case of my sorting tools, I determined that every algorithm needed to compare the values of two array elements. Such comparisons, however, are very type-specific, and to act upon generic data in a polymorphic fashion, I defined a superinterface named `SortTool`:

```
public interface SortTool
{
  // comparison values
  public final static int COMP_LESS  = -1;
  public final static int COMP_EQUAL =  0;
  public final static int COMP_GRTR  =  1;

  IllegalArgumentException err1 =
    new IllegalArgumentException("incompatible objects
        in sort");

  // compare two values
  int compare
    (
    Object x1,
    Object x2
    );
}
```

The `compare` method returns one of three integer values based on the relationship of object `x1` to `x2`. For example, if `x1` is less than `x2`, compare should return `COMP_LESS`. A type specific implementation of compare would throw an `err1` exception if the either of the parameters is not of the expected type. You can see how this works in the following class, where I've implemented `SortTool` to handle the comparison of `Integer` values:

```
public class IntegerSortTool
   implements SortTool
{
  // compare two values
  public int compare
    (
    Object x1,
    Object x2
    )
```

```
  {
    if ((x1 instanceof Integer)
    && (x2 instanceof Integer))
    {
      int n1 = ((Integer)x1).intValue();
      int n2 = ((Integer)x2).intValue();

      if (n1 < n2)
        return COMP_LESS;
      else
        if (n1 > n2)
          return COMP_GRTR;
        else
          return COMP_EQUAL;
    }
    else
      throw SortTool.err1;
  }


}
```

The following code snippet shows how an `IntegerSortTool` could be used in comparing a pair of `Integer` values:

```
// create a pair of integers
Integer i1 = new Integer(1701);
Integer i2 = new Integer(463);

// create an object for comparing Integers
IntegerSortTool ist = new IntegerSortTool();

// now compare the two Integers
int result = ist.compare(i1,i2);
```

Why don't I sort "real" `int`s instead of `Integer`s, using standard numeric comparison operators like < and ==? In the real world, programs rarely sort arrays of simple types; in most cases, applications must sort arrays of reference objects, where the standard operators don't apply. And our purpose is to develop *generic* tools applicable to a variety of types; if I were to define a sorting routine in terms of `int`, I'd be forced to duplicate my algorithm code with minor changes

for `floats`, `Strings`, and other object types. But the *algorithm* isn't
type dependent — what is unique about a type is how its objects
compare to each other. Each type to be sorted will have unique comparison requirements, which can be quickly implemented via a subclass of `SortTool`. For example, to define a `SortTool` for `String`
objects, I created the following class:

```
public class StringSortTool
  implements SortTool
{

  // compare two values
  public int compare
    (
    Object x1,
    Object x2
    )
  {
    if ((x1 instanceof String)
    &&  (x2 instanceof String))
    {
      int c = ((String)x1).compareTo((String)x2);

      if (c < 0)
        return COMP_LESS;
      else
        if (c > 0)
          return COMP_GRTR;
        else
          return COMP_EQUAL;
    }
    else
      throw SortTool.err1;
  }

}
```

Another advantage to my design is that sorting can be added to
any class without having to change or subclass it. Many object-oriented libraries define a `Sortable` interface to be implemented by
any class that will be sorted. To sort arrays of `Integers`, we would

need to derive a new class that implements `Sortable` — but Java defines `Integer` (and other numeric classes) as `final`, preventing them from being subclassed. In my experience, it seems best to make sorting something that is *applied* to an array of objects, rather than a characteristic of the objects themselves.

On the enclosed CD-ROM, I've included `SortTool` subclasses for the following basic types: `Short`, `Integer`, `Long`, `Float`, `Double`, and `String`.

To see how `SortTool` operates, review my `Sorter` class, which defines the polymorphic interface for all sorting algorithms:

```
public abstract class Sorter
{
  public void Sort
    (
    Object [] list,
    SortTool tool
    )
  {
    Sort(list,tool,false);
  }

  public abstract void Sort
    (
    Object [] list,
    SortTool tool,
    boolean descending
    );
}
```

The first version of the `Sort` method is defined in terms of the second; in both cases, the calling code passes an array of `Objects` and a `SortTool` that compares the elements of that array. Assuming that the `SortTool` is correctly implemented, a given implementation of `Sort` can operate on the `Objects` without knowing anything about their actual type. This design accomplishes one of the primary goals of object-oriented programming: the creation of a single algorithm that acts on polymorphic data.

Elementary Sorts

Almost every basic course in programming will do students a great
disservice by teaching them the infamous *Bubble Sort*. Essentially,
the Bubble Sort algorithm makes several passes through an array,
exchanging adjacent items as necessary; the sorting process is complete when no exchanges occur during a pass. Essentially, items
"slide" through the array, one element per pass, until they reach
their appropriate location. While Bubble Sort *does* work, other algorithms are faster and simpler. I won't be implementing Bubble Sort
here, since better tools are available.

Notes

For the sake of discussion, I'll be talking about an ascending
*sort, where the smallest item comes first and the largest item
last. A* descending *sort, of course, rearranges the elements in
the opposite order from an ascending sort. These algorithms
work the same way for both ordering directions; just substitute
"larger" for "small" and vice versa when thinking of a descending sort.*

Selection Sort

The Selection Sort is uncomplicated: find the smallest element in the
array and exchange it with the first element; then find the second-
smallest element and exchange it with the second element, and so
on. Continuing this process will produce a sorted file, by selecting
the items that will be exchanged into their proper location. Defining
a `Sorter` class for Selection Sort is rather easy:

```
public class SelectionSorter
  extends Sorter
{

  public void Sort
    (
    Object [] list,
    SortTool tool,
    boolean descending
```

```
    )
  {
    int comp;

    if (descending)
      comp = SortTool.COMP_GRTR;
    else
      comp = SortTool.COMP_LESS;

    for (int i = 0; i < list.length - 1; ++i)
    {
      int min = i;

      for (int j = i + 1; j < list.length; ++j)
      {
        if (tool.compare(list[j],list[min]) == comp)
          min = j;
      }

      Object t   = list[min];
      list[min] = list[i];
      list[i]   = t;
    }
  }
}
```

As you can see, `SelectionSorter` is both small and simple, using a pair of nested loops to find and exchange elements. One feature applies to other subclasses of `Sorter`: the local variable `comp` is set to control the direction of the sort, based on the value of the descending parameter. In the case of `SelectionSorter`, `comp` is set to `COMP_GRTR` for a descending sort, and to `COMP_LESS` for ascending order. In an ascending sort, `SelectionSorter.Sort` exchanges the element `list[i]` with the smallest element in the range `list[i]`…`list[list.length - 1]`.

Let's see how these pieces, based on `SortTool` and `Sorter`, fit together in an application. The following piece of code creates a 100-element array of `Integer` objects, and sorts it with a `SelectionSorter`:

```
Random randGen = new Random();

int i;

Integer [] iArray = new Integer [100];

for (i = 0; i < 100; ++i)
  iArray[i] = new Integer(randGen.nextInt());

IntegerSortTool ist = new IntegerSortTool();
Sorter sort = new SelectionSorter();

sort.Sort(iArray,ist);
```

If I were to change the last line of code to `sort.Sort(iArray,ist, true)`, the algorithm would apply a descending order to the elements.

Insertion Sort

Selection Sort works, but it isn't the most efficient algorithm of its type by far. Another algorithm is one that you've probably used without even realizing it. When most people play a card game, they reorder their hand by looking at each card in turn, pulling it out and reinserting it at the proper location relative to the values of other cards. We can implement this *Insertion Sort* in Java by examining each element in sequence moving larger elements to make room. My `InsertionSorter` class looks like this:

```
public class InsertionSorter
  extends Sorter
{

  public void Sort
    (
    Object [] list,
    SortTool tool,
    boolean descending
    )
  {
    int comp;
```

```
      if (descending)
        comp = SortTool.COMP_LESS;
      else
        comp = SortTool.COMP_GRTR;

      for (int i = 1; i < list.length; ++i)
      {
        Object t = list[i];

        int j = i;

        while ((j > 0) && (tool.compare(list[j-1],t) ==
            comp))
        {
          list[j] = list[j-1];
          --j;
        }

        list[j] = t;
      }
    }
  }
```

The Insertion Sort algorithm scans the array from its second element through the last, moving the element i to its proper position in the sorted segment list[0]…list[i-1]. Essentially, the process shifts sorted elements larger than list[i] one position "up" in the array, making room to insert list[i].

In the example of using SelectionSorter, you can select algorithms by changing the type of allocated Sorter objects. To use the InsertionSorter, replace the line:

```
Sorter sort = new SelectionSorter();
```

with:

```
Sorter sort = new InsertionSorter();
```

See how polymorphism allows us to treat processes in a generic fashion? Abstraction isn't just for data types.

Insertion Sort is usually a bit faster than Selection Sort, and it's nearly as small. Computer science tells us that the average invocation of Selection Sort performs `list.length`$^{2/2}$ comparisons and `list.length` exchanges, while the Insertion Sort requires only `list.length`$^{2/4}$ comparisons and `list.length`$^{2/8}$ exchanges on average. Even so, Insertion Sort suffers when the target array is "almost" sorted, since it then performs many unnecessary shifts and exchanges. This is the central inefficiency of Insertion Sort, where it shifts an element into a nearly-sorted group, forcing the algorithm to shift the item back again.

Shell Sort

A still better sorting algorithm is the Shell Sort. Here we have our introduction to the divide and-conquer tactic that produces so many efficient algorithms. Where Insertion Sort treats an array as one piece, Shell Sort divides the data into segments, sorting each by insertion and then making a final pass to move objects into their proper places. The subsidiary sorts arrange elements quickly within a limited range.

Let's say that we're sorting 8 numbers with Shell Sort. First, we sort the subranges (0..1), (2..3), (4..5) and (6..7). Once that pass is complete, we sort two groups of four: (0..3) and (4..7). Finally, we make a pass through the entire list. What Shell Sort has done is to presort sections of the array, moving elements closer to their final destination and eliminating needless shifting.

No one has determined the optimal segment sizes, which are usually called *increments*. Powers of two, as used in my example above, have actually proven to be poor choices. For practical purposes, increment sizes of 1, 4, 13, 40, etc. — calculated as $(3^k - 1)/2$ — work well. Even for the worst possible ordering of data, that sequence of increments will require no more than `list.length`$^{3/2}$ comparisons, which is a considerable improvement on the Insertion Sort's worst-case performance of `list.length`^{2} comparisons.

```java
public class ShellSorter
  extends Sorter
{
  public void Sort
    (
    Object [] list,
    SortTool tool,
    boolean descending
    )
  {
  int inc, comp;

  if (descending)
    comp = SortTool.COMP_LESS;
  else
    comp = SortTool.COMP_GRTR;

  for (inc = 1; inc <= list.length / 9; inc = 3 *
      inc + 1) ;

  for ( ; inc > 0; inc /= 3)
    {
    for (int i = inc + 1; i <= list.length; i += inc)
      {
      Object t = list[i - 1];

      int j = i;

      while ((j > inc)
        && (tool.compare(list[j - inc - 1],t) == comp))
        {
        list[j - 1] = list[j - inc - 1];
        j -= inc;
        }

      list[j - 1] = t;
      }
    }
  }
}
```

As you can see, `ShellSorter` is more complex than either `Selec-tionSorter` or `InsertionSorter`, although it is by no means incomprehensible. The `Sort` method begins by calculating the largest increment in the sequence $(3^k - 1) / 2$ that is less than `list.length`. Each pass through the array sorts `inc`-sized segments, decreasing the size of the increment until it equals 1 for the final pass.

QuickSort

Where Shell Sort is small and generally efficacious on small data sets, QuickSort is more complicated and faster for larger tasks. Sorting involves two actions: comparing values and exchanging values; an efficient sorting routine will minimize the number of comparisons and exchanges. QuickSort is just such an algorithm, invented by C. A. R. Hoare in 1960. While several minor improvements have been made to QuickSort since then, no one has developed a sorting algorithm that is faster or more elegant.

The Basic Algorithm

The QuickSort algorithm can be stated simply, even if its implementation is complex when compared to earlier algorithms. The process begins by selecting an array element as the *pivot* value. All elements less than the pivot value are moved to its left; all of the elements that come after the pivot value are placed on the right. Then the elements to the left of the pivot are processed using the same technique, as are the elements to the right of the pivot. This goes on, with smaller and smaller sections being processed, until the entire array is sorted.

Let's see how this works, using a simple 11-element array of characters.

index:	0	1	2	3	4	5	6	7	8	9	10
value:	S	T	A	N	J	F	U	B	X	R	G

Any element can be chosen for the pivot value; in this case, I'll use the right-most element in the array, or G. Two indices will scan the array; one begins with the leftmost element, and the other starts with the element just to the left of the pivot value. So, the left index begins at 0 and the right index begins at 9.

index:	0	1	2	3	4	5	6	7	8	9	10
value:	S	T	A	N	J	F	U	B	X	R	G

⇧ left   ⇧ right   ⇧ pivot

The left index is incremented while the element it references is less than the pivot value. In other words, all the elements that are already less than the pivot value are ignored; what we're looking for is an element that is out of place by virtue of being greater than the pivot value G. In the example above, the very first element is S, so the left index simply stays at 0. The right index is decremented until it references an element that is less that the pivot value; in this case, it stops on B with a value of 7.

index:	0	1	2	3	4	5	6	7	8	9	10
value:	S	T	A	N	J	F	U	B	X	R	G

⇧ left   ⇧ right   ⇧ pivot

B and S are out of order; therefore, they need to be swapped. Then, the left and right indices must be moved to start scanning anew. Now the array and its indices look like this:

index:	0	1	2	3	4	5	6	7	8	9	10
value:	B	T	A	N	J	F	U	S	X	R	G

⇧ left   ⇧ right   ⇧ pivot

The left and right indices begin scanning again from their new positions. The left index stays on element 1 (*T*) and the right index moves to element 5 (*F*).

index:	0	1	2	3	4	5	6	7	8	9	10
value:	B	T	A	N	J	F	U	S	X	R	G
		⇧				⇧					⇧
		left				right					pivot

Again, the elements are swapped, and the indices are moved to continue the scanning.

index:	0	1	2	3	4	5	6	7	8	9	10
value:	B	F	A	N	J	T	U	S	X	R	G
			⇧		⇧						⇧
			left		right						pivot

The scan continues. The left index will stop at element 3 (*N*) and the right index will stop at 2 (*A*).

index:	0	1	2	3	4	5	6	7	8	9	10
value:	B	F	A	N	J	T	U	S	X	R	G
			⇧	⇧							⇧
			right	left							pivot

At this point, the indices have passed each other, and the scanning is complete. All that remains is to swap the pivot element with the element in the position where the left index stopped.

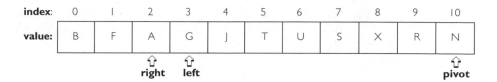

All of the elements to the left of *G* are smaller than it; all of the elements larger than *G* are now on its right. The partially sorted array can now be viewed as two pieces that need to be sorted further by partitioning: the elements to the right of *G*, and the elements to its left. It doesn't matter which section is partitioned first; for example's sake, I'll use the right partition. When partitioning begins, the section looks like this:

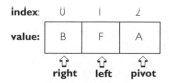

This section doesn't take much time to partition! The right index stays just where it is, pointing to *B* (which is larger than the pivot value, *A*). The left index moves to point to *B* also, ending the partitioning process. *A* is then swapped with *B* as the final act of the partitioning process.

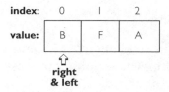

This leaves two sections: *A* by itself, and *B* with *F*. A single-element section can be ignored, since it can't be sorted. So, the two-element section needs to be partitioned, beginning with these indices:

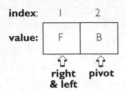

The right and left indices have nowhere to go; all that needs to be done is to swap the pivot value, *B*, with the value pointed to by the left index, *F*. This ends the processing of everything to the left of *G*, and the array now contains the following:

index:	0	1	2	3	4	5	6	7	8	9	10
value:	A	B	F	G	J	T	U	S	X	R	N

Now, the elements to the left of *G* need to be processed by the partitioning routine. Here's how the pivot and indices start out:

index:	4	5	6	7	8	9	10
value:	J	T	U	S	X	R	N

The left index will scan to element 5, *T*, and the right index will scan to element 4, *J*, ending the scanning process. The pivot element *N* is exchanged with *T*.

index:	4	5	6	7	8	9	10
value:	J	N	U	S	X	R	T

⇧ right ⇧ left

Since *J* is in a section by itself, it doesn't need further processing. The algorithm now proceeds to partitioning the section containing elements 6 through 10:

index:	6	7	8	9	10
value:	U	S	X	R	T

⇧ left ⇧ right ⇧ pivot

The indices start out referencing elements that need to be exchanged. After the exchange, the next scan begins:

index:	6	7	8	9	10
value:	R	S	X	U	T

⇧ left ⇧ right ⇧ pivot

After scanning, the indices will be positioned:

index:	6	7	8	9	10
value:	R	S	X	U	T

⇧ right ⇧ left ⇧ pivot

The left and right indices have crossed, and the scanning ends. To complete the partitioning, element 8, *X*, will be exchanged with the pivot value *T*.

index:	6	7	8	9	10
value:	R	S	T	U	X

           ⇧ ⇧   ⇧
     right left   pivot

While the entire array is sorted, the two-element sections will still be partitioned since the programs doesn't know that they are already in order. The end result is that the array now looks like this:

index:	0	1	2	3	4	5	6	7	8	9	10
value:	A	B	F	G	J	N	R	S	T	U	X

It may not be obvious that QuickSort is efficient. Sections that are already sorted are sometimes partitioned, which is useless. Indices scan back and forth through the data, often scanning over the same item several times. But QuickSort is fast because it performs very few comparisons and exchanges. Incrementing and decrementing indices does not use significant CPU time; comparing values and moving data, however, are time-consuming operations. In the example, only seven swaps were required to sort eleven elements. Overall, empirical testing has shown that QuickSort is by far the fastest sorting routine so far invented — unless the wrong circumstances get it into trouble.

Avoiding SlowSort

QuickSort has an Achilles heel that turns it into SlowSort: sorted arrays and QuickSort do not get along. For example, let's say that we tried to QuickSort this array:

index:	0	1	2	3	4	5	6	7	8	9	10
value:	A	B	C	D	E	F	G	H	I	J	K

While it may seem silly to sort sorted data, it often happens that incoming data is either sorted or nearly-sorted. QuickSort will begin as it did before, by picking a pivot value and the starting points for right- and left-scanning indices.

index:	0	1	2	3	4	5	6	7	8	9	10
value:	A	B	C	D	E	F	G	H	I	J	K

⇑
left
                                                                ⇑   ⇑
                                                              right   pivot

The left index will scan forward until it reaches the first element greater than or equal to the pivot element; the right index will stay right where it is, since J is less than K.

index:	0	1	2	3	4	5	6	7	8	9	10
value:	A	B	C	D	E	F	G	H	I	J	K

                                                                ⇑   ⇑
                                                              right   pivot
                                                                      & left

The left and right indices have passed each other, ending the partitioning process. Since the left index now points to the pivot element, no exchanges took place. Since there are no elements to the right of the pivot element, QuickSort will proceed to partition the elements on the left (0 through 9).

index:	0	1	2	3	4	5	6	7	8	9
value:	A	B	C	D	E	F	G	H	I	J

⇧ left   ⇧ right   ⇧ pivot

Again, the left index will slide all the way over to the left, and the right index will remain stationary. No exchanges take place.

index:	0	1	2	3	4	5	6	7	8	9
value:	A	B	C	D	E	F	G	H	I	J

⇧ right   ⇧ pivot & left

If you see a pattern developing, you're right! QuickSort continues to partition sections of the array that are one element smaller than the last section. *Lots* of comparisons will be performed, but no exchanges will take place. The end result? QuickSort takes a very long time to sort sorted information. It doesn't matter which element is selected as the pivot value; changing the pivot selection changes the order of partitioning, but it doesn't reduce the amount of work that is done.

All is not lost, however. A simple improvement to QuickSort can make it perform very quickly on sorted arrays. The solution involves finding a better way of selecting the pivot element. Two techniques have been presented in various texts:

- Use a random number generator to pick an element for the pivot value. Picking a random element avoids the possibility that a consistent selection (e.g. always using the right-most element in a section) will generate lots of partitions.

- Pick three elements, sort them, and pick the middle-most element for the pivot value. This is known as *median-of-three partitioning*.

I don't select the pivot randomly for several reasons. To begin with, random number functions use multiplication or division to generate values; those are generally the slowest mathematical operators on any processor. Also, I don't like hit or-miss techniques for solving problems.

I prefer to use an empirical method that leaves as little as possible to chance. So I implement median-of-three partitioning. In the following example, let L represent the index of the left-most argument, R the index of the right-most argument, and M the index of the middle element.

index:	0	1	2	3	4	5	6	7	8	9	10
value:	S	T	A	N	J	F	U	B	X	R	G
	⇧L					⇧M					⇧R

I begin by sorting L, M, and R into order relative to each other.

index:	0	1	2	3	4	5	6	7	8	9	10
value:	F	T	A	N	J	G	U	B	X	R	S
	⇧L					⇧M					⇧R

Then, the middle-most element is exchanged with the element just to the left of the right-most element.

index:	0	1	2	3	4	5	6	7	8	9	10
value:	F	T	A	N	J	R	U	B	X	G	S
	⇧L					⇧M					⇧R

Partitioning now proceeds, with the left scan starting at $L + 1$ and the right scan at $R - 2$.

index:	0	1	2	3	4	5	6	7	8	9	10
value:	F	T	A	N	J	R	U	B	X	G	S

⇧ left (at index 1) ⇧ right (at index 8) ⇧ pivot (at index 9)

It may not seem obvious that median-of-three partitioning could improve QuickSort's performance. Why does shuffling a few elements make the algorithm run faster? QuickSort performs best when the pivot value is the median of the values in a section. The original algorithm always picked the right-most element in a section as the pivot element. For an unordered section, any element has an equal chance of being close to the median value; thus, always picking the right-most element (or any other element, for that matter) works well. When a section is sorted or almost sorted, the right-most element will be the largest value, causing a SlowSort to occur.

Median-of-three selects the median of three values in a section, increasing the chance of picking a good pivot value. It's easier to see how this helps when we look at how median-of-three partitioning affects a sorted array like this one:

index:	0	1	2	3	4	5	6	7	8	9	10
value:	A	B	C	D	E	F	G	H	I	J	K

After performing the median-of-three operation, the array and its scanning indices look like this before partitioning begins:

index:	0	1	2	3	4	5	6	7	8	9	10
value:	A	B	C	D	E	K	G	H	I	F	K

⇧ left (at index 1) ⇧ right (at index 8) ⇧ pivot (at index 9)

Without a median-of-three set-up, partitioning would begin like this:

index:	0	1	2	3	4	5	6	7	8	9	10
value:	A	B	C	D	E	F	G	H	I	J	K

⇧ left   ⇧ right   ⇧ pivot

Median-of-three selects a pivot value of *F*, which is closer to being a median value than is the element *K* selected without median-of-three. Strange as it may seem, median-of-three partitioning improves sorting performance by "unsorting" sorted data! Of course, for small sections, the added overhead for median-of-three partitioning overshadows the benefits. In testing, I found that I saw the best performance when I used median-of-three partitioning for sections with 8 or more elements. I defined a variable named `Threshold`, which defines the size of the largest section that will not be partitioned with median-of-three. `Threshold` should not be set to a value less than 3, because you need at least three elements (right, left, and middle) for median-of-three partitioning.

Removing Recursion

QuickSort is easiest to implement when you use recursion, having the algorithm call itself for successively-smaller partitions. But recursion is expensive, requiring arguments to be pushed onto the stack before each function call is executed. When each invocation of QuickSort ends, those arguments must be removed from the stack. Pushing, calling, popping, and returning all take time; in any environment, this is expensive in terms of processor power and resources. While this may not be a concern for some applications, Java requires programmers to consider every efficiency when writing their programs.

Removing recursion isn't difficult. Analysis by computer scientists has shown that any algorithm that can be expressed recursively can be also be expressed iteratively. So, we need to replace recursion with a loop that tracks the sizes of partitions. Let's look at a simple example before removing recursion from QuickSort.

A *factorial* is the value obtained when multiplying a whole number by all of the whole numbers that proceed it in sequence. For example, the factorial of 4 (4! in mathematical notation) is 4 x 3 x 2 x 1, or 24. And, 5! is $5 \times 4 \times 3 \times 2 \times 1$, or 120. An observant person will notice a pattern:

$$\text{for } x > 1, x! = x \text{ x } (x - 1)!$$
$$\text{for } x = 1, x! = 1;$$

In other words, the factorial of 1 is defined explicitly as 1; all other factorials can be defined in terms of other factorials, leading to this recursive implementation of a factorial function:

```
int factorial(int n)
{
  if (n == 1)
    return 1;
  else
    return n * factorial(n - 1);
}
```

The function calls itself with successively smaller values of n, until n equals 1. When n equals 1, the recursion "unfolds," providing the correct answer.

While the recursive implementation is very simple, it isn't fast. Assuming a large range for an `int`, it's possible that the factorial of a very large number could cause a stack overflow. And, as I mentioned before, function calls are not generally efficient. A solution is to remove the recursion by implementing `factorial` as an iterative function:

```
int factorial(int n)
{
  int result = 1;

  while (n > 1)
  {
```

```
        result *= n;
        --n;
    }

    return result;
}
```

The iterative version of `factorial` is longer, and it looks more complex than does its recursive cousin. But by removing the need for function calls and stack overhead, the iterative `factorial` runs much faster than does the recursive method.

Notes

The factorial *function could be implemented as a table look-up, removing the need for repeated multiplications at the expense of allocating static memory for the table.*

The same principles can be applied in creating an iterative version of QuickSort; what we need is a mechanism that will allow us to store information on sections that have not yet been partitioned. Information on one section can be imparted through loop variables, while the bounds of the other section will need to be stored for later processing. To save partition information, I use a simple internal stack, using an array of objects defined by the inner class `StackItem`. Each `StackItem` objects contains the left and right bounds of sections that need to be partitioned. The index `stackPtr` points to the top of the stack, indicating the number of sections stored in the array. Once partitioning is complete, the bounds of one partition are stored in the internal stack; I replace the recursive calls with a loop, and use the other bounding indices to reset the parameters for each iteration.

The Code

My `QuickSorter` class implements all of the ideas above, providing a powerful, if somewhat complicated, generic sorting tool.

```
public class QuickSorter
  extends Sorter
{
  private IllegalArgumentException err1 =
    new IllegalArgumentException("stack overflow in
        QuickSort");

  private class StackItem
  {
    public int left;
    public int right;
  }

  public void Sort
    (
    Object [] list,
    SortTool tool,
    boolean descending
    )
  {
    // create stack
    final int stackSize = 32;
    StackItem [] stack = new StackItem [stackSize];

    for (int n = 0; n < 32; ++n)
      stack[n] = new StackItem();

    int stackPtr = 0;

    // determine direction of sort
    int comp;

    if (descending)
      comp = SortTool.COMP_GRTR;
    else
      comp = SortTool.COMP_LESS;

    // size of minimum partition to median-of-three
    final int Threshold = 7;
```

```
                    // sizes of left and right partitions
                    int lsize, rsize;

                    // create working indices
                    int l, r, mid, scanl, scanr, pivot;

                    // set initial values
                    l = 0;
                    r = list.length - 1;

                    Object temp;

                    // main loop
                    while (true)
                    {
                      while (r > l)
                      {
                        if ((r - l) > Threshold)
                        {
                          // "median-of-three" partitioning
                          mid = (l + r) / 2;

                          // three-sort left, middle, and right elements
                          if (tool.compare(list[mid],list[l]) == comp)
                          {
                            temp  = list[mid];
                            list[mid] = list[l];
                            list[l]   = temp;
                          }

                          if (tool.compare(list[r],list[l]) == comp)
                          {
                            temp= list[r];
                            list[r] = list[l];
                            list[l] = temp;
                          }

                          // three-sort left, middle, and right elements
                          if (tool.compare(list[r],list[mid]) == comp)
                          {
```

```
         temp      = list[mid];
         list[mid] = list[r];
         list[r]   = temp;
      }

   // set-up for partitioning
   pivot = r - 1;

   temp  = list[mid];
   list[mid]   = list[pivot];
   list[pivot] = temp;

   scanl = l + 1;
   scanr = r - 2;
}
else
{
   // set-up for partitioning
   pivot = r;
   scanl = l;
   scanr = r - 1;
}

for (;;)
{
   // scan from left for element >= to pivot
   while ((tool.compare(list[scanl],list[pivot])
      == comp)
      && (scanl < r))
      ++scanl;

   // scan from right for element <= to pivot
   while ((tool.compare(list[pivot],list[scanr])
       == comp)
      && (scanr > l))
      --scanr;

   // if scans have met, exit inner loop
   if (scanl >= scanr)
      break;
```

```
                 // exchange elements
         temp  = list[scanl];
         list[scanl] = list[scanr];
         list[scanr] = temp;

         if (scanl < r)
           ++scanl;

         if (scanr > l)
           --scanr;
      }

      // exchange final element
      temp  = list[scanl];
      list[scanl] = list[pivot];
      list[pivot] = temp;

      // place largest partition on stack
      lsize = scanl - l;
      rsize = r - scanl;

      if (lsize > rsize)
      {
        if (lsize != 1)
        {
          ++stackPtr;

          if (stackPtr == stackSize)
            throw err1;

          stack[stackPtr].left  = l;
          stack[stackPtr].right = scanl - 1;
        }

        if (rsize != 0)
          l = scanl + 1;
        else
          break;
      }
      else
      {
```

```
            if (rsize != 1)
            {
              ++stackPtr;

              if (stackPtr == stackSize)
                throw err1;

              stack[stackPtr].left  = scanl + 1;
              stack[stackPtr].right = r;
            }


            if (lsize != 0)
              r = scanl - 1;
            else
              break;
          }
        }


        // iterate with values from stack
        if (stackPtr != 0)
        {
          l = stack[stackPtr].left;
          r = stack[stackPtr].right;

          --stackPtr;
        }
        else
          break;
      }
    }
  }
```

Unlike the other sorting algorithms, `QuickSorter` can throw an
exception. Since QuickSort is a binary algorithm, a stack containing
32 elements should be sufficient for sorting any array with up to 2^{32}
elements. It will be some years, I suspect, before we're asking our
algorithms to work with arrays of more than 4 billion elements.

Other Considerations

Some texts talk about using alternate sorting routines for small partitions, essentially implementing other sorts within QuickSort. It makes logical sense to handle small sections using simpler sorts; for example, a two-element section can be sorted with a simple `if` statement; three-element partitions can be sorted used the three-sort method I showed at the beginning of the chapter. Some texts suggest that for partitions of less than 20 elements, a simple insertion or selection sort will be faster than the partitioning process.

I wrote versions of QuickSort that used alternate sorts for array elements ranging in size from 2 to 10 elements. In every case, the internal sorts contributed to a slower QuickSort. Profiling the results, I found that the overhead of additional conditional statements was sufficient to cancel the advantage of having little sorts for small sections.

Array Conversions

Let's go back to a problem mentioned at the beginning of the chapter. In sorting arrays of `Objects`, we render the `Sorter` classes incapable of sorting an array of a simple type, such as `long` or `float`. I've encountered this problem before with polymorphic tools, since the simple types do not derive from Object, and thus do not exist in Java's hierarchy of classes. To solve this problem, I created a set of static methods, inside the `Translator` class, to convert between arrays of simple types and arrays of wrapper classes.

```java
public class Translator
{

  public static Short [] toShort(short [] a)
  {
    Short [] result = new Short [a.length];

    for (int n = 0; n < a.length; ++n)
      result[n] = new Short(a[n]);
```

```java
    return result;
}

public static short [] fromShort(Short [] a)
{
  short [] result = new short [a.length];

  for (int n = 0; n < a.length; ++n)
    result[n] = a[n].shortValue();

  return result;
}

public static Integer [] toInteger(int [] a)
{
  Integer [] result = new Integer [a.length];

  for (int n = 0; n < a.length; ++n)
    result[n] = new Integer(a[n]);

  return result;
}

public static int [] fromInteger(Integer [] a)
{
  int [] result = new int [a.length];

  for (int n = 0; n < a.length; ++n)
    result[n] = a[n].intValue();

  return result;
}

public static Long [] toLong(long [] a)
{
  Long [] result = new Long [a.length];

  for (int n = 0; n < a.length; ++n)
    result[n] = new Long(a[n]);

  return result;
}
```

```java
public static long [] fromLong(Long [] a)
{
  long [] result = new long [a.length];

  for (int n = 0; n < a.length; ++n)
    result[n] = a[n].longValue();

  return result;
}

public static Float [] toFloat(float [] a)
{
  Float [] result = new Float [a.length];

  for (int n = 0; n < a.length; ++n)
    result[n] = new Float(a[n]);

  return result;
}

public static float [] fromFloat(Float [] a)
{
  float [] result = new float [a.length];

  for (int n = 0; n < a.length; ++n)
    result[n] = a[n].floatValue();

  return result;
}

public static Double [] toDouble(double [] a)
{
  Double [] result = new Double [a.length];

  for (int n = 0; n < a.length; ++n)
    result[n] = new Double(a[n]);

  return result;
}

public static double [] fromDouble(Double [] a)
```

```
    {
      double [] result = new double [a.length];

      for (int n = 0; n < a.length; ++n)
        result[n] = a[n].doubleValue();

      return result;
    }
}
```

Onward

These sorting tools should provide you with a choice between speed and simplicity. Generally, I choose Shell Sort for any array with fewer than fifty elements, and let QuickSort handling larger arrays. Being polymorphic, I can pick and choose algorithms with little effort, selecting the best tool for a given task.

In the next chapter, we'll examine tools for advanced numeric work, including classes to implement polynomials and complex numbers.

Chapter 2

Mathematical Components

I programmed my first numerical applications in FORTRAN, on a DEC PDP-8 back in the late 1970s. For many years, FORTRAN was the only practical tool for developing high-end mathematical software; Pascal, BASIC, and C/C++ just didn't measure up to FORTRAN's built in library of tools and intrinsic support for complex numbers. So where does Java stand as a mathematical tool? Let's take a look.

Java Does Math

In terms of numeric data types, Java is unlike C++ in many ways. Here's a quick list of the differences:

- Java does not support `unsigned` types.

- There is no `long double` type in Java.

- A char in Java is an unsigned 16-bit value, because Java implicitly uses the 16-bit Unicode character set.

- Java includes support for 64-bit signed integers (type `long`).

- Java type sizes (the number of bits in a value) are constant across all platforms. Table 2.1 shows the different types and their ranges.

- The Virtual Machine throws an `ArithmeticException` for integer division by zero — but for floating point number, Java produces an infinity result (see the section below on "Special Values").

- Java introduces a new operator, `>>>`, that performs an unsigned right shift. The `>>` operator performs a signed right shift.

Table 2.1
Numeric Data Types in Java

Type	Bits	Minimum Value	Maximum Value
byte	8	-128	127
short	16	-32,768	32,767
int	32	-2,147,483,648	2,147,483,647
long	64	-9,223,372,036,854,775,808	9,223,372,036,854,775,807
char	16	'\u0000'	'\uffff'
float	32	$\pm1.40130\times10^{-45}$	$\pm3.40282\times10^{38}$
double	64	$\pm4.94066\times10^{-324}$	$\pm1.79769\times10^{308}$

Conversions

Automatic conversions in Java work much as they do in C/C++; an expression has the type of its "largest" value, with "smaller" values converted to the larger type. In other words, if an expression involves a `short`, an `int`, and a `float`, the result will be a `float`, with the `short` and the `int` promoted to `float` during calculation. Java does not support the function style casting used in C++; the following statement from a C++ program:

```
float f = 1.0f;
int n = int(f);
```

would need to be written in Java using the older C-style syntax:

```
int n = (int)f;
```

Java doesn't support conversion between integral and `boolean` types. In other words, Java rejects any attempt at using an integer value in a logical statement. In C++, this code fragment uses a common coding convention to continue execution of a loop while an integer value is not zero:

```
int flag = 1;

while (flag)
{
    // do something
}
```

In Java, you would need to change the code to explicitly compare the value of flag to zero:

```
while (flag != 0)
```

Or, better yet, change flag's type from `int` to `boolean`. (Also note that a boolean value cannot be converted to an integer).

Floating Point Bestiary

Java conforms to an IEEE standard for numeric data types. The float type corresponds to an IEEE 754 single-precision value, and the double implements the IEEE 754 double-precision type. This isn't so much different from C/C++, which also implement the IEEE floating-point types. Where the difference lies is in the subtleties, and in special values. For example, execute the following line of code in C/C++:

```
double f = 1.0/0.0;
```

The result of the above will vary substantially between platforms; on a PC, floating-point division by zero generates a hardware exception in the numeric coprocessor. Java, however, understands the concept of *infinity*, which is the result of dividing a finite value by zero. The standard classes `java.lang.Double` and `java.lang.Float` define the public constants `POSITIVE_INFINITY` and `NEGATIVE_INFINITY` for their respective primitive types.

This also brings up the concept of *signed zeros*. In Java, zero may be positive or negative. These two values are equal in terms of comparison operators; +0.0 is not greater than -0.0. Some operations can distinguish between positive and negative zeros, however; for example, `1.0/0.0` equals positive infinity, while `1.0/-0.0` equals negative infinity. Furthermore, the two variants of zero are treated differently by the `min` and `max` methods in the `java.lang.Math` class.

If you divide zero by zero, the result is a value known as *Not-a-Number* (or *NaN* for short). Any numerical operation involving a NaN results in a NaN; this is known as the propagation of NaNs. I've found NaNs to be incredibly useful; for example, I may initialize a table with NaNs to catch any unfilled elements. Initializing the table with zeros is often problematic, since zero may be a valid value. By using NaNs, I know which elements have been assigned and which haven't. Several of the trigonometric and logarithmic methods in `java.lang.Math` will return NaN results when given invalid parameters. The standard classes `java.lang.Double` and `java.lang.Float` define the public constant `NaN` for their respective primitive types.

The Math Class

In C/C++, floating-point mathematical functions — `sin`, `atan`, and `log`, for example — are standalone functions defined in the standard library. Java requires all methods to be defined within a class; this, the trigonometric, logarithmic, and transcendental methods are all defined in the `java.lang.Math` class. Where in C++ you would say:

```
double d = atan(1.2345);
```

Java requires that you specify a class identifier:

```
double d = Math.atan(1.2345);
```

In math, Java declares methods for both `float` and `double` types; unlike C, which treated `float` as a second-class type, Java provides full support for both single- and double-precision operations.

Now it's time for a practical example of how numerical work can be accomplished in Java. The remainder of this chapter focuses on implementing a basic system for manipulating polynomials, and includes an introduction to complex numbers and the Fast Fourier Transform (FFT).

Polynomials

A *polynomial* is a formula that sums the products of corresponding coefficients and powers of a variable, as in:

$$7x^5 - 2x^4 + x^2 + 3x - 9 = y$$

Essentially, a polynomial defines a complex curve on a two-dimensional x-y coordinate grid. You probably graphed some polynomials when you were in high school; they're often used in engineering applications. Since **x** is a constant factor, a polynomial class need only maintain a list of a polynomial's coefficients. For example, the polynomial above could be (and is in my implementation) stored as the following array:

```
{-9, 3, 1, 0, -2, 7}
```

Notice that the order of the coefficients is "backwards." This is because the zero element of an array is the leftmost element, and I store coefficients so that their index corresponds to the power of **x**. Thus, -2 is placed at index location 4 in the coefficient array.

Adding two polynomials is easy; simply add their corresponding coefficients. For example, adding the following two polynomials

$$f(x) = -3x^3 + x^2 - 6$$
$$g(x) = 5x^3 + x + 1;$$

results in the new polynomial:

$$g(x) + f(x) = 2x^3 + x^2 + x - 5$$

We use the same algorithm when subtracting polynomials, where corresponding coefficients are subtracted. For example:

$$f(x) - g(x) = -8x^3 + x^2 - x - 7$$

As you might expect, multiplying two polynomials is a bit more complicated. In algebraic terms, every coefficient in $f(x)$ is multiplied by every coefficient in $g(x)$, producing a new polynomial that potentially has twice as many coefficients as the largest of its multiplicands. In the case of $f(x)$ and $g(x)$:

$$h(x) = f(x) \bullet g(x) = -15x^6 + 5x^5 - 3x^4 - 32x^3 + x^2 - 6x - 6$$

Any polynomial class will need to allow the function to be evaluated for a given value of x. The fastest way to evaluate a polynomial involves a looping technique known as *Horner's rule*, which alternates addition and multiplication. For example, to evaluate $h(x)$ using Horner's rule, I would implement this formula:

$$f(x) = (x(x(x(x(x(x(-15) + 5) - 3) - 32) + 1) - 6) - 6)$$

A Java Implementation

I began by considering how I had used polynomials in various applications. My first insight was that I had never used any other type of `Polynomial` except that based on `double` or `complex double`, so that immediately simplified the design of my Java class. For now, I'll talk about my `Polynomial` class for `double`, saving the `Complex-Polynomial` class for the next section.

Notes

While many Java texts will tell you to use generic objects to replace templates, it doesn't always work that way in practice. The Number *class, for example, allows you to treat any number as a class object—say, handling* ints *through* Integer *and doubles through* Double, *both of those class wrappers being derived from* Number. *Also, I find working with* Number *cumbersome; it seems more suited as an abstraction of a number and less as a computational value.*

In C++, my `Polynomial` class implements several methods that implement operators such as + and –, making numerical code more understandable. Alas, Java does not allow for defining operator methods. This required me to define methods with names for various operations. I've settled on the standard names `add`, `sub`, `mul`, and `div` for the four basic methods.

```java
package coyote.math;

//
//
// Polynomial
//
//
public class Polynomial
{
  // fields
  protected int m_nDegree;
  protected double [] m_dCoeff;

  // constructors
  public Polynomial(int n)
  {
    if (n <= 1)
      throw new IllegalArgumentException
        ("Bad # of polynomial coefficients");

    m_nDegree = n;
    m_dCoeff = new double [m_nDegree];

    for (int i = 0; i < m_nDegree; ++i)
      m_dCoeff[i] = 0.0D;
  }

  public Polynomial(double [] c)
  {
    m_nDegree = c.length;

    if (m_nDegree <= 1)
      throw new IllegalArgumentException
          ("Bad # of polynomial coefficients");
    m_dCoeff = new double [m_nDegree];
```

```
      for (int i = 0; i < m_nDegree; ++i)
        m_dCoeff[i] = c[i];
    }

    public Polynomial(Polynomial p)
    {
      m_nDegree = p.m_nDegree;

      m_dCoeff = new double [m_nDegree];

      for (int i = 0; i < m_nDegree; ++i)
        m_dCoeff[i] = p.m_dCoeff[i];
    }

    // get coefficients in an array
    public double [] asArray()
    {
      return m_dCoeff;
    }

    // get number of coefficients
    public int getDegree()
    {
      return m_nDegree;
    }

    // get and set coefficients
    public double getCoeff(int n)
    {
      return m_dCoeff[n];
    }

    public double setCoeff(int n, double c)
    {
      double result = m_dCoeff[n];

      m_dCoeff[n] = c;

      return result;
    }
```

```
// increase degree
public Polynomial stretch(int newN)
{
  if (newN <= m_nDegree)
    return new Polynomial(this);

  Polynomial result = new Polynomial(newN);

  for (int i = 0; i < m_nDegree; ++i)
    result.m_dCoeff[i] = m_dCoeff[i];

  return result;
}


// evaluate for value n
public double evaluate(double x)
{
  double y = m_dCoeff[m_nDegree - 1];

  for (int i = m_nDegree - 2; i >= 0; - i)
    y = x * y + m_dCoeff[i];

  return y;
}


// operations
public Polynomial negate()
{
  Polynomial result = new Polynomial(this);

  for (int i = 0; i < m_nDegree; ++i)
    result.m_dCoeff[i] *= -1.0;

  return result;
}


public Polynomial add(Polynomial p)
{
  Polynomial result;
```

```
      if (m_nDegree > p.m_nDegree)
      {
        result = new Polynomial(this);

        for (int i = 0; i < p.m_nDegree; ++i)
          result.m_dCoeff[i] += p.m_dCoeff[i];
      }
      else
      {
        result = new Polynomial(p);

        for (int i = 0; i < m_nDegree; ++i)
          result.m_dCoeff[i] += m_dCoeff[i];
      }

      return result;
    }

    public Polynomial sub(Polynomial p)
    {
      Polynomial result;

      if (m_nDegree > p.m_nDegree)
      {
        result = new Polynomial(this);

        for (int i = 0; i < p.m_nDegree; ++i)
          result.m_dCoeff[i] -= p.m_dCoeff[i];
      }
      else
      {
        result = new Polynomial(p);

        for (int i = 0; i < m_nDegree; ++i)
          result.m_dCoeff[i] -= m_dCoeff[i];
      }

      return result;
    }
```

```
public Polynomial mul(Polynomial p)
{
  if (m_nDegree != p.m_nDegree)
    throw new ArithmeticException
      ("Can't multiply polynomials of different
          degrees");

  Polynomial result = new Polynomial
      (2 * m_nDegree - 1);

  for (int i = 0; i < m_nDegree; ++i)
  {
    for (int j = 0; j < m_nDegree; ++j)
      result.m_dCoeff[i + j] += m_dCoeff[i] *
          p.m_dCoeff[j];
  }

  return result;
}
}
```

A programmer has many choices in selecting the exceptions to be thrown by a class. Many of this book's classes define a class-specific exception class to allow selective error handling by exception handlers. In the case of `Polynomial` and my other numeric classes, I decided to integrate my exceptions with those already thrown by existing numeric classes like `Integer` and `Double`. Often, making such a choice is a matter of programmer perception; you need to decide how exceptions will be handled for your classes, and design accordingly.

I throw the system-defined `ArithmeticException` when something goes wrong. Because the Java Virtual Machine manages objects, I don't need destructors to delete arrays, nor do I need to manually check each object creation (memory allocation) for success. If my program runs out of memory, Java notifies me by throwing an exception. This is just one way in which Java simplifies programming over C/C++; another is in how it handles arrays. Since an array is an object, and its length is known intrinsically, I can dispense with manual range checking and the passing of array lengths to methods like the constructor.

Complex Numbers

In implementing a version of `Polynomial` for complex numbers, I encountered a big problem: FORTRAN implements complex numbers as intrinsic types, and C++ includes a `complex` class in its standard library. Java, however, does not support complex numbers in its standard packages. What follows is a simplified version of the `Complex` class that I've developed, containing only those methods necessary for implementing complex `Polynomials`. The full version of the class — which implements trigonometric methods, logarithms, and other features — is provided on this book's source code CD-ROM.

```
package coyote.math;

//
//
// Complex
//
//
public final class Complex
{

   // real and imaginary numeric fields
   private double m_dR;
   private double m_dI;

   // constructors
   public Complex()
   {
      m_dR = 0.0D;
      m_dI = 0.0D;
   }

   public Complex(double r, double i)
   {
      m_dR = r;
      m_dI = i;
   }
```

```java
        public Complex(double r)
        {
          m_dR = r;
          m_dI = 0.0D;
        }

        public Complex(Complex z)
        {
          m_dR = z.m_dR;
          m_dI = z.m_dI;
        }

        // methods to return fields
        public double real()
        {
          return m_dR;
        }

        public double imag()
        {
          return m_dI;
        }

        // conversion to a string
        public String toString()
        {
          StringBuffer s = new StringBuffer("(");

          s.append(m_dR);
          s.append(",");
          s.append(m_dI);
          s.append(")");

          return s.toString();
        }

        // basic arithmetic
        public Complex negate()
        {
          return new Complex(-m_dR,-m_dI);
        }
```

```
public Complex add(double x)
{
   return new Complex(m_dR + x, m_dI);
}

public Complex add(Complex z)
{
   return new Complex(m_dR + z.m_dR, m_dI + z.m_dI);
}

public Complex sub(double x)
{
   return new Complex(m_dR - x, m_dI);
}

public Complex sub(Complex z)
{
   return new Complex(m_dR - z.m_dR, m_dI - z.m_dI);
}

public Complex mul(double x)
{
   return new Complex(m_dR * x, m_dI * x);
}

public Complex mul(Complex z)
{
   return new Complex
     (
     m_dR * z.m_dR - m_dI * z.m_dI,
     m_dI * z.m_dR + m_dR * z.m_dI
     );
}

public Complex div(double x)
{
   return new Complex(m_dR / x, m_dI / x);
}

public Complex div(Complex z)
{
```

```
        Complex result = new Complex();
        double d, n;

        if (Math.abs(z.m_dR) >= Math.abs(z.m_dI))
          {
          n = z.m_dI / z.m_dR;
          d = z.m_dR + n * z.m_dI;

          result.m_dR = (m_dR + n * m_dI) / d;
          result.m_dI = (m_dI - n * m_dR) / d;
          }
        else
          {
          n = z.m_dR / z.m_dI;
          d = z.m_dI + n * z.m_dR;

          result.m_dR = (m_dR * n + m_dI) / d;
          result.m_dI = (m_dI * n - m_dR) / d;
          }

        return result;
    }

    // absolute value
    public double abs()
    {
        double r, i, a, t;

        r = Math.abs(m_dR);
        i = Math.abs(m_dI);

        if (r == 0.0D)
          a = i;
        else
          {
          if (i == 0.0D)
            a = r;
          else
            {
            if (r > i)
              {
```

```
            t = i / r;
            a = r * Math.sqrt(1.0D + t * t);
            }
        else
            {
            t = r / i;
            a = i * Math.sqrt(1.0D + t * t);
            }
        }
    }

  return a;
}


// conversion of polar coordinates to complex
public static Complex cpolar(double radius, double
    theta)
{
  return new Complex(radius * Math.cos(theta),
                     radius * Math.sin(theta));
}

// natural logarithmic method
public Complex exp()
{
  return cpolar(Math.exp(Math.abs(m_dR)),m_dI);
}
}
```

You might wonder why I haven't designed a `NumericOperations` interface to encapsulate a generic version of the basic math operators. In practice, such an interface is less useful than it might appear to be in practice. For example, `NumericOperations` would define its methods in terms of generic `Objects`; any class implementing this interface would then define its methods as taking and return `Object` references, forcing any calculation to use numerous casts to `Complex` and `Polynomial`. Also, the operation methods would need to perform runtime type checking to ensure that their `Object` arguments were, indeed, `Complex` or `Polynomial` objects. That simply adds too much overhead to Java's already slow numeric support.

I've maintained the pattern of function names (e.g., `add`, `mul`, etc.) in implementing `Complex`. For the purposes of the Fast Fourier Transform (which I'll be describing later), the class also includes the `exp` method to calculate the natural exponentiation of a complex value. The `cpolar` method calculates a complex value from a polar coordinate given by an angle (`theta`) and a length (`radius`). You'll also notice that `Complex`. supports the basic mathematical operations on `Complex`. objects and with `double` values.

Complex Polynomials

The `ComplexPolynomial` class is very similar to `Polynomial`, but since `Complex` is a reference type and `double` is a primitive one, the two classes have some substantial differences in how they manipulate their array of coefficients. The trickiest part of implementing `ComplexPolynomial` in Java is in ensuring that objects themselves are being copied, and not just their references. I didn't want multiple `Polynomials` using the same list of `Complex` objects, so I needed to be careful in allocating new arrays when creating or copying objects

```java
public class ComplexPolynomial
{
  // fields
  int m_nDegree;
  Complex [] m_dCoeff;

  // constructors
  public ComplexPolynomial(int n)
  {
    if (n <= 1)
      throw new IllegalArgumentException
        ("Bad # of ComplexPolynomial coefficients");

    m_nDegree = n;
    m_dCoeff = new Complex [m_nDegree];
  }

  public ComplexPolynomial(Complex [] c)
  {
    m_nDegree = c.length;
```

```
    if (m_nDegree <= 1)
      throw new IllegalArgumentException
        ("Bad # of ComplexPolynomial coefficients");

  m_dCoeff = new Complex [m_nDegree];

  for (int i = 0; i < m_nDegree; ++i)
    m_dCoeff[i] = new Complex(c[i]);
}

public ComplexPolynomial(ComplexPolynomial p)
{
  m_nDegree = p.m_nDegree;

  m_dCoeff = new Complex [m_nDegree];

  for (int i = 0; i < m_nDegree; ++i)
    m_dCoeff[i] = new Complex(p.m_dCoeff[i]);
}

// get coefficients in an array
public Complex [] asArray()
{
  return m_dCoeff;
}

// get number of coefficients
public int getDegree()
{
  return m_nDegree;
}

// get and set coefficients
public Complex getCoeff(int n)
{
  return m_dCoeff[n];
}

public Complex setCoeff(int n, Complex c)
{
  Complex result = m_dCoeff[n];
```

```
    m_dCoeff[n] = new Complex(c);

    return result;
}

public Complex setCoeff(int n, double c)
{
    Complex result = m_dCoeff[n];

    m_dCoeff[n] = new Complex(c);

    return result;
}

// increase degree
public ComplexPolynomial stretch(int newN)
{
    if (newN <= m_nDegree)
        return new ComplexPolynomial(this);

    ComplexPolynomial result = new
            ComplexPolynomial(newN);

    for (int i = 0; i < m_nDegree; ++i)
        result.m_dCoeff[i] = new Complex(m_dCoeff[i]);

    return result;
}

// evaluate for value n
public Complex evaluate(Complex x)
{
    Complex y = m_dCoeff[m_nDegree -- 1];

    for (int i = m_nDegree - 2; i >= 0; -- i)
    {
        y = x.mul(y);
        y = y.add(m_dCoeff[i]);
    }

    return y;
```

```
}

// operations
public ComplexPolynomial negate()
{
  ComplexPolynomial result = new
        ComplexPolynomial(this);

  for (int i = 0; i < m_nDegree; ++i)
    result.m_dCoeff[i] =
        result.m_dCoeff[i].negate();

  return result;
}

public ComplexPolynomial add(ComplexPolynomial p)
{
  ComplexPolynomial result;

  if (m_nDegree > p.m_nDegree)
  {
    result = new ComplexPolynomial(m_nDegree);

    for (int i = 0; i < p.m_nDegree; ++i)
      result.m_dCoeff[i] = m_dCoeff[i].add
          (p.m_dCoeff[i]);
  }
  else
  {
    result = new ComplexPolynomial(p.m_nDegree);

    for (int i = 0; i < m_nDegree; ++i)
      result.m_dCoeff[i] = p.m_dCoeff[i].add
          (m_dCoeff[i]);
  }

  return result;
}

public ComplexPolynomial sub(ComplexPolynomial p)
{
```

```
        ComplexPolynomial result;

        if (m_nDegree > p.m_nDegree)
        {
          result = new ComplexPolynomial(m_nDegree);

          for (int i = 0; i < p.m_nDegree; ++i)
            result.m_dCoeff[i] = m_dCoeff[i].sub
                (p.m_dCoeff[i]);
        }
        else
        {
          result = new ComplexPolynomial(p.m_nDegree);

          for (int i = 0; i < m_nDegree; ++i)
            result.m_dCoeff[i] = p.m_dCoeff[i].sub
                (m_dCoeff[i]);
        }

        return result;
    }

    public ComplexPolynomial mul(ComplexPolynomial p)
    {
      if (m_nDegree != p.m_nDegree)
        throw new ArithmeticException
          ("Can't multiply polynomials of different
              degrees");

      ComplexPolynomial result = new ComplexPolynomial
          (2 * m_nDegree - 1);

      for (int i = 0; i < m_nDegree; ++i)
      {
        for (int j = 0; j < m_nDegree; ++j)
          result.m_dCoeff[i + j] =
            result.m_dCoeff[i + j].add
                (m_dCoeff[i] .mul(p.m_dCoeff[j]));
      }
      return result;
    }
```

```
public ComplexPolynomial mulFFT(ComplexPolynomial p)
{
   return this;
}
}
```

The Fast Fourier Transform

The Fast Fourier Transform (FFT) may be the most efficacious algorithm ever discovered; its applicability is incredibly broad. From signal processing and data compression to earthquake analysis and image enhancement, the FFT provides a powerful tool by converting information between domains. Much has been written about the FFT; for this book, I'll show how the FFT can improve the performance of polynomial multiplication.

So far, I've presented polynomials in coefficient form; some applications, however, work best with a polynomial represented in `point-value` form. Any polynomial of degree `n` can be represented by `n` pairs of points and values, where `value` is the polynomial evaluated at a given `point`. Many mathematical applications rely on the Fast Fourier Transform, which implements an efficient conversion between point-value and coefficients.

To quickly multiply two polynomials, `A` and `B`, follow this procedure:

1. Use a single set of values in converting both `A` and `B` from coefficient to point-value forms `pA` and `pB`.

2. Multiply the corresponding point-values of `pA` and `pB`, creating `pC`.

3. Interpolate `pC` to obtain the coefficient polynomial `C`, equaling `A` multiplied by `B`.

On the surface, the above technique appears no more efficient — and is more complicated — than the direct multiplication scheme I used for `mul`. However, a clever selection of evaluation values can make point-value multiplication very fast.

The mathematics underlying the selection of points is outside the scope of this book. The Discrete Fourier Transform (DFT), and its inverse, are the salient equations that map N coefficient values to and from point-value form at specific data values. The DFT converts coefficients to point values using this summation:

$$H_n = \sum_{k=0}^{N-1} h_k e^{2\pi i k n / N}$$

The inverse DFT (designated DFT^{-1}) implements a slightly different formula to convert point-values to coefficients:

$$h_k = \frac{1}{N} I \sum_{n=0}^{N-1} H_n e^{-2\pi i k n / N}$$

Notice the simple differences between the DFT and its inverse. If a DFT can be effectively implemented, its inverse can be constructed simply by reversing the sign of the exponent and dividing each element of the result by N.

The Fast Fourier Transform takes advantage of the properties of the DFT summations. In algorithmic terms, the `mul` function requires $O(N^2)$ operations to multiply two polynomials; the same multiplication can be accomplished by the FFT in only $O(N \log_2 N)$ operations. The larger the polynomials involved, the better the FFT performs in comparison to the `mul` technique.

Here's how the FFT works. In both the DFT and DFT^{-1}, a constant can be extracted:

$$W \equiv e^{2\pi i / N}$$

Allowing the DFT, for example, to be rewritten as:

$$H_n = \sum_{k=0}^{N-1} h_k W^{kn}$$

The DFT^{-1} is then expressed as:

$$H_n = \frac{1}{N} \sum_{k=0}^{N-1} \frac{h_k}{W^{kn}}$$

In the 1960s, the FFT emerged as a divide-and-conquer approach to calculating DFTs. The FFT is based on the ability to rewrite a DFT of length `N` as the sum of two DFTs of length `N/2`. From that fact, the most obvious implementation of an FFT would involve recursion, successively processing halves-of-halves to calculate a DFT. Recursion, however, has high overhead from nested function calls; an iterative version of the FFT is required to obtain full speed.

The iterative FFT works by rearranging the input values to match their order of processing under the recursive algorithm. This can be accomplished by bit-reversing the indexes of the input values. For example, in an order-16 polynomial, the values would be rearranged as follows:

index	binary	flip	new index
0	0000	0000	0
1	0001	1000	8
2	0010	0100	4
3	0011	1100	12
4	0100	0010	2
5	0101	1010	10
6	0110	0110	6
7	0111	1110	14
8	1000	0001	1
9	1001	1001	9
10	1010	0101	5
11	1011	1101	13
12	1100	0011	3
13	1101	1011	11
14	1110	0111	7
15	1111	1111	15

Reversing the order of the bits in a coefficient's index gives the index for the coefficient in the reordered array. So we'll need functions to both reverse the set of bits, and to copy coefficients from the initial array into the one used for the FFT. The algorithm also relies on N being a power of two; this doesn't present much of a problem, since we can simply extend the length of any polynomial by adding coefficients with a value of zero.

Conversion of `PolynomialFFT` into Java was relatively straight-forward. The Java class looks much likes its C++ counterpart; the primary difference is in how I handle the copying of array elements, taking into consideration differences in how the two languages handle object assignment.

```
package coyote.math;

/*
 *
 * PolynomialFFT
 *
 */
public class PolynomialFFT extends Polynomial
{
  // utility field
  final protected static Complex PI2I =
              new Complex(0.0D, 6.283185307179586D);

  // utility methods
  protected static int log2(int n)
  {
    int x = 1;
    int c = 0;

    while (true)
    {
      if (x >= n) break;

      ++c;
      x <<= 1;

      if (x == 0) break;
    }

    return c;
  }

  protected static int FlipBits(int k, int bits)
  {
```

```
            int lm = 1 << (bits - 1);
            int rm = 1;
            int  r = 0;

            while (lm != 0)
            {
              if ((k & rm) != 0)
                r |= lm;

              lm >>= 1;
              rm <<= 1;
            }

            return r;
        }

    // increase degree to power of two!
    protected static PolynomialFFT stretchFFT
        (PolynomialFFT p)
    {
      int n = 1;
      int d = p.m_nDegree;

      while (true)
      {
        if (d <= n) break;

        n <<= 1;

        if (n == 0)
          throw new ArithmeticException
              ("stretchFFT failed");
      }

      n <<= 1;

      return new PolynomialFFT(p.stretch(n));
    }

    // reverse-bit copy of a Polynomial into a
        ComplexPolynomial
```

```
protected static ComplexPolynomial BitRevCopy
    (PolynomialFFT p)
{
  int n = p.getDegree();
  int b = log2(n);

  ComplexPolynomial a = new ComplexPolynomial(n);

  for (int k = 0; k < n; ++k)
    a.setCoeff(FlipBits(k,b),p.getCoeff(k));

  return a;
}

// reverse-bit copy of one ComplexPolynomial into
    another
protected static ComplexPolynomial BitRevCopy
  (ComplexPolynomial p)
{
  int n = p.getDegree();
  int b = log2(n);

  ComplexPolynomial a = new ComplexPolynomial(n);

  for (int k = 0; k < n; ++k)
    a.setCoeff(FlipBits(k,b),p.getCoeff(k));

  return a;
}

// FFT of a Polynomial into a ComplexPolynomial
protected static ComplexPolynomial FFT
    (PolynomialFFT p)
{
  int n = p.getDegree();
  int nl = log2(n);
  int j, k, l, m, m2, s;
  Complex wm, w, t, u;

  ComplexPolynomial a = BitRevCopy(p);
```

```
        m  = 2;
        m2 = 1;

        for (s = 0; s < n1; ++s)
        {
          wm = PI2I.div(m);
          wm = wm.exp();
          w  = new Complex(1.0D);

          for (j = 0; j <= (m2 - 1); ++j)
          {
            for (k = j; k <= n - 1; k += m)
            {
              t = w.mul(a.getCoeff(k + m2));
              u = a.getCoeff(k);
              a.setCoeff(k,u.add(t));
              a.setCoeff(k + m2,u.sub(t));
            }

          w = w.mul(wm);
          }


          m  <<= 1;
          m2 <<= 1;
        }


        return a;
}


// inverse FFT of ComplexPolynomial into another
protected static ComplexPolynomial InvFFT
      (ComplexPolynomial p)
{
  int n = p.getDegree();
  int n1 = log2(n);
  int j, k, l, m, m2, s;
  Complex wm, w, t, u;

  ComplexPolynomial a = BitRevCopy(p);
```

```
m  = 2;
m2 = 1;

for (s = 0; s < nl; ++s)
{
  wm = PI2I.div(m);
  wm = wm.negate();
  wm = wm.exp();
  w  = new Complex(1.0D);

  for (j = 0; j <= (m2 - 1); ++j)
  {
    for (k = j; k <= n - 1; k += m)
    {
      t = w.mul(a.getCoeff(k + m2));
      u = a.getCoeff(k);
      a.setCoeff(k,u.add(t));
      a.setCoeff(k + m2,u.sub(t));
    }

  w = w.mul(wm);
  }

  m  <<= 1;
  m2 <<= 1;
}

for (j = 0; j < n; ++j)
  a.setCoeff(j,a.getCoeff(j).div(n));

return a;
}

// constructors
public PolynomialFFT(int n)
{
  super(n);
}

public PolynomialFFT(double [] c)
{
```

```
      super(c);
  }

  public PolynomialFFT(PolynomialFFT p)
  {
    super(p);
  }

  public PolynomialFFT(Polynomial p)
  {
    super(p);
  }

  // FFT multiply
  public PolynomialFFT mulFFT(PolynomialFFT p)
  {
    int n2;
    int k;

    // duplicate original polynomials
    PolynomialFFT a1 = new PolynomialFFT(this);
    PolynomialFFT a2 = new PolynomialFFT(p);

    // expand polynomials to next-largest power of two
    if (a1.getDegree() > a2.getDegree())
    {
      a1 = stretchFFT(a1);
      a2 = new PolynomialFFT(a2.stretch
        (a1.getDegree()));
    }
    else
    {
      a2 = stretchFFT(a2);
      a1 = new PolynomialFFT(a1.stretch
        (a2.getDegree()));
    }

    n2 = a1.getDegree();

    // FFT polynomials
    ComplexPolynomial dft1 = FFT(a1);
    ComplexPolynomial dft2 = FFT(a2);
```

```
// multiply coefficients
for (k = 0; k < n2; ++k)
  dft1.setCoeff(k,dft1.getCoeff(k).mul
      (dft2.getCoeff(k)));

// inverse DFT to obtain result
dft2 = InvFFT(dft1);

// create result
PolynomialFFT result = new PolynomialFFT(n2 - 1);

for (k = 0; k < n2 - 1; ++k)
  result.setCoeff(k,dft2.getCoeff(k).real());

// done
return result;
  }
}
```

In testing my Java code, I found that it performed about 20% slower than my C++ code. This is probably due to the overhead of the Java Virtual Machine, and to the increased complexities of some methods due to the need to create new objects rather than simply copy them. Overall, I found the Java implementation to be quite satisfactory. Certainly, there are advantages in flexibility and code conservation when using the parameterized version of the C++ **Polynomial** and **complex** classes. While all of the polynomial classes were implemented in a single C++ header and source file pair, the Java implementation required me to make each individual class a separate .java file.

Onward

In the next chapter, I'm going to look at enhancing Java's built-in String and text classes with advanced algorithms for searching. Java provides a number of different text tools; my goal is to show how to add new functionality with high-powered algorithms and components.

3

Java Strings and Text

Any significant application will manipulate text information, yet most programming languages treat text management as an afterthought. FORTRAN barely handles character data, while C simply defines strings as arrays of characters. Java's designers wisely decided to make string support intrinsic; while the `String` type is defined as a class, the Java compiler treats strings in a special way, recognizing the + operator for concatenation and enforcing incompatibility with character arrays.

Brute Force

Still, Java's `String` class is very basic, lacking, for instance, robust searching tools. The `indexOf` methods will return the position of a pattern within a target string, but these use simple brute-force algorithms unsuited to large-scale applications. The JavaSoft JDK 1.1.3, for example, implements the `indexOf` method as:

```java
public int indexOf(String str, int fromIndex)
{
  char v1[] = value;
  char v2[] = str.value;

  int max = offset + (count - str.count);

  if (fromIndex < 0)
  {
    fromIndex = 0;
  }
  else
    if (fromIndex >= count)
      {
      // Note: fromIndex might be near -1>>>1.
      return -1;
      }

  test:

  for (int i = offset + ((fromIndex < 0) ? 0 :
      fromIndex); i <= max ; i++)
  {
    int n = str.count;
    int j = i;
    int k = str.offset;

    while (n-- != 0)
    {
      if (v1[j++] != v2[k++])
      {
        continue test;
      }
    }

    return i - offset;
  }

  return -1;
}
```

Let's assume that I've written an application which searches an electronic copy of Dante's *The Divine Comedy*. When a brute-force algorithm is asked to find the pattern string "unto" in the target string "Pure and disposed to mount unto the stars" (from canto XXXIII, line 145), the search begins like this:

```
target:   Pure, disposed to mount unto the stars
pattern:  unto
```

The algorithm can best be understood by placing the pattern parallel to the target. The algorithm compares the characters in the pattern to those directly above it in the target. For example, the *u* in "unto" does not match the corresponding *p* in the target. This is not a match, and the algorithm moves the pattern right one character.

```
target:   Pure, disposed to mount unto the stars
pattern:   unto
```

The *u* characters in both strings match — but the second character of the pattern, *n*, does not match the corresponding character in the target, *r*. So it moves the pattern right one more character.

```
target:   Pure, disposed to mount unto the stars
pattern:    unto
```

The brute-force algorithms keeps looking for the pattern string by sliding it to the right one character every time the pattern is not found. After several more comparisons, the pattern is situated below the *u* in mount:

```
target:   Pure, disposed to mount unto the stars
pattern:                  unto
```

Four comparisons (one for each character in the pattern) are made before the algorithm realizes it hasn't got a match. The pattern is moved right four more times before it finally lands under the matching word.

```
target:   Pure, disposed to mount unto the stars
pattern:                       unto
```

In the example, the brute-force algorithm performs 32 comparisons to find the pattern string. In a worst case situation — where the pattern isn't found in target — the brute-force algorithm will need to perform a *strlen(target) – strlen(pattern)* comparison, and more comparisons if there are any partial matches. When performing a search many times, or when the target string is very large, the brute force algorithm is brutally slow.

Boyer-Moore String Searching

The best algorithms in computer science use intelligent algorithms to increase their efficiency. In the case of string searching, Robert S. Boyer and J. Strother Moore developed a very efficient string searching algorithm in 1977, using a simple finite state machine (FSM) to control "movement" through the target string. The FSM is implemented as an array with a number of elements equal to the size of the character set being used. Java uses Unicode, a 16-bit international character set. To account for any type of Unicode string search, the FSM table would need to contain 65,536 entries. However, since the first 128 characters of Unicode are the 7-bit ASCII character set, you could define the table as having only 128 entries — assuming, of course, that your Java code will never be expected to process Unicode.

Initially, the array should contain zeros in all entries. Then, a "delta" value is computed for each character in the pattern, as shown by this pseudo-code:

```
for index = 1 to (pattern_length)
    delta [pattern [ index - 1 ] ] =
        pattern_length - index
```

The delta value for a character is the position leftmost occurrence of that character, relative to the end of pattern. For the word "unto," *u* would be assigned 3, *n* would be assigned 2, *t* would be assigned 1, and *o* would be assigned zero.

In the brute-force algorithm, comparisons are performed from left to right; the first character of the pattern is compared against the first search position in the target, then the second character in the pattern is compared against the second target character, and so on. The Boyer-Moore algorithm is a right-to-left algorithm; it begins by comparing the *last* character in the pattern to the corresponding character in the target.

```
target:  Pure, disposed to mount unto the stars
pattern: unto
```

o is not equal to *e*; the pattern must be moved to the right. The pattern is moved to the right the number of characters from the entry in the delta table that corresponds to the target character from the mismatch. Since *e* does not appear in the pattern string its delta value is four (the length of the pattern), and the pattern is moved four characters left relative to the target string.

```
target: Pure, disposed to mount unto the stars
pattern:     unto
```

Again, the *o* in pattern fails to match the corresponding character in target. Since *i* is not in the pattern, the pattern is again moved four positions right.

```
target: Pure, disposed to mount unto the stars
pattern:         unto
```

Another mismatch. Again, the pattern is shifted right by its length, where it reaches this position.

```
target: Pure, disposed to mount unto the stars
pattern:             unto
```

While the pattern's *o* does not match the corresponding *u* in the target string, the *t* does match a character in the pattern. Again, the pattern is shifted right by the delta value for *t*, which is 1.

```
target: Pure, disposed to mount unto the stars
pattern:              unto
```

The last two characters of pattern match the target, but *n* does not match a space. The pattern is once again shifted by its length.

```
target: Pure, disposed to mount unto the stars
pattern:               unto
```

The *o* does not match the *u* in the target. u is a member of the string "unto", and its table entry has a delta value of 3. So the pattern is shifted right by three characters, placing the *u* characters in the target and pattern strings together.

```
target: Pure, disposed to mount unto the stars
pattern:                  unto
```

The *o* in "unto" does not match the corresponding space in the target. Again, the pattern is shifted right by its length.

```
target: Pure, disposed to mount unto the stars
pattern:                      unto
```

And the pattern is found! Where the brute-force algorithm required more than 30 comparisons for finding the pattern, the Boyer-Moore algorithm need only 13.

The Boyer-Moore algorithm is faster because it has information about the pattern string, stored in the delta table. The character that caused the mismatch in the target string tells Boyer-Moore how to move the pattern in relation to the target. If the mismatching character in the target does not exist in the pattern, Boyer-Moore can safely move the pattern its length to the right, since it is a waste of time to compare the pattern against a character it doesn't contain. When the mismatched character in the target is also resident in the pattern, the delta value for that character aligns the rightmost occurrence of that character in the pattern with the character in target.

Classes for Searching

Once the delta table has been created, it can be used to search for the pattern string in any target string. The overhead of creating the table is sufficient that I wanted to create the table once, and use it again and again. In the case where searches are being performed for several patterns, I wanted to be able to define unique delta tables for each pattern. A class is a great tool for encapsulating a data item and associated process, which is what we have with the Boyer-Moore algorithm.

A Generic Base

I began with a generic string-searching superclass that can be extended to define a variety of string-searching algorithms. The `StringSearchTool` class provides a basis for any searching tool you might devise, allowing you to use `BoyerMoore` with other algorithms in a polymorphic fashion using generic `StringSearchTool` objects.

```java
package coyote.tools;

//
//
// StringSearchTool
//
//
public abstract class StringSearchTool
{
  //-------------------------
  // constants
  //-------------------------
  public static int NOT_FOUND = -1;

  public static int SEARCH_EXACT    = 0;
  public static int SEARCH_CASELESS = 1;


  //-------------------------
  // fields
  //-------------------------
  protected String pattern;
  protected int search;


  //-------------------------
  // constructors
  //-------------------------
  public StringSearchTool()
```

```
{
  search  = SEARCH_CASELESS;
  pattern = null;
}

public StringSearchTool
  (
  final String p
  )
{
  search = SEARCH_CASELESS;
  setPattern(p);
}

public StringSearchTool
  (
  final String p,
  int type
  )
{
  search = type;
  setPattern(p);
}

//-------------------------
// properties
//-------------------------

public synchronized String getPattern()
{
  return pattern;
}

public synchronized void setPattern
  (
  final String p
  )
{
  if (search == SEARCH_CASELESS)
    pattern = p.toUpperCase();
  else
```

```
        pattern = new String(p);
}

public synchronized int getPatternLength()
{
  return pattern.length();
}

public int getSearchType()
{
  return search;
}

//--------------------------
// methods
//--------------------------
public int find
  (
  final String target
  )
{
  // search from begining
  return find(target,0);
}

public abstract int find
  (
  final String target,
  int start
  );
}
```

The `StringSearchTool` class defines the essential characteristics of any `String` searching algorithm. Each `StringSearchTool` object will contain pattern and search type properties, defining, respectively, the text being sought and whether the search ignores the differences between upper and lower case letters. These properties can be set when the `StringSearchTool` is constructed, or later via the `get`/`set` property-management methods.

A pair of `find` methods perform the actual searching of a target `String`. The first `find` is implemented in terms of the `second`, explicitly beginning a search at the beginning of the target `String`. The second method includes parameters for both a target and a starting position, allowing a search to begin from any point within a `String`. This second `find` is an abstract method defined by subclasses implementing specific searching algorithms.

The BoyerMoore Class

Extending `StringSearchTool` to implement the Boyer-Moore algorithm is a matter of implementing `find` and constructing a shift table.

```
package coyote.tools;
//
//
// BoyerMoore
//
//
public class BoyerMoore
  extends StringSearchTool
{

  //-------------------------
  // fields
  //-------------------------
  protected int [] delta;

  // base the following value on character set size
  //   for Unicode, DELTA_SIZE = 65536
  //   for ASCII-8, DELTA_SIZE =   256
  //   for ASCII-7, DELTA_SIZE =   128
  private final static int DELTA_SIZE = 65536; //
          assume Unicode

  //-------------------------
  // constructors
  //-------------------------
```

```java
public BoyerMoore()
{
  super();
}

public BoyerMoore
  (
  final String p
  )
{
  super(p);
}

public BoyerMoore
  (
  final String p,
  int type
  )
{
  super(p,type);
}


//-------------------------
// properties
//-------------------------

public synchronized void setPattern
  (
  final String p
  )
{
  super.setPattern(p);

  int n;

  // allocate and generate delta table
  delta = new int [DELTA_SIZE];

  for (n = 0; n < DELTA_SIZE; ++n)
    delta[n] = pattern.length();
```

```
      for (n = 1; n < pattern.length(); ++n)
        delta[(int)pattern.charAt(n - 1)] =
            pattern.length() - n;

    delta[(int)pattern.charAt(pattern.length() - 1)]
        = 1;
}


//-------------------------
// methods
//-------------------------
public int find
  (
  final String target,
  int start
  )
{
  // exit if pattern is null (blank)
  if ((pattern == null) || (start < 0))
    return NOT_FOUND;

  // prepare a temporary string for the search
  String target2;

  if (search == SEARCH_CASELESS)
    target2 = target.toUpperCase();
  else
    target2 = target; // just assign reference

  // index into target
  int t = start + pattern.length();

  while (t <= target2.length())
  {
    // index into pattern
    int p = pattern.length();

    // search while corresponding characters match
    while (pattern.charAt(p - 1) ==
        target2.charAt(t - 1))
    {
```

```
            if (p > 1)
            {
              // move left one character
              --p;
              --t;
            }
            else
            {
              // pattern found
              return t - 1;
            }
          }

          // move target index based on delta table
          t += delta[(int)target2.charAt(t - 1)];
        }

      // pattern not found
      return NOT_FOUND;
    }
  }
```

To the properties inherited from StringSearchTool, BoyerMoore adds an array of characters — the `delta` shift table — that will be allocated with a number of elements equal to the setting of the constant `DELTA_SIZE`. As defined above, `DELTA_SIZE` handles the entire UniCode character set of 65,536 characters; I've also provided comments that give constants for other character set sizes, including 7- and 8-bit ASCII. Supporting UniCode is probably not an issue today, since most Java Virtual Machines are still locked into an ASCII environment — but in the future, UniCode will become increasingly common, and your applications will need to handle searching that involves extended characters.

To build `delta`, `BoyerMoore` overrides the superclass method `setPattern`. This puts all of the algorithm set-up code in one place, since the superclass constructors will call `BoyerMoore`'s `setPattern` method automatically. In `setPattern`, `BoyerMoore` allocates the `delta` array and calculates the offsets for characters in the given `pattern`.

BoyerMoore's `find` method begins at a given position within a target string, and begins moving based on the values in the `delta` table. The constant `NOT_FOUND`, defined by the superclass, will be returned if the pattern is not found. Because Java does define all array indexes as `int`s (which can be negative), the algorithm verifies that the starting index is greater than or equal to zero.

Using `BoyerMoore` is simply a matter of defining a text string and a search tool object, as in this example:

```
String strRaven =
  "THE RAVEN\n" +
  "by Edgar Allen Poe\n" +
  "\n" +
  "Once upon a midnight dreary,\n" +
  "  while I pondered, weak and weary,\n" +
  "Over many a quaint and curious\n" +
  "  volume of forgotten lore -\n" +
  "While I nodded, nearly napping,\n" +
  "  suddenly there came a tapping,\n" +
  "As of some one gently rapping,\n" +
  "  rapping at my chamber door.\n" +
  "'Tis some visiter, I muttered,\n" +
  "  tapping at my chamber door -\n" +
  "Only this and nothing more.";

// create tool
BoyerMoore tool = new BoyerMoore("napping");

// find pattern in target, starting at beginning
int n = tool.find(strRaven);
```

Tools for Searching Text Areas

In searching a `TextArea`, we not only want to find a string, but we want to highlight it as well. I extended the `BoyerMoore` class to implement this feature for `TextArea`s:

```java
package coyote.tools;

import java.awt.*;
import java.awt.event.*;

//
//
// MarkTextArea
//
//
public class MarkTextArea
  extends BoyerMoore
  implements ActionListener
{
  //-------------------------
  // fields
  //-------------------------
  private TextArea target; // area to be searched


  //-------------------------
  // constructors
  //-------------------------
  public MarkTextArea
    (
    TextArea t
    )
  {
    super();

    target = t;
  }


  public MarkTextArea
    (
    final String p,
    TextArea t
    )
  {
    super(p);
```

```
    target = t;
}

public MarkTextArea
  (
  final String p,
  int type,
  TextArea t
  )
{
  super(p,type);

  target = t;
}


//------------------------
// properties
//------------------------
public TextArea getTarget()
{
  return target;
}

public void setTarget
  (
  TextArea t
  )
{
  target = t;
}


//------------------------
// events
//------------------------
public void actionPerformed
  (
  ActionEvent e
  )
{
  // locate the specified text
```

```
      int n = find(target.getText(),
          arget.getCaretPosition());

      if (n != NOT_FOUND)
      {
        // mark it
        target.setCaretPosition(n);
        target.select(n, n + pattern.length());
      }
    }
  }
```

Essentially, `MarkTextArea` extends a `BoyerMoore` object for a specific `TextArea` that is given during object construction. The class implements the `ActionListener` interface; to use it, you assign a `MarkTextArea` object as a listener for a control, such as a button. When the button is clicked, an action event will be passed to the `MarkTextArea` object. This will search the target's content `String` beginning at the current caret position, marking the pattern text if it is found. Here's a quick example applet showing how this works:

```
import java.applet.*;
import java.awt.*;
import java.awt.event.*;
import coyote.tools.*;

public class Chapter03
  extends Applet
{
  //-------------------------
  // fields
  //-------------------------
  private TextArea taRaven;
  private Button   findChamber;
  private Button   findDreary;

  private String strRaven =
    "THE RAVEN\n" +
    "by Edgar Allen Poe\n" +
    "\n" +
    "Once upon a midnight dreary,\n" +
```

```
        "   while I pondered, weak and weary,\n" +
        "Over many a quaint and curious\n" +
        "   volume of forgotten lore -\n" +
        "While I nodded, nearly napping,\n" +
        "   suddenly there came a tapping,\n" +
        "As of some one gently rapping,\n" +
        "   rapping at my chamber door.\n" +
        "'Tis some visiter, I muttered,\n" +
        "   tapping at my chamber door -\n" +
        "Only this and nothing more.";

    //-------------------------
    // constructors
    //-------------------------
    public Chapter03()
    {
        // see init()
    }

    public void init()
    {
        // set applet properties
        resize(240, 160);
        setLayout(new BorderLayout(5,5));
        setBackground(Color.lightGray);

        // create search buttons
        findChamber = new Button("Find 'chamber'");
        add("North",findChamber);

        findDreary = new Button("Find 'dreary'");
        add("South",findDreary);

        // text area to be searched
        taRaven = new TextArea(strRaven,1,1,
            TextArea.SCROLLBARS_BOTH);
        add("Center",taRaven);

        // padding for text area
        add("East",new Label());
        add("West",new Label());
```

```
        // create tools for searching text area
        findChamber.addActionListener(new MarkTextArea
            ("chamber",taRaven));
        findDreary.addActionListener(new MarkTextArea
          ("DrEaRy",StringSearchTool.SEARCH_CASELESS,
            taRaven));
    }


    //------------------------
    // applet-specific methods
    //------------------------
    public String getAppletInfo()
    {
      return "Java Algorithms and Components:
          Chapter Three\r\n" +
           "Copyright 1997 Scott Robert Ladd\r\n" +
           "All rights reserved\r\n";
    }
}
```

Figure 3-1 shows how the applet looks when executed by Sun's HotJava browser.

Figure 3-1

The Applet in
the Browser

Clicking on the **Find 'chamber'** button invokes the find method for the `findChamber` object, scrolling the `TextArea` to show the highlighting text "chamber." To search forward from the current position, simply move the caret one position right in the string, as shown in Figure 3-2.

Figure 3-2

More of the Applet

Onward

`TextArea`s are often parts of complex user interfaces. Java, unlike other programming languages, is defined with built-in support for the development of graphical user interfaces. In the next chapter, I'll explore how you can create your own layout managers to control the visual impact of your applets and applications.

Layout Managers

The Java Abstract Window Toolkit (AWT) is a complex system designed for the development of platform-independent graphic interfaces. To implement this independence, the AWT defines the concept of *layout managers*, objects that control the positioning of components within a container. While the AWT provides a standard set of layout manager classes, you may need to develop a custom layout manager for your applications.

Types of Layout Managers

Layout managers come in two flavors, based on two interfaces defined by the **java.awt** package. The simplest implement is the **LayoutManager** interface. This declares several **public abstract** methods, which will be called by the container that is associated with a given layout manager. You will not call any of these methods for the layout manager objects you create; they are only for the internal use of the associated container.

- **void addLayoutComponent(String name, Component comp)**
  The container calls this method to add a specified component, with a given name, to the layout. This method can have an empty implementation for any layout manager that does not maintain an internal list of components.

- **void removeLayoutComponent(Component comp)**
  The counterpart to `addLayoutComponent`, this method removes the specified component from the layout. It should have an empty implementation if `addLayoutComponent` is also empty.

- **Dimension preferredLayoutSize(Container parent)**
  Returns the preferred dimensions for the container given the components to be managed by the layout.

- **Dimension minimumLayoutSize(Container parent)**
  Returns the minimum dimensions for the container given the components to be managed by the layout.

- **void layoutContainer(Container parent)**
  The workhorse method for any layout manager, `layoutContainer` resizes and moves components based on a given design. For example, a `GridLayout` object will place components into a define number of rows and columns.

Examples of `LayoutManager`s include `FlowLayout` and `GridLayout`.

The `LayoutManager2` subinterface, derived from `LayoutManager`, defines methods that associate some parameter `Object` with a `Component`. Classes that implement `LayoutManager2` can be thought of as *constrained*, in that an object individually controls the way in which elements are presented. In addition to methods inherited from `LayoutManager`, this interface declares these methods:

- **void addLayoutComponent(Component comp, Object constraints)**
  This method adds the specified component to the layout, using the specified constraint object. When implementing `LayoutManager2`, you can (and probably should) implement the single-argument version of this method as a call to the two-argument method, passing a default `constraints` object as the second parameter.

- `Dimension maximumLayoutSize(Container target)`
  Returns the maximum dimensions for the container given the components to be managed by the layout.

- `float getLayoutAlignmentY(Container target)`
  `float getLayoutAlignmentX(Container target)`
  These methods return the "alignment" of the layout along the x and y axes. The value should be a number between 0 and 1, where 0 represents alignment along the origin, 1 is aligned the furthest away from the origin, 0.5 is centered, etc. In most layout managers, these methods return 0.5.

- `void invalidateLayout(Container target)`
  The target container calls this method to invalidate a layout; if the layout manager has cached information (for example, some precomputed value), that data should be discarded or recalculated either in this method or in `layoutContainer`.

The `GridBagLayout`, `CardLayout`, and `BorderLayout` classes implement `LayoutManager2`.

When designing a layout manager, you need to consider several factors. First, you must decide if your layout manager will maintain an internal list of constituent components, or if it will instead use a list of components obtained from its associated container. The `FlowLayout` class, for example, provides empty implementations of the `addLayoutComponent` and `removeLayoutComponent` methods; when called upon to organize components, `FlowLayout` interrogates the target container for a list of components. Other layout managers, such as `BorderLayout`, need to track which component is in which named position. In such cases, implementing an internal set of `Component` references allows the layout manager to control the locations of components.

Also think in terms of how your manager will display components. Do you need to allow for vertical and horizontal padding space between components? Should some components have precedence over others in terms of their dimensions? For constrained layouts, what factors will influence the organization of components? Your best guide is to examine existing layout managers — those in this book, and those that come with the Abstract Window Toolkit.

`GridBagLayout`, for example, provides an excellent example of a constrained layout manager that uses a complex object to control the placement of components.

Above all else, think *generic*. A layout manager should always base the locations and sizes of components on the size of the target container. Never assume how much space you have; never expect that fonts, buttons, or other components will have identical characteristics on different platforms. If possible, check your layout managers on a variety of platforms — I often wander down to the local high school on Thursday nights just to verify my code on their Macintosh computers. The goal in building a layout manager is to create a tool for presenting an application in any environment in which it might run, without requiring your application to have foreknowledge of its host operating system.

Building a Vertical Flow Layout

The AWT's `FlowLayout` organizes components horizontally, creating a new row when the current line runs of out space. This is a useful layout for toolbars and menus; for some applications, you may want to organize components vertically, (in columns). Building such a "vertical flow" layout manager is relatively simple once you understand how the AWT organizes components.

In creating the `VFlowLayout` class, I looked to `FlowLayout` for guidance. `FlowLayout` is a simple manager that implements the `LayoutManager` interface. As defined by the JDK, `FlowLayout` does not maintain its own list of components; instead, it interrogates its target container during the layout processes, relocating and sizing each component according to the container's size. Internally, `FlowLayout` maintains values for vertical and horizontal separation between components, in addition to a value that determines whether components will be justified left, right or centered within a row. The class defines public constants for the valid justification flags. In the case of `VFlowLayout`, the equivalent component justifications would be *top*, *centered*, and *bottom*.

`VFlowLayout` begins by declaring constants and defining its fields and exceptions.

```
package coyote.ui;

import java.awt.*;

//
//
// VFlowLayout
//
//
public class VFlowLayout
  implements LayoutManager
{
  //------------------------
  // constants
  //------------------------
  public static final int TOP = 0;
  public static final int CENTER = 1;
  public static final int BOTTOM = 2;


  //------------------------
  // fields
  //------------------------
  private int m_align;
  private int m_hgap;
  private int m_vgap;


  //------------------------
  // exceptions
  //------------------------
  private static final IllegalArgumentException err1 =
    new IllegalArgumentException("invalid VFlowLayout
        alignment");

  private static final IllegalArgumentException err2 =
    new IllegalArgumentException("invalid VFlowLayout
        hgap");

  private static final IllegalArgumentException err3 =
    new IllegalArgumentException("invalid VFlowLayout
        vgap");
```

The constructors for `VFlowLayout` correspond to those declared by `FlowLayout`. A `VFlowLayout` can be constructed entirely with default values, with only a justification value, or with parameters defining padding and justification.

```
//------------------------
// constructors
//------------------------
public VFlowLayout()
{
  this(CENTER,5,5);
}

public VFlowLayout
  (
  int align
  )
{
  this(align,5,5);
}

public VFlowLayout
  (
  int align,
  int hgap,
  int vgap
  )
{
  // verify parameters
  if ((align < TOP) || (align > BOTTOM))
    throw err1;

  if (hgap < 0)
    throw err2;

  if (vgap < 0)
    throw err3;

  // store parameters
  m_align = align;
```

```
   m_hgap   = hgap;
   m_vgap   = vgap;
}
```

A set of property methods provides access to the parameters of a
`VFlowLayout`.

```
//-------------------------
// properties
//-------------------------
public void setAlignment
   (
   int align
   )
{
   // verify parameters
   if ((align < TOP) || (align > BOTTOM))
     throw err1;

   // save parameter
   m_align = align;
}

public int getAlignment()
{
   return m_align;
}

public void setHgap
   (
   int hgap
   )
{
   // verify parameters
   if (hgap < 0)
     throw err2;

   // store parameters
   m_hgap   = hgap;
}
```

```
public int getHgap()
{
  return m_hgap;
}

public void setVgap
  (
  int vgap
  )
{
  // verify parameters
  if (vgap < 0)
    throw err3;

  // store parameters
  m_vgap  = vgap;
}

public int getVgap()
{
  return m_vgap;
}
```

VFlowLayout does not maintain an internal list of components, so it implements empty versions of the addLayoutComponent or removeLayoutComponent methods defined by LayoutManager. You must define these empty methods to fulfill the contract defined by the LayoutManager interface.

```
//-------------------------
// methods
//-------------------------
public void addLayoutComponent
  (
  String name,
  Component comp
  )
{
  // does nothing in this class
}
```

```
public void removeLayoutComponent
  (
  Component comp
  )
{
  // does nothing in this class
}
```

VFlowLayout calculates its preferred layout size from the pre-ferred sizes of the components in the target Container. The algorithm calculates the preferred width of the layout as the width of the widest Component plus insets and horizontal padding. The preferred height is the sum total of all component heights plus any vertical padding and insets.

```
public Dimension preferredLayoutSize
  (
  Container target
  )
{
  // create a zero dimension
  Dimension dim = new Dimension(0,0);

  // how many components in container?
  int n = target.getComponentCount();

  // compute width and height
  for (int i = 0; i < n; ++i)
  {
    // reference target component
    Component m = target.getComponent(i);

    // only compute for visible components
    if (m.isVisible())
    {
      Dimension d = m.getPreferredSize();

      dim.width  = Math.max(dim.width,d.width);
      dim.height += d.height + m_vgap;
    }
  }
```

```
        // include insets in dimensions
        Insets ins = target.getInsets();

        dim.width  += ins.left + ins.right + 2 * m_hgap;
        dim.height += ins.top + ins.bottom + m_vgap;

        // return results
        return dim;
    }
```

The `minimumLayoutSize` method is almost identical to `preferredLayoutSize`; the only difference between the two routines is in using the `getMinimumSize` method in calculating component heights.

```
    public Dimension minimumLayoutSize
      (
      Container target
      )
    {
      // create a zero dimension
      Dimension dim = new Dimension(0,0);

      // how many components in container?
      int n = target.getComponentCount();

      // compute width and height
      for (int i = 0; i < n; ++i)
      {
        // reference target component
        Component m = target.getComponent(i);

        // only compute for visible components
        if (m.isVisible())
        {
          Dimension d = m.getMinimumSize();

          dim.width  = Math.max(dim.width,d.width);
          dim.height += d.height + m_vgap;
        }
      }
```

```
    // include insets in dimensions
    Insets ins = target.getInsets();

    dim.width  += ins.left + ins.right + 2 * m_hgap;
    dim.height += ins.top + ins.bottom + m_vgap;

    // return results
    return dim;
}
```

The central method of any layout manager is layoutContainer. VFlowLayout implements this method using a loop that distributes components in columns.

```
public void layoutContainer
  (
  Container target
  )
{
  Insets ins = target.getInsets();
  int maxH = target.getSize().height -
      (ins.top + ins.bottom
                              + m_vgap * 2);
  int n = target.getComponentCount();
  int x = ins.left + m_vgap;
  int y = 0;
  int c = 0;
  int start = 0;

  for (int i = 0; i < n; ++i)
  {
    Component m = target.getComponent(i);

    if (m.isVisible())
    {
      Dimension d = m.getPreferredSize();
      m.setSize(d.width,d.height);

      if ((y == 0) || ((y + d.height) <= maxH))
      {
```

```
              if (y > 0)
                y += m_vgap;

              y += d.height;

              c = Math.max(c,d.width);
          }
          else
          {
            moveComponents(target, x, ins.top + m_vgap,
                       c, maxH - y, start, i);
            y  = d.height;
            x += m_hgap + c;
            c  = d.width;
            start = i;
          }
        }
      }

      moveComponents(target, x, ins.top + m_vgap, c,
          maxH - y, start, n);
    }
```

The central loop cycles through the Components stored in target, adding their height and the vertical gap to a total stored in y, and tracking the maximum width in c. When y is greater than the maximum available height in target, the algorithm calls the private moveComponent algorithm to distribute elements from start through i. Once a group of components have been located in their container, the loop resets itself to begin distributing the next group of elements in another column. The actual sizing and positioning of Components is carried out by the moveComponents method:

```
    private void moveComponents
        (
        Container target,
        int x,
        int y,
        int width,
        int height,
        int colStart,
```

```
      int colEnd
      )
{
  switch (m_align)
  {
  case TOP:
    break;
  case CENTER:
    y += (height / 2);
    break;
  case BOTTOM:
    y += height;
    break;
  }

  for (int i = colStart; i < colEnd; ++i)
  {
    Component m = target.getComponent(i);
    Dimension d = m.getSize();

    if (m.isVisible())
    {
      m.setLocation(x + (width - d.width) / 2, y);
      y += m_vgap + d.height;
    }
  }
}
```

In practice, the `VFlowLayout` will organize Components into columns, just as the `FlowLayout` places `Components` into rows. For example, the following applet fragment shows how a `VFlowLayout` works in practice:

```
private String [] ButtonName =
{
  "One",
  "Two",
  "Three",
  "Four",
  "Five",
  "Six",
```

```
        "Seven",
        "Eight",
        "Nine",
        "Ten",
        "Eleven"
    };

    private boolean vertical = true;

    public void init()
      {
      // set applet size
      setSize(160, 160);

      if (vertical)
        setLayout(new VFlowLayout(VFlowLayout.TOP));
      else
        setLayout(new FlowLayout(FlowLayout.LEFT));


      // create an add buttons to applet display
      for (int n = 0; n < ButtonName.length; ++n)
        add(new Button(ButtonName[n]));
      }
```

As the code is written, a `VFlowLayout` will be created for the applet display, resulting in the buttons appearing as they do in Figure 4-1.

Figure 4-1
Buttons Displayed
with VFlowLayout

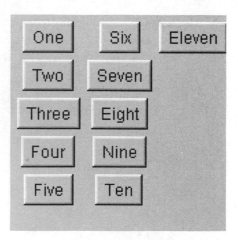

Changing the `vertical` flag to `false` will make the applet use the AWT's `FlowLayout` to organize the components in left-justified rows, as shown in Figure 4-2.

Figure 4-2
Buttons Displayed with
AWT FlowLayout

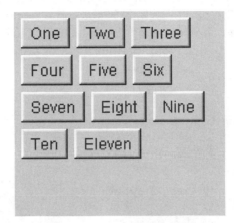

I've used `VFlowLayout` in several of my applications, usually for creating vertical toolbars at one edge of an applet display. You can also use a `VFlowLayout` as a simple grid layou, to display text fields or checkboxes in neat columns.

Building a Clock Layout

`VFlowLayout` is a simple but useful layout manager based on the `LayoutManager` interface. For many applications, you'll want to use a layout manager that allows you to provide specific information for each component. This requires your layout manager to be based on the `LayoutManager2` interface, which is used by the `BorderLayout` and `GridBagLayout` standard classes.

In writing one applet, I needed to lay out the components in a clock-like pattern, with buttons located at the twelve hour positions. I could have done this manually, explicitly positioning elements inside my container. But object-oriented programming is, in many ways, the art of building reusable tools. The purpose of layout managers is to provide universal tools for organizing graphic interfaces — and so I set about creating a `ClockLayout` object. My goal was to have thirteen possible components laid out in a twelve-point circle, with an additional item at the center.

Like BorderLayout, the components in a ClockLayout will be positioned at named locations; where BorderLayout has locations named after the four directions, the ClockLayout places its components based on strings that name the numbers on a clock's face: "2" for two o'clock, "10" for ten o'clock, and so on. The "0" (zero) position is the center of the object. To facilitate using these location strings, ClockLayout defines a set of public constants.

```
package coyote.ui;

import java.awt.*;

//
//
// ClockLayout
//
//
public class ClockLayout
  implements LayoutManager2
{
  //-------------------------
  // constants
  //-------------------------
  private static final String [] POS_NAME =
  {
    "0","1","2","3","4","5","6","7","8","9","10",
    "11","12"
  };

  public static final String CENTER  = "0";
  public static final String CLOCK01 = "1";
  public static final String CLOCK02 = "2";
  public static final String CLOCK03 = "3";
  public static final String CLOCK04 = "4";
  public static final String CLOCK05 = "5";
  public static final String CLOCK06 = "6";
  public static final String CLOCK07 = "7";
  public static final String CLOCK08 = "8";
  public static final String CLOCK09 = "9";
  public static final String CLOCK10 = "10";
  public static final String CLOCK11 = "11";
```

```
public static final String CLOCK12 = "12";
public static final String CLOCK00 = CLOCK12;


//------------------------
// fields
//------------------------
private Component [] m_comp;


//------------------------
// exceptions
//------------------------
private static final IllegalArgumentException err1 =
    new IllegalArgumentException("invalid ClockLayout
        radius");
```

The constructor's only task is to allocate space for the array of `Components` maintained by the layout.

```
//------------------------
// constructors
//------------------------
public ClockLayout()
{
  // allocate component array
  // automatically initialized to null references
  m_comp = new Component [13];
}
```

Unlike `VFlowLayout`, `ClockLayout` maintains an array of references to components at specific locations; if no `Component` is assigned to a given location, the corresponding reference will be `null` and nothing will be displayed in that place. The `addLayout-Component` methods will be called for a layout by its container to include a new component; `ClockLayout` implements these methods to assign the component reference to an element of the `m_comp` array, based on the content of a `String` argument. `removeLayoutComponent` searches the array and replaces a specified component with a null reference (deleting that `Component` from the layout).

```
//-------------------------
// methods
//-------------------------
public void addLayoutComponent
  (
  Component comp,
  Objectobj
  )
{
  // convert the object to a string
  if (obj instanceof String)
    addLayoutComponent((String)obj,comp);
  else
    addLayoutComponent(CENTER,comp);
}

public void addLayoutComponent
  (
  Stringname,
  Component comp

  )
{
  // default value
  if (name == null)
    name = CENTER;

  // find position and assign component
  for (int i = 0; i < 13; ++i)
  {
    if (name.equals(POS_NAME[i]))
    {
      m_comp[i] = comp;
      break;
    }
  }
}

public void removeLayoutComponent
  (
  Component comp
```

```
        )
    {
      // find position and assign component
      for (int i = 0; i < 13; ++i)
      {
        if (m_comp[i] == comp)
        {
          m_comp[i] = null;
          break;
        }
      }
    }
```

For the most part, `ClockLayout` implements simple versions of many methods defined by `LayoutManager2`. For example, `Clock-Layout` uses the display area of its target container, so it returns the size of target for its preferred, minimum, and maximum sizes. The `ClockLayout` should be centered within its container, so `getLay-outAlignmentX` and `getLayoutAlignmentY` both return 0.5F. And the class has nothing to do when its `invalidateLayout` method is called, since it does not maintain any precalculated values or objects.

```
    public Dimension preferredLayoutSize
      (
      Container target
      )
    {
      return target.getSize();
    }

    public Dimension minimumLayoutSize
      (
      Container target
      )
    {
      return preferredLayoutSize(target);
    }

    public Dimension maximumLayoutSize
      (
      Container target
```

```
       )
     {
       return preferredLayoutSize(target);
     }

     public float getLayoutAlignmentX
       (
       Container parent
       )
     {
       return 0.5F;
     }


     public float getLayoutAlignmentY
       (
       Container parent
       )
     {
       return 0.5F;
     }


     public void invalidateLayout
       (
       Container target
       )
     {
       // not used
     }
```

Finally, we come to `layoutContainer`, where the real work occurs. `ClockLayout` uses the dimensions and insets of its associated container to define the bounds of the clock's circle. If the enclosing container is not square, `ClockLayout` places components in an ellipse. The `layoutContainer` method loops through the 13 elements of `m_comp`; for those elements that are non-`null` and visible, a `switch` statement determines the coordinates. Calculations are quite simple for the "orthogonal" components at the center, twelve-, three-, six-, and nine-o'clock positions; for the other eight positions, which are on the edge of the circle, I use the trigonometric Law of Sines to calculate x-y coordinates.

```
public void layoutContainer
  (
  Container target
  )
{
  // get target container size
  Dimension dim = target.getSize();

  // get parameters
  Insets ins = target.getInsets();
  // compute center of area
  int h = (dim.height - ins.top  - ins.bottom) / 2;
  int w = (dim.width  - ins.left - ins.right)  / 2;

  // clockwise angle for this component
  double angle = 0.0;
  final double INCR = 0.52359877559; // 30 degrees
      in radians

  for (int i = 0; i < 13; ++i)
  {
    if ((m_comp[i] != null) &&
        (m_comp[i].isVisible()))
    {
      // set component to its preferred size
      Dimension d = m_comp[i].getPreferredSize();
      m_comp[i].setSize(d);

      // coordinates for component
      int x, y;

      switch (i)
      {
      case 1:
      case 2:
      case 4:
      case 5:
      case 7:
      case 8:
      case 10:
      case 11:
```

```java
            // use sine law to compute coordinates
            x = (int)(w + Math.sin
                (angle) * w - d.width / 2);
            y = (int)(h - Math.sin(1.57079632679 - angle)
                    * h - d.height / 2);
            break;


        case 3:
          // right side
          x = 2 * w - d.width;
          y = h - d.height / 2;
          break;


        case 6:
          // bottom
          x = w - d.width  / 2;
          y = 2 * h - d.height;
          break;


        case 9:
          // left side
          x = 0;
          y = h - d.height / 2;
          break;


        case 12:
          // top of area
          x = w - d.width  / 2;
          y = 0;
          break;


        default: // put in center
          x = w - d.width  / 2;
          y = h - d.height / 2;
        }


        m_comp[i].setLocation(x + ins.left,
            y + ins.top);
    }
```

```
        angle += INCR;
    }
}
```

The following applet fragment shows how a `ClockLayout` works in a real program. I create thirteen buttons, one for each position.

```
private String [] ClockName =
{
  "Center",
  "One",
  "Two",
  "Three",
  "Four",
  "Five",
  "Six",
  "Seven",
  "Eight",
  "Nine",
  "Ten",
  "Eleven",
  "Twelve"
};

private String [] ClockPos =
{
  "0","1","2","3","4","5","6","7","8","9","10",
    "11","12"
};

public void init()
{
  setSize(320, 320);
  setLayout(new ClockLayout());

  for (int n = 0; n < ClockName.length; ++n)
    add(ClockPos[n],new Button(ClockName[n]));
}
```

In Sun's HotJava browser, the display looks like Figure 4-3.

Figure 4-3
Example of a
ClockLayout

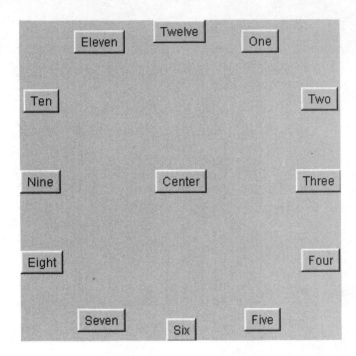

ClockLayout does not require you to place a component at every possible position. If you don't assign a `Component` to a location, the corresponding reference in `m_comp` will be `null`, and nothing will appear.

Onward

In the next chapter, I move from fundamental types and tools into the development of classes to implement data structures. While Java does a fine job of defining classes for information display, it lacks a robust set of classes for manipulating that data in the first place. In the next four chapters, you'll see how to create tree structures, array-based containers, and finite state machines — all important elements of powerful applications.

Chapter

High-Performance Containers

Not all algorithms require complex logic and long class definitions. The concepts of simple data structures — linked lists, stacks, and queues — fall into a category of algorithms I think of as "useful tools:" program components that provide the essential gears and widgets of an application.

Most data structures create a container that organizes a collection of objects. Java uses the term *container* to refer to a graphic construct that encapsulates a set of components. In the world of computer science, however, container means something more generic: an object that contains and organizes other objects. From linked lists to queues and heaps, containers are among the most important and useful data structures. Unfortunately, the standard Java packages do not provide a sophisticated set of container types; in fact, the language hardly provides any data structures at all!

In `java.lang`, you'll find the `Vector` class, which defines a dynamic array that resizes itself according to the number of objects you store therein. Derived from `Vector` is `Stack`, a last-in, first-out container. Neither of these classes were built for speed. `Vector` was designed to be a jack-of-all-trades container, trading speed and conciseness for flexibility and general applicability. `Stack` specializes `Vector` but retains all of its superclass' overhead. Even if performance isn't your primary concern, you'll find that the Java packages fail to implement some very useful data structures, including queues and heaps.

Over the years, I've developed more types of containers than I care to remember. In this chapter, I'll be showing you some generic stack, queue, deque, and heap templates based on fixed-length arrays. For most of the fundamental container types, using an array is shorter and faster than a dynamic memory implementation.

Garbage Collection Issues

Garbage collection occurs when the Java Virtual Machine removes unreferenced objects from memory. In C++, it is the programmer's responsibility to explicitly delete any dynamic objects from the heap; Java puts this onus on the VM. While garbage collection adds some overhead to a program, it also makes code easier to read and less prone to memory overflow caused by inadvertent failures to manually free the memory occupied by unused objects.

In converting my code from C/C++ to Java, I needed to make some changes in how I handled the storage of object references. Due to garbage collection, I needed to ensure that my lists of `Objects` did not keep unused references to objects that have been removed. For example, it would be wrong for a stack to simply decrement a stack point after returning the top value; doing so would leave a reference on the stack to the returned object. In the eyes of the garbage collector, the object would still be on the stack, even if I'd popped it! So I replace references to removed objects with `null`.

Exceptions

When developing a set of related classes, there are advantages to creating a specific exception type for those classes. In the case of my array-based containers, I created a common exception type, `Fixed-ContainerException`, derived from `RuntimeException`. Container types will throw exceptions for invalid parameters or when code attempts the impossible — as when trying to pop a value from an empty stack, for example. Like most of the exceptions already defined by the Java packages, `FixedContainerException` simply provides a shell over its superclass, so that catch blocks can selectively handle errors by group.

```
package coyote.tools;

public class FixedContainerException
  extends RuntimeException
{

  public FixedContainerException()
  {
    super();
  }

  public FixedContainerException(String s)
  {
    super(s);
  }

}
```

Stacks

A stack places new items at the top of a list, "pushing" the other items in the list down. Instead of traveling through a stack element-by-element, information is retrieved from a stack by "popping" the top item and removing it from the list. Items pushed onto a stack are popped in reverse order. If I push the numbers 1, 2, 3 and 4 onto a stack in that order, and then pop the top item, I will receive 4 and the list will contain 3, 2 and 1. Popping again retrieves 3, leaving 2 and 1 in the stack. A stack only lets you retrieve the last item you stored — and when you pop an item, it is deleted from the stack, reducing the stack size by one. In essence, using a stack is like traveling backward in history, seeing the most recent events before past ones.

The `FixedStack` class begins with the definition of fields and exceptions. The `stack` array contains the data, and `top` points to the top item in the structure.

```
package coyote.tools;

//
//
// FixedStack
//
//
public class FixedStack
{
  //-------------------------
  // Fields
  //-------------------------

  private Object [] stack;
  private int top;

  //-------------------------
  // exceptions
  //-------------------------

  private FixedContainerException err_empty  =
    new FixedContainerException("pop on empty stack");

  private FixedContainerException err_full=
    new FixedContainerException("push on full stack");

  private FixedContainerException err_invalid =
    new FixedContainerException("invalid stack
      parameters");
```

The constructor allocates memory for the stack data and sets the top of the stack to zero.

```
public FixedStack
  (
  int capacity
  )
{
  if (capacity < 1)
    throw err_invalid;

  stack = new Object [capacity];
  top = 0;
}
```

Pushing a new value onto a `FixedStack` is simply a matter of adding it as the last item in the array, incrementing `top` to reflect the new stack size.

```
public void push
  (
  Object x
  )
{
  if (top == stack.length)
    throw err_full;

  stack[top] = x;
  ++top;
}
```

To examine the data in a stack, I implement both `peek` and `pop` methods. `peek` returns a reference to the `top` item but leaves it on the `stack`, while pop removes the top `Object` before removing it.

```
public Object peek()
{
  if (top == 0)
    throw err_empty;
```

```
    return stack[top - 1];
  }

  public Object pop()
  {
    if (top == 0)
      throw err_empty;

    --top;

    Object result = stack[top];
    stack[top] = null;

    return result;
  }
```

A set of property interrogation methods complete FixedStack.

```
  public int getCount()
  {
    return top;
  }

  public int getCapacity()
  {
    return stack.length;
  }

  public boolean isEmpty()
  {
    return top == 0;
  }
}
```

In terms of size, FixedStack is a clear improvement over the standard Stack class. While both classes compile to roughly the same size, Stack must also load the large (4K or bigger) Vector class.

Queues

Outside the United States, a line of people — such as a group waiting to buy a plane ticket — is known as a *queue*. A queue appends new items to the end of a list and retrieves items from the head; thus the last item stored is the last item retrieved. If I store 1, 2, 3 and 4 in a queue, I'll retrieve them in the order 1, 2, 3, 4. Implementing such a structure is a bit more complicated than creating a stack; since both ends of the list change, both a head and tail index must be managed. The head index moves "up" in the array, being incremented as items are removed; the tail index also moves up, as new items are added. In a very active queue, the head and tail indices may wrap around the end of the array.

My `FixedQueue` class begins by defining data members and exceptions:

```
package coyote.tools;

//
//
// FixedQueue
//
//
public class FixedQueue
{
  //-------------------------
  // Fields
  //-------------------------

  private Object [] queue;
  private int head;
  private int tail;
  private int count;

  //-------------------------
  // exceptions
  //-------------------------
```

```
private FixedContainerException err_empty  =
   new FixedContainerException("pop on empty queue");

private FixedContainerException err_full=
   new FixedContainerException("push on full queue");

private FixedContainerException err_invalid =
   new FixedContainerException("invalid queue
       parameters");
```

The constructor allocates the array of elements and sets the indices for an empty queue.

```
public FixedQueue
   (
   int capacity
   )
{
   if (capacity < 1)
     throw err_invalid;

   queue = new Object [capacity];
   head = 0;
   tail = 0;
   count = 0;
}
```

The push method adds a new item in the tail position. If the queue is empty, the new item will be placed in the first element of the array, and head and tail will both be zero. If the queue already contains elements, the algorithm increments tail and places the new element in that position.

```
public void push
   (
   Object item
   )
{
   if (count == queue.length)
     throw err_full;
```

```
        if (count == 0)
        {
          tail = 0;
          head = 0;
          queue[0] = item;
        }
        else
        {
          ++tail;

          if (tail == queue.length)
            tail = 0;

          queue[tail] = item;
        }

        ++count;
      }
```

To retrieve a reference to the first item in a queue, call the peek method. If you want to obtain the reference and remove the item, call pop.

```
    public Object peek()
    {
      if (count == 0)
        throw err_empty;

      return queue[tail - 1];
    }

    public Object pop()
    {
      if (count == 0)
        throw err_empty;

      Object result = queue[head];
      queue[head] = null;

      --count;
```

```
      if (count != 0)
      {
        ++head;

        if (head == queue.length)
          head = 0;
      }

      return result;
    }
```

The `FixedQueue` property methods are almost the same as those I defined for `FixedStack`.

```
    public int getCount()
    {
      return count;
    }

    public int getCapacity()
    {
      return queue.length;
    }

    public boolean isEmpty()
    {
      return count == 0;
    }
  }
```

By allowing the indexes to wrap the array, I make available the full capacity of the `queue` array, no matter how many pushes and pops have been made.

Deques

The *deque* is a hybrid container implementing the concepts of both stack and queue. The name comes from the phrase "double-ended queue," meaning that a deque allows elements to be pushed and popped from both ends of the same list. Array-based deques require some tricky handling of indexes, since both head and tail indexes can wrap either end of the data array. Whenever a new node is added, I check to see if the structure is full; if so, I throw an exception. If the deque still has room, I decrement head or increment tail; the indices move in opposite directions, and can't "overrun" each other so long as I watch the number of elements in the deque.

Definitions of indexes, the data array, and exceptions will be found in the first part of the `FixedDeque` class definition.

```
package coyote.tools;

//
//
// FixedDeque
//
//
public class FixedDeque
{
  //----------------------------
  // Fields
  //------------------------

  private Object [] deque;
  private int head;
  private int tail;
  private int count;


  //------------------------
  // exceptions
  //------------------------

  private FixedContainerException err_empty  =
    new FixedContainerException("pop on empty deque");

  private FixedContainerException err_full=
    new FixedContainerException("push on full deque");

  private FixedContainerException err_invalid =
    new FixedContainerException("invalid deque
        parameters");
```

The constructor sets values and allocates the element array.

```
public FixedDeque
    (
    int capacity
    )
{
  if (capacity < 1)
    throw err_invalid;

  deque = new Object [capacity];
  head = 0;
  tail = 0;
  count = 0;
}
```

Unlike `FixedStack` and `FixedQueue`, `FixedDeque` implements two versions each of the pop, peek, and push methods, to handle both ends of the list. While `pushHead` adds new elements at the beginning of the list, `pushTail` stores elements at the end.

```
public void pushHead
  (
  Object item
  )
{
  if (count == deque.length)
    throw err_full;

  if (count == 0)
  {
    tail = 0;
    head = 0;
    deque[0] = item;
  }
  else
  {
    if (head == 0)
      head = deque.length - 1;
    else
      --head;
```

```
      deque[head] = item;
    }

    ++count;
  }

  public void pushTail
    (
    Object item
    )
  {
    if (count == deque.length)
      throw err_full;

    if (count == 0)
    {
      tail = 0;
      head = 0;
      deque[0] = item;
    }
    else
    {
      ++tail;

      if (tail == deque.length)
        tail = 0;

      deque[tail] = item;
    }

    ++count;
  }
```

The `peekHead` and `peekTail` methods return references to `Object`s at opposite ends of the list.

```
  public Object peekHead()
  {
    if (count == 0)
      throw err_empty;
```

```
    return deque[head];
  }

  public Object peekTail()
  {
    if (count == 0)
      throw err_empty;

    return deque[tail];
  }
```

And then we have the `popHead` and `popTail` methods, which return references and remove items from a `FixedDeque`.

```
  public Object popHead()
  {
    if (count == 0)
      throw err_empty;

    Object result = deque[head];
    dequeue[head] = null;

    --count;

    if (count > 0)
    {
      ++head;

      if (head == deque.length)
        head = 0;
    }

    return result;
  }

  public Object popTail()
  {
    if (count == 0)
      throw err_empty;
```

```
      Object result = deque[tail];
      dequeue[tail] = null;

      --count;

      if (count > 0)
      {
        if (tail == 0)
          tail = deque.length - 1;
        else
          --tail;
      }

      return result;
    }
```

Finally, the ubiquitous property methods return information on the capacity and state of a `FixedDeque`.

```
    public int getCount()
    {
      return count;
    }

    public int getCapacity()
    {
      return deque.length;
    }

    public boolean isEmpty()
    {
      return count == 0;
    }
```

Heaps & Priority Queues

One of the most useful algorithmic tools is the priority queue, in which items are extracted in order of a value. Scheduling applications use priority queues to automatically organize data in order of creation time or priority. In simulation programs, a priority queue ensures that events occur in a specified order, even when new events join the queue. In most cases, a priority queue is a binary heap — usually just called a *heap* — which is an array of elements organized like a binary tree. Each array element corresponds to a tree node, and every level in the tree is completely filled before elements are added to the next level. The first array element is the root, and it always contains the largest value in the heap. Simple math calculates the indexes of parent and child nodes. For element i,

```
Parent index = i /2
Lesser child = 2 * i
Greater child = 2 * i + 1
```

Every node is less than or equal to its parent, a characteristic known as the *heap property*. The largest element is stored in the root, and subtrees contain progressively smaller values. This is a valid heap containing twelve letters:

X T O G S M N A E R A I

Operations on heaps include creation, insertion of new nodes, and the extraction of the largest (root) value. Inserting a new value involves a simple search through the tree, moving the new key upward from the root until the heap condition is met. Whenever the heap changes, it must be adjusted so that the heap property is maintained. This involves recursively exchanging larger child values with smaller parent nodes until the parent is larger than its children. This process is known by a number of names; I prefer to use the term *heapify* that I've found in several texts.

Extracting the largest value from a heap is quite simple: return the data in the heap's first element, then swap the last item in the heap into the first element. This reduces the size of the heap by one, and requires the *heapify* process to be invoked. Thus, as elements are removed from a heap, the highest value "sifts" down to the root. In this context, a heap acts as a priority queue, and the two are one and the same.

The `FixedHeap` class is an array-based container, just like the other types introduced in this chapter. The `heap` array contains references to elements, and the `count` field tracks the number of elements stored.

```
package coyote.tools;

//
//
// FixedHeap
//
//
public class FixedHeap
{
  //------------------------
  // fields
  //------------------------

  private Object [] heap;
  private int    count;
  private SortTool tool;

  //------------------------
  // exceptions
  //------------------------

  private FixedContainerException err_empty  =
    new FixedContainerException("pop on empty heap");

  private FixedContainerException err_full=
    new FixedContainerException("push on full heap");

  private FixedContainerException err_invalid =
    new FixedContainerException("invalid heap
        parameters");
```

A FixedHeap must be able to compare elements so that they can be properly sorted; to do so, I fall back upon the SortTool class developed for the sorting algorithms in Chapter 1. When calling the Fixed-Heap constructor, you must provide a reference for an object that will implement the SortTool interface for the type of data you'll be storing. In addition, the constructor requires you to specify the number of elements you want the heap to contain. The actual capacity of the heap will be the next largest power of two greater than the requested size, minus one. That value is chosen because, as a binary structure, a heap will contain one "root" element and an even number of children.

```
public FixedHeap
  (
  int capacity,
  SortTool tool
  )
{
  // verify parameters
  if ((capacity < 1) || (tool == null))
    throw err_invalid;

  // compute a power of two greater than capacity
  int c = 1;

  while (c < capacity)
    c *= 2;

  --c;

  // allocate data space
  heap = new Object [c];

  count = 0;

  this.tool = tool;
}
```

`FixedHeap` uses several utility methods to find the child and parent nodes of a specified element. The `get…` family of methods perform simple index calculations, and will be compiled as inline code by a sophisticated Java compiler.

```
protected int getBeforeIndex
  (
  int i
  )
{
  return ((i + 1) * 2) - 1;
}

protected int getAfterIndex
  (
```

```
  int i
  )
{
  return ((i + 1) * 2);
}


protected int getParentIndex
  (
  int i
  )
{
  return ((i + 1) / 2) - 1;
}
```

The `heapify` method performs the heapify operation. This is a recursive method, calling itself to "sift" the array into order.

```
protected void heapify
  (
  int i
  )
{
  // set beginning indexes
  int b = getBeforeIndex(i);
  int a = getAfterIndex(i);
  int largest;

  // choose greater of "less" child or current
  if ((b < count)
  && (tool.compare(heap[b],heap[i]) ==
      SortTool.COMP_GRTR))
    largest = b;
  else
    largest = i;

  // choose greater of "more" child and largest
  if ((a < count)
  && (tool.compare(heap[a],heap[largest]) ==
      SortTool.COMP_GRTR))
    largest = a;
```

```
  // if one of the children was greater, swap
  if (largest != i)
  {
    Object temp = heap[i];
    heap[i] = heap[largest];
    heap[largest] = temp;

    // recurse to further adjust heap
    heapify(largest);
  }
}
```

To insert a new object into the heap, the push method finds an insertion point and shifts elements to make room.

```
public void push
  (
  Object obj
  )
{
  // verify parameters
  if (count == heap.length)
    throw err_full;

  if (obj == null)
    throw err_invalid;

  // insertion sort
  int i = count;

  ++count;

  while ((i > 0)
  && (tool.compare(heap[getParentIndex(i)],obj) ==
      SortTool.COMP_LESS))
  {
    heap[i] = heap[getParentIndex(i)];
    i = getParentIndex(i);
  }

  heap[i] = obj;
}
```

The first element in a heap is always the greatest; the `peek` method returns a reference to `heap[0]`; `pop` not only returns the reference, but removes it from the list, swapping in the last element of the list into the first and calling `heapify` to reorganize the array.

```
public Object peek()
{
  // if heap is empty, complain
  if (count == 0)
    throw err_empty;

  return heap[0];
}

public Object pop()
{
  // if heap is empty, complain
  if (count == 0)
    throw err_empty;

  // remember largest item
  Object result = heap[0];
  heap[0] = null;

  // swap in last item in list
  heap[0] = heap[count - 1];
  --count;

  // adjust heap
  if (count > 0)
    heapify(0);

  // return stored result
  return result;
}
```

The interrogation methods require little explanation (and are probably getting a bit monotonous by now).

```
public int getCount()
  {
    return count;
  }

  public int getCapacity()
  {
    return heap.length;
  }

  public boolean isEmpty()
  {
    return count == 0;
  }
}
```

You'll find heaps most useful in implementing structures such as print queues, where you want to organize data based on a priority or time of submission. Remember that the SortTool interface allows you to customize the order of any type based on the requirements of a given application.

An Example

I built a basic applet to exercise the classes above. The display contains paired Labels and Lists, one pair for each of the four container types. The Lists contain the output from using a specific kind of container.

```
import java.applet.*;
import java.awt.*;
import java.util.*;

import coyote.tools.*;
import coyote.ui.*;

public class Chapter05
  extends Applet
{
```

```
        private List stackList;
        private List queueList;
        private List dequeList;
        private List heapList;
        private FixedStack stack;
        private FixedQueue queue;
        private FixedDeque deque;
        private FixedHeap heap;

        private boolean simple = false;

        private final int CAPACITY = 32;
        private final int TEST_SIZE = 25;
```

All the important action takes place in the init method; the applet will take a few seconds to load as it goes through its paces. I begin init by creating the labels and containers, adding them to the applet window. I use a VFlowLayout (defined in Chapter 4) to organize the components into a column. For the FixedHeap, I create a StringSortTool (defined in Chapter 1) to compare objects.

```
    public void init()
    {
      setSize(140, 400);
      setLayout(new VFlowLayout());
      setBackground(Color.lightGray);

      Dimension d;

      // set up stack and display components
      add(new Label("Stack List:"));
      stackList = new List();
      add(stackList);

      stack = new FixedStack(CAPACITY);

      // set up queue and display components
      add(new Label("Queue List:"));
```

```
queueList = new List();
add(queueList);
queue = new FixedQueue(CAPACITY);

// set up deque and display components
add(new Label("Deque List:"));
dequeList = new List();
add(dequeList);

deque = new FixedDeque(CAPACITY);

// set up heap and display components
add(new Label("Heap List:"));
heapList = new List();
add(heapList);

heap = new FixedHeap(CAPACITY,new
    StringSortTool());
```

The first loop loads twenty-five numbers into each container. For deque, I load odd numbers at the head and even numbers at the tail; I convert the integers to Strings for storage in the heap.

```
int n;

// store values
for (n = 0; n < TEST_SIZE; ++n)
{
  stack.push(new Integer(n));
  queue.push(new Integer(n));

  if ((n & 1) == 1)
    deque.pushHead(new Integer(n));
  else
    deque.pushTail(new Integer(n));

  heap.push(String.valueOf(n));
}
```

The `boolean` value `simple` determines the rest of the test. When true, `simple` specifies that the test just pop elements and store their `String` representation in the appropriate `List`. When `simple` is `false` (as it is in this example), I perform fifty random operations on `stack`, `queue`, and `heap`, reporting the results in their `Lists`. For `heap`, I simply pop all the stored values.

```
if (simple)
{
  // retrieve and load values into lists
  for (n = 0; n < TEST_SIZE; ++n)
  {
    // reverse order
    Integer i = (Integer)stack.pop();
    stackList.add(i.toString());


    // in order
    i = (Integer)queue.pop();
    queueList.add(i.toString());


    // alternate order
    if ((n & 1) == 1)
      i = (Integer)deque.popTail();
    else
      i = (Integer)deque.popHead();


    dequeList.add(i.toString());
  }
}
else
{
  Random rand = new Random();

  for (n = 0; n < TEST_SIZE * 2; ++n)
  {
    int v = (n + 1) * 100 + 1;
    int choice;
    Integer i;
```

```
// stack operation
choice = rand.nextInt();


try
{
  if ((choice & 1) == 1)
  {
    stack.push(new Integer(v));
    stackList.add("Pushing " + v);
  }
  else
  {
    i = (Integer)stack.pop();
    stackList.add("Popping " + i.toString());
  }
}
catch (FixedContainerException x)
{
  stackList.add("XXX: " + x.getMessage());
}


// queue operation
choice = rand.nextInt();


try
{
  if ((choice & 1) == 1)
  {
    queue.push(new Integer(v));
    queueList.add("Pushing " + v);
  }
  else
  {
    i = (Integer)queue.pop();
    queueList.add("Popping " + i.toString());
  }
}
catch (FixedContainerException x)
{
```

```
                 queueList.add("XXX: " + x.getMessage());
             }
             // deque operation
             choice = rand.nextInt() % 4;

             try
             {
               switch (choice)
               {
               case 0:
                 deque.pushHead(new Integer(v));
                 dequeList.add("PushHead " + v);
                 break;
               case 1:
                 deque.pushTail(new Integer(v));
                 dequeList.add("PushTail " + v);
                 break;
               case 2:
                 i = (Integer)deque.popHead();
                 dequeList.add("PopHead " + i.toString());
                 break;
               case 3:
                 i = (Integer)deque.popTail();
                 dequeList.add("PopTail " + i.toString());
                 break;
               }
             }
             catch (FixedContainerException x)
             {
               dequeList.add("XXX: " + x.getMessage());
             }
           }
         }

         for (n = 0; n < TEST_SIZE; ++n)
           heapList.add((String)heap.popMax());
```

When executed, the applet display will look something like Figure 5-1. Results will vary, depending on how the Random class is implemented for your version of Java.

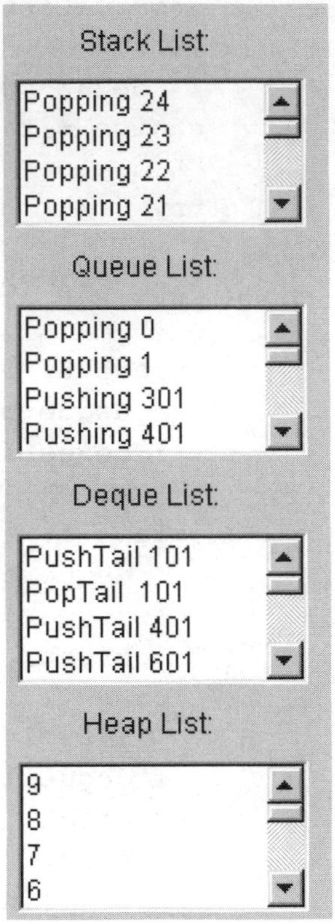

Figure 5-1
A Container Example

I've found these classes to be very effective in many applications; they're small, fast, and reliable. Perhaps their only weakness is a common one they share with many Java classes: their reliance on `Object` for managing generic objects. In using `Object`, these containers require that you convert simple data types to class objects like `Integer`. However, since few applications will be building containers for simple types, I don't see this as a serious limitation.

Onward

Containers come in many types; this chapter looked into some of the fundamental types. Now I'll move on to looking at binary trees, including types that "balance" their elements to provide efficient access.

Chapter 6

Tree Structures

A *binary tree* is a container that provides access to its elements in a specific order based on its internal structure and algorithms. Such a structure may be the perfect choice when your program must automatically store data in sorted order. You build a binary tree from *nodes* that contain objects; each node has a link to two *child* nodes, representing subtrees of greater and lesser objects. The *root* node marks the base of the tree; at the ends of the tree lie the *leaf* nodes, which have no children. By following the links from parent to child, a program can access the stored objects in sorted order.

Binary Trees

In this chapter's figures, each node is a box; we'll assume, for the sake of discussion, that each node contains an object, or *key*, holding a single alphabetic character. Lines show links by connecting the lower left- and right-hand corners of a parent node to the center top of a child node. Lesser nodes are linked on the left; greater nodes are linked on the right.

Figure 6-1 shows a binary tree. K is the root of the tree, and it is the parent of G and M. Notice that a node can be both a parent and a child; G is a child of K and the parent of D and H. The nodes containing the A, E, H, N, and S keys are leaf nodes.

Figure 6-1
A Binary Tree

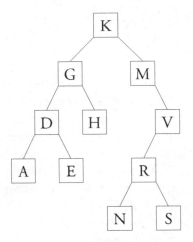

Searching

The algorithm for finding a key in a binary tree begins by comparing the search key to the key stored in the root node. If the keys don't match, the algorithm follows the links to other nodes in the tree based on the relationship between the search key and the keys in the nodes. For example, if the search key is less than the root key, we follow the left link to the next node; if the search key is greater than the root key, we follow the right link. The newly-selected node is now treated just as the root was, by comparing the search key against the node key and selecting the next search node. If the link to be followed does not connect to a child node, the search key is not in the tree.

The arrows in Figure 6-2 show the links followed by the algorithm in searching for the key E. Since E is less than the root node key K, the algorithm follows the left link. E is less than G, so again we follow the left link. E is greater than D, and we follow the right link to the node that contains E.

Figure 6-2

Searching for *E* in a
Binary Tree

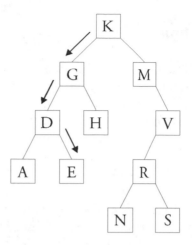

Figure 6-3 shows the procedure followed when searching for the
non-existent key *T*. The search begins again at the root, and travels
down through the tree until it reaches the *S* node. *T* would be connected to the right of *S* if it were in the tree. Instead, the algorithm
encounters a null link in node *S*, and knows that *T* is not resident in
the tree.

Figure 6-3

Searching for a
Non-Existent Node

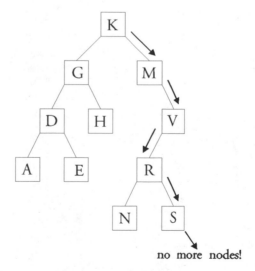

no more nodes!

The binary tree search is recursive. Start at the root node, compare keys, and select another node. Compare keys, and select another node, and so on, until a null link is reached or the key is found.

Insertion

The first node inserted into a binary tree becomes the root node. Inserting subsequent nodes involves searching the tree for the proper location. If the key being inserted is not found, the search will end at a null link. When a null link is encountered, a new leaf node is constructed and linked to that part of the tree.

Figure 6-4 assumes that insertion begins with an empty tree, and shows the results of inserting each of the keys C, A, R, K, D, and U, in that order. The first key inserted, C, becomes the root node. A is less than C, so it is attached to the left of C as a new node; R is greater than C and it links to C's right side. K is greater than C but less than R, placing it left of R. D is greater than C and less than R and K, so it is attached to K's left link. The U is greater than C and R, and it goes on R's right side.

Figure 6-4
Binary Tree
Insertion

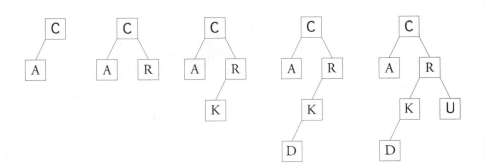

Figure 6-5 shows the tree after adding the additional keys P, B, E, N, X, Z, and S. You may notice that more nodes are greater than the root, giving the tree a lopsided appearance. For now, we'll ignore this problem; I'll be addressing it later in the chapter.

Figure 6-5

The Result of Inserting
More Nodes

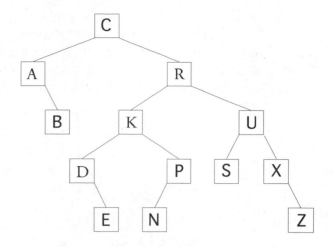

Deletion

Deleting a node from a tree requires that we handle one of three situations. The node will be childless, or it will have one or two links to
child nodes; the algorithm must adjust the tree's nodes to ensure
that all remaining keys have the proper, in-order connections.

Figure 6-6 shows how deletion of the *H* node affects the tree. Since
H is a leaf node, it is deleted simply by setting the link from its parent to `null`. Deleting a leaf node does not require us to change the
organization of other nodes. When a parent node is deleted from a
binary tree, all of its child nodes must be relinked to the tree.

Figure 6-6

Deleting a leaf node

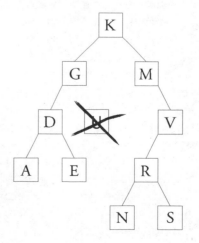

In Figure 6-7, you can see what happens when a single child is deleted from a binary tree. The deleted node is replaced by its child; in this case, G is replaced by D. All children of a node have the same relationship to the node's parent as does the node, so replacing a deleted node with its child maintains the integrity of the tree's organization.

Figure 6-7
Deleting a Parent
Node with One Child

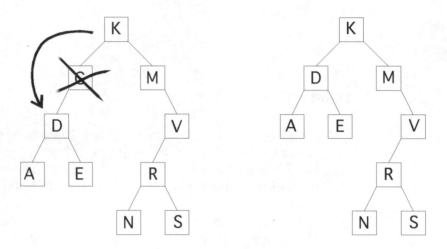

When deleting a two-child node from the tree, we need to use a more complicated algorithm, as shown in Figure 6-8. The deleted node is replaced by its immediate successor, which is defined as the node that immediately follows the deleted node in sequence. The successor node is found by moving to the "greater" child's node, and then travelling from there along the "lesser" children until a leaf is reached. In Figure 6-8, N immediately follows M and is therefore its successor. The data stored in N — such as the key value — is transferred to the deleted node M. All of M's links, however, remain intact. Once the successor node has replaced the deleted node, the algorithm deletes the original successor node from the tree. In the case above, M is removed from the tree and replaced with spliced-in node N. The relationship of the keys remains intact.

Figure 6-8

Deleting a
Parent Node
with Two
Children

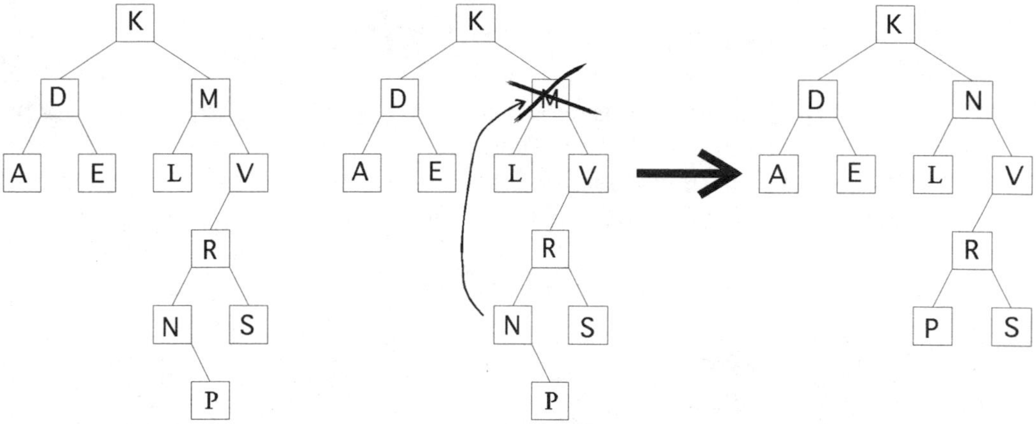

Exceptions

Now it's time to implement binary trees in Java. To track all
exceptions thrown from these classes, I derived a class from
`RuntimeException`.

```
package coyote.tools;

import java.lang.RuntimeException;

public class BinaryTreeException
  extends RuntimeException
{

  public BinaryTreeException()
  {
    super();
  }

  public BinaryTreeException(String s)
  {
    super(s);
  }

}
```

Implementing a Binary Tree

The `BinaryTree` class begins by creating an inner class named `Node` that defines the structure of the linked nodes in the tree. `Node` is a protected class; new `Node` objects cannot be created outside the context of the `BinaryTree` class.

```
package coyote.tools;

//
//
// BinaryTree
//
//
public class BinaryTree
  implements Iterable
{
  // class-global constant
  public final Node SENTINEL = new Node();

  //------------------------
  // inner classes
  //------------------------
  protected class Node
  {
    //------------------------
    // fields
    //------------------------
    public Node prev;
    public Node next;
    public Node parent;

    public Object content;

    //------------------------
    // constructors
    //------------------------

    // construct sentinel node
    protected Node()
```

```
      {
        prev= this;
        next= this;
        parent  = null;

        content = null;
      }

      // construct new node
      public Node
        (
        Object obj
        )
      {
        prev    = SENTINEL;
        next    = SENTINEL;
        parent = SENTINEL;

        content = obj;
      ]
    }
```

The **prev** member points to a child node containing a lesser key; the **next** member points to a child node containing a greater key. The **parent** pointer is a backward link to the node's parent; deletion of nodes from the tree is greatly simplified when a link provides the address of the parent node. A reference to the node's **Object** data is stored in **content**.

The binary tree identifies null node links as those for which the **prev** or **next** pointers reference a special node called a **SENTINEL**. The **SENTINEL** could be **null**, which is the way most binary trees indicate empty nodes — but in the case of more advanced binary tree types (such as the red-black trees shown later in this chapter) the sentinel is actually a special node that points to itself. As you'll see later, use of a sentinel node greatly simplifies the implementation of red-black trees. In the case of **BinaryTree**, the constant **SENTINEL** is unique for each tree, defined at compile time by a call to the protected constructor **Node()**.

Notes

Some purists may argue that Node *should define its data members as private, allowing access only through property methods. In the case of utilitarian inner classes, I consider such practices to be unnecessary and confusing.* Node *is an integral part of* BinaryTree, *never used outside the scope of the enclosing class' methods. In essence,* Node *acts very much like a C or C++* struct — *providing a basic tool for combining several pieces of related data into a single object.*

Iterators

Unlike an array, the elements of a binary tree can't easily be retrieved using an integer index, since the data isn't stored in a linear fashion. To access the content of a binary tree, an iterator is an excellent tool. Essentially, an iterator is an object that knows how the information is stored in a given container; the iterator can "move" through the data in order, just as an index can move backward and forward through the elements of an array. The concept of iterators is applicable to any container type, particular a complex container like a binary tree.

While all iterators have common features, each container will implement a unique iterator type based on its internal structure. In Java, I implemented an interface to describe the iterator type; each container class will then define its own type implementing this interface.

```
package coyote.tools;

public interface Iterator
{
  // move to first element
  void goFirst();

  // move to last element
  void goLast();

  // move to next (greater) element
  void next();
```

```
    // move to previous (lesser) element
    void prev();

    // true if this iterator points to a valid object
    boolean isValid();

    // return reference to current object
    Object getObject();
}
```

For a binary tree, an iterator would point to some node in the tree. The iterator interface declares a `getObject` method to return a reference to the current object. The `goFirst` and `goLast` methods set the iterator to respective ends of the list, while the `next` and `prev` methods move the iterator's reference forward and backward in the container's content. Using these methods, an iterator can traverse the container from end to end, in order and in reverse order.

Most iterators will access the internal fields and methods of its associated class; this makes iterators excellent candidates for implementation as inner classes. Each container type then implements the interface `Iterable`, returning a reference to an instance of the inner class in the `makeIterator` method.

```
package coyote.tools;

public interface Iterable
{
    Iterator makeIterator();
}
```

The inner class `BinaryTreeIterator` defines the implementation of iterators for the `BinaryTree` class.

```
    protected class BinaryTreeIterator
        implements Iterator
    {
        //-------------------------
        // fields
        //-------------------------
        protected Node    current;
```

```
//-----------------------
// constructors
//-----------------------
public BinaryTreeIterator()
{
  ++locks;
  goFirst();
}

protected void finalize()
{
  --locks;
}


//-----------------------
// methods
//-----------------------

// move to first element
public void goFirst()
{
  current = minimum(root);
}

// move to last element
public void goLast()
{
  current = maximum(root);
}

// move to next (greater) element
public void next()
{
  current = successor(current);
}

// move to previous (lesser) element
public void prev()
{
  current = predecessor(current);
}
```

```
    // true if this iterator points to a valid object
    public boolean isValid()
    {
      return current != SENTINEL;
    }

    // return reference to current object
    public Object getObject()
    {
      return current.content;
    }
  }
```

As an inner class, a `BinaryTreeIterator` "knows" which `Binary-Tree` object it is associated with, and can freely reference enclosing class methods and fields. In this case, `BinaryTreeIterator` uses utility methods defined by `BinaryTree` in positioning the content reference.

```
public Iterator makeIterator()
  {
    return new BinaryTreeIterator();
  }
```

With its inner classes defined, `BinaryTree` declares four fields, including a reference to the `root` node, a `SortTool` (see Chapter 1) for comparing objects, a `count` of items stored, and a lock count.

```
    //------------------------
    // fields
    //--------------------------

    // root node
    protected Node root;

    // tool for sorting
    protected SortTool tool;

    // number of elements resident
    protected int count;

    // number of iterator locks
    protected int locks;
```

The lock count is necessary because more than one iterator can exist contemporaneously, allowing different sections of a program to examine the same container in different ways. A problem arises if an iterator references a node that is changed by some manipulation — insertion or deletion, for example — of its tree. To prevent that problem, I've incorporated the theory of "locks" into my binary trees. The creation of an iterator object increments the lock count; when an iterator is destroyed, its `finalize` method decrements the lock count. If the lock count is greater than zero, a binary tree will throw an exception for an operation that might potentially affect an iterator. In this way, I prevent items from being inserted into or deleted from a binary tree for which an active iterator exists. This design isn't meant to handle multi-threaded synchronization; the goal is to prevent modifcations to the tree that could disrupt the actions of an iterator.

The two exceptions that can be thrown from a `BinaryTree` are:

```
//--------------------------
// exceptions
//--------------------------

protected BinaryTreeException err_not_found =
  new BinaryTreeException("item not found in binary
        tree");

protected BinaryTreeException err_locked=
  new BinaryTreeException("binary tree locked");
```

Constructors and Properties

The constructor for a `BinaryTree` requires a single parameter: a reference to a `SortTool` object that handles comparisons between the types of objects that will be stored. I also provide property methods to return the number of objects stored in a tree and the number of iterator locks in place.

```
//--------------------------
// constructors
//--------------------------
```

```
public BinaryTree
  (
  SortTool tool
  )
{
  this.tool = tool;

  root  = SENTINEL;
  count = 0;
  locks = 0;
}


//------------------------
// properties
//------------------------
public int getLocks()
{
  return locks;
}

public int getCount()
{
  return count;
}
```

Utility Methods

I created a set of **protected** utility methods that provide services to **BinaryTree** and its iterator class. These methods follow the algorithms described at the beginning of the chapter, providing tools for finding nodes relative to each other.

```
//------------------------
// internal utility methods
//------------------------
protected Node minimum
  (
  Node n
  )
{
```

```
    if (n != SENTINEL)
      while (n.prev != SENTINEL)
        n = n.prev;


    return n;
}


protected Node maximum
  (
  Node n
  )
{
  if (n != SENTINEL)
    while (n.next != SENTINEL)
      n = n.next;


  return n;
}


protected Node predecessor
  (
  Node n
  )
{
  Node x, y;

  if (n.prev != SENTINEL)
    return maximum(n.prev);
  else
  {
    x = n;
    y = n.parent;

    while ((y != SENTINEL) && (x == y.prev))
    {
      x = y;
      y = y.parent;
    }
  }
```

```
        return y;
    }

    protected Node successor
      (
      Node n
      )
    {
      Node x, y;

      if (n.next != SENTINEL)
        return minimum(n.next);
      else
      {
        x = n;
        y = n.parent;

        while ((y != SENTINEL) && (x == y.next))
        {
          x = y;
          y = y.parent;
        }
      }

      return y;
    }

    protected Node search
      (
      Object item
      )
    {
      Node n = root;

      while ((n != SENTINEL) && (n.content != item))
      {
        if (tool.compare(item,n.content) ==
            SortTool.COMP_LESS)
          n = n.prev;
        else
          n = n.next;
      }
```

```
      if (n.content == item)
        return n;
      else
        throw err_not_found;
  }
```

The `search` utility function finds the node that contains a specific data item. Beginning at the root, `search` follows the node links by comparing the requested item against node contents using a `Sort-Tool`. If `search` finds a `SENTINEL` node, it has reached the end of the tree; it throws an exception if the item was not found.

Adding and Removing Objects

The `add` function calls the internal `insert` method to perform a standard binary tree insertion. Why not implement the `insert` code in `add` and eliminate a method call? Because subclasses of `Binary-Tree` will need to reference the node where new data was inserted into the tree. Since I don't want `add` to return a `Node` (the latter being an inner class), I created `insert` to create a new `Object` and return a reference to its `Node`. Subclasses of `BinaryTree` will override `add`, calling `insert` before implementing additional capabilities.

```
protected Node insert
  (
  Object item
  )
{
  if (locks > 0)
    throw err_locked;

  Node y = SENTINEL;
  Node x = root;

  while (x != SENTINEL)
  {
    y = x;

    if (item.equals(x.content))
      return null;
```

```
      else
      {
        if (tool.compare(item,x.content) ==
            SortTool.COMP_LESS)
          x = x.prev;
        else
          x = x.next;
      }
    }

    Node z = new Node(item);
    z.parent = y;

    if (y == SENTINEL)
      root = z;
    else
    {
      if (tool.compare(z.content,y.content) ==
          SortTool.COMP_LESS)
        y.prev = z;
      else
        y.next = z;
    }

    return z;
  }
```

After it creates a node, **insert** searches the tree for the data value. If a match is found, the new node replaces the existing one using the original links and parent. Otherwise, the search ends at a sentinel link that is to be replaced by the new node.

```
public void add
  (
  Object item
  )
{
  insert(item);
}
```

Deleting an item involves the removal of nodes with zero, one, or two links. Provided with an Object reference, remove begins by searching for its target. If the given Object isn't found, remove throws an exception. Otherwise, the located node is deleted and the tree adjusted. If the deleted node is the only node in the tree, remove leaves an empty tree. If the node has only one child, that child replaces the deleted node, becoming the new root if the root node is being deleted. If both of the previous two cases aren't true, the node has two children and is replaced by its immediate successor.

```
public void remove
  (
  Object item
  )
{
  if (locks > 0)
    throw err_locked;

  // find node
  Node z = search(item);

  if (z == SENTINEL)
    throw err_not_found;

  // locate node to be sliced out
  Node x, y;

  if ((z.prev == SENTINEL) || (z.next == SENTINEL))
    y = z;
  else
    y = successor(z);

  // find child to replace with y
  if (y.prev == SENTINEL)
    x = y.next;
  else
    x = y.prev;

  // splice child onto parent
  if (x != SENTINEL)
    x.parent = y.parent;
```

```
            if (y.parent == SENTINEL)
              root = x;
            else
            {
              // splice child node
              if (y == y.parent.prev)
                y.parent.prev = x;
              else
                y.parent.next = x;
            }

            // do we need to save y?
            if (y != z)
              z.content = y.content;
          }
```

Limitations

Binary trees sort information as it is inserted, making them very useful for application where dynamic information must be organized. Binary trees, however, have a problem with balance. Figure 6-9 shows a tree constructed from the keys *C, A, R, K, D, U, P, B, E, N, X, Z,* and *S,* inserted in that order. The tree has two nodes left of the root and 10 nodes to its right. Searching for a key greater than *C* can require up to five comparisons, while an optimal tree would require only three comparisons.

Figure 6-9
An Unbalanced
Binary Tree

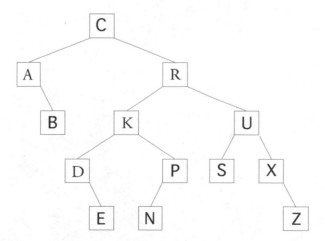

A tree is balanced when it has equal numbers of nodes on both sides of its root. For example, inserting the same set of keys in a different order will result in a perfectly balanced tree. Figure 6-10 shows the keys inserted in the order *NCUBADEKRPSXZ*. *N* is a good root value, since it is near the median value of all keys; *C* was a bad root value in Figure 6-9, because it tended toward one end of the range of values.

Figure 6-10
A Balanced
Binary Tree

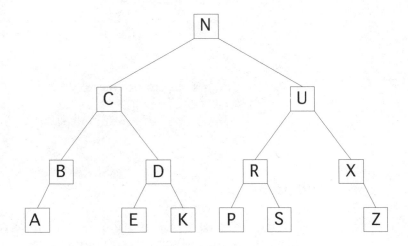

Figure 6-11 shows a binary tree generated from the keys *A*, *B*, *C*, *D*, *E*, and *F*. Since each subsequent node is greater than its predecessor, the binary tree degenerates into a linked list. A search on a linked list is very inefficient, and all benefits of a binary tree are lost.

Figure 6-11
A Degenerate
Binary Tree

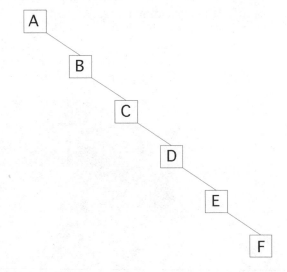

Sorted and almost-sorted data is common, and, as with QuickSort, computer scientists have developed several schemes for lessening the impact of sorted data. Balancing and nearly balancing binary trees requires sophisticated rearrangement of the tree as nodes are added and deleted.

Red Black Trees

Red black trees are a binary tree derivative which use a marking technique to ensure that portions of the tree do not become massively imbalanced with other parts of the tree. Each red-black tree node contains a color marker, which can be either "red" or "black." All red-black nodes follow this set of rules:

1. Every node is either red or black.

2. Every leaf (sentinel) node is considered black.

3. If a node is red, its children are black.

4. All paths from a node to descendant leaves will contain the same number of black nodes.

The number of black nodes in any path is that path's "black height." The rules above ensure that a red-black tree is approximately balanced; no path through the tree can be more than twice as long as its sibling path.

Red Black Tree Class

For the most part, red-black trees operate exactly like standard binary trees; only insertion and deletion change substantially, because they need to maintain the four color rules specified above. Red-black trees, then, should be derived from `BinaryTrees`.

```
package coyote.tools;

public class RedBlackTree
   extends BinaryTree
```

```
{
  //-------------------------
  // inner classes
  //-------------------------

  protected class RBData
  {
    // fields
    public boolean red;
    public Object  content;

    // constructors
    public RBData
      (
      Object item
      )
    {
      red = false;
      content = item;
    }
  }
```

Each red-black node contains a color indicator not found in standard binary nodes. The most effective way I've found to do this is by
creating a template for an auxiliary data structure, RBData, that
combines a data item and color indicator. The red field is true when
the node is "red," and false when the node is "black." The actual
object for a node is referenced by content. When a RedBlackTree
creates a node, it does so by allocating a new RBTree object and
inserting that into the tree structure.

Iterators

Since the data elements in a RedBlackTree reside within RBData
structures, I created RedBlackIterator to add an extra level of
indirection to BinaryTree. The getObject method dereferences the
current Node's content pointer to an RBTree object and returns a
reference to the actual object being stored.

```
protected class RBTreeIterator
   extends BinaryTreeIterator
{
  // constructors
  public RBTreeIterator()
  {
    super();
  }

  // return reference to current object
  public Object getObject()
  {
    return ((RBData)(current.content)).content;
  }
}
```

BinaryTreeIterator is a protected inner class of BinaryTree, allowing it to be extended by BinaryTree's subclass RedBlackIterator. RedBlackTree overrides the makeIterator method to return a RedBlackIterator.

```
public Iterator makeIterator()
{
  return new RBTreeIterator();
}
```

Sorting Tools

When creating a BinaryTree, the constructor requires a reference to a SortTool that will compare the relative values of the Objects being stored in the container. With RedBlackTree, the use of RBData objects complicates the matter, since the SortTool will need to compare the content of RBData items and not the RBData objects themselves. I created the RBDataSortTool inner class to solve this problem, providing a layer of indirection over the SortTool much as RedBlackIterator provides access to the inner data of nodes containing RBData objects.

```
protected class RBDataSortTool
  implements SortTool
{
  // fields
  SortTool tool;

  // constructor
  public RBDataSortTool
    (
    SortTool tool
    )
  {
    tool = tool;
  }

  // comparison method
  public int compare
    (
    Object x1,
    Object x2
    )
  {
    return tool.compare(((RBData)x1).content,
        ((RBData)x2).content);
  }
}
```

Constructors and Destructors

The constructor creates an RBDataSortTool from the given Sort-
Tool, and calls the superclass constructor.

```
public RedBlackTree
  (
  SortTool tool
  )
{
  super(null);

  this.tool = new RBDataSortTool(tool);
}
```

Utility Functions

RedBlackTree requires several utility methods in addition to those inherited from BinaryTree. The rotateLeft and rotateRight methods exchange (in opposite directions) the two subtrees of a node, in keeping the red-black tree organized according to its special rules.

```
protected void rotateLeft
  (
  Node n
  )
{
  Node y = n.next;

  // turn y's left subtrree into n's right subtree
  n.next = y.prev;

  if (y.prev != SENTINEL)
    y.prev.parent - n;

  // link n's parent to y
  y.parent = n.parent;

  if (n.parent == SENTINEL)
    root = y;
  else
  {
    if (n == n.parent.prev)
      n.parent.prev = y;
    else
      n.parent.next = y;
  }

  // put n on y's left
  y.prev    = n;
  n.parent = y;
}

protected void rotateRight
  (
```

```
    Node n
    )
{
  Node y = n.prev;

  // turn y's left subtrree into n's right subtree
  n.prev = y.next;

  if (y.next != SENTINEL)
    y.next.parent = n;

  // link n's parent to y
  y.parent = n.parent;

  if (n.parent == SENTINEL)
    root = y;
  else
  {
    if (n == n.parent.next)
      n.parent.next = y;
    else
      n.parent.prev = y;
  }

  // put n on y's left
  y.next   = n;
  n.parent = y;
}


protected void deleteFixup
  (
  Node n
  )
{
  Node w, x = n;

  while ((x != root) && (!((RBData)(x.content)).red))
  {
    if (x == x.parent.prev)
    {
      w = x.parent.next;
```

```
                    if (((RBData)(w.content)).red)
                    {
                      ((RBData)(w.content)).red          = false;
                      ((RBData)(x.parent.content)).red = true;
                      rotateLeft(x.parent);
                      w = x.parent.next;
                    }

                    if ((!((RBData)(w.prev.content)).red)
                    && (!((RBData)(w.next.content)).red))
                    {
                      ((RBData)(w.content)).red = true;
                      x = x.parent;
                    }
                    else
                    {
                      if (!((RBData)(w.next.content)).red)
                      {
                        ((RBData)(w.prev.content)).red = false;
                        ((RBData)(w.content)).red        = true;
                        rotateRight(w);
                        w = x.parent.next;
                      }

                      ((RBData)(w.content)).red =
                              ((RBData)(x.parent.content)).red;
                      ((RBData)(x.parent.content)).red = false;
                      ((RBData)(w.next.content)).red    = false;
                      rotateLeft(x.parent);
                      x = root;
                    }
                  }
                  else
                  {
                    w = x.parent.prev;

                    if (((RBData)(w.content)).red)
                    {
                      ((RBData)(w.content)).red          = false;
                      ((RBData)(x.parent.content)).red = true;
                      rotateRight(x.parent);
```

```
            w = x.parent.prev;
        }

        if ((!((RBData)(w.next.content)).red)
        && (!((RBData)(w.prev.content)).red))
        {
          ((RBData)(w.content)).red = true;
          x = x.parent;
        }
        else
        {
          if (!((RBData)(w.prev.content)).red)
          {
            ((RBData)(w.next.content)).red = false;
            ((RBData)(w.content)).red        = true;
            rotateLeft(w);
            w = x.parent.prev;
          }

          ((RBData)(w.content)).red =
                ((RBData)(x.parent.content)).red;
          ((RBData)(x.parent.content)).red = false;
          ((RBData)(w.prev.content)).red   = false;
          rotateRight(x.parent);
          x = root;
        }
      }
    }

    ((RBData)(x.content)).red = false;
  }
```

Insertion

The add method begins by calling insert to insert a new node into
the tree. Then the RedBlackTree.add function moves up the tree,
rotating subtrees to restore the red-black tree conditions.

```
public void add
  (
  Object item
  )
{
  // create a new item
  RBData rbitem = new RBData(item);

  // insert the item into the tree
  Node y, x = insert(rbitem);

  // mark new node as true;
  ((RBData)(x.content)).red = true;

  // adjust the tree
  while ((x != root) && (((RBData)(x.parent.
      content)).red))
  {
    if (x.parent == x.parent.parent.prev)
    {
      y = x.parent.parent.next;

      if (((RBData)(y.content)).red)
      {
        ((RBData)(x.parent.content)).red = false;
        ((RBData)(y.content)).red         = false;
        ((RBData)(x.parent.parent.content)).red =
            true;
        x = x.parent.parent;
      }
      else
      {
        if (x == x.parent.next)
        {
          x = x.parent;
          rotateLeft(x);
        }

        ((RBData)(x.parent.content)).red= false;
        ((RBData)(x.parent.parent.content)).red =
            true;
```

```
            rotateRight(x.parent.parent);
        }
    }
    else
    {
      y = x.parent.parent.prev;

      if (((RBData)(y.content)).red)
      {
        ((RBData)(x.parent.content)).red = false;
        ((RBData)(y.content)).red        = false;
        ((RBData)(x.parent.parent.content)).red =
            true;
        x = x.parent.parent;
      }
      else
      {
        if (x == x.parent.prev)
        {
          x = x.parent;
          rotateRight(x);
        }

        ((RBData)(x.parent.content)).red = false;
        ((RBData)(x.parent.parent.content)).red =
            true;
        rotateLeft(x.parent.parent);
      }
    }
  }
}
```

Deletion

When a black node is deleted from the tree, it causes any path containing the removed node to have one fewer black node, thus possibly violating the red-black tree conditions. The problem is corrected by pretending that an extra "black" node is connected to x; this artificial "blackness" is moved toward the root until a red node is found or the root is encountered. If a red node is found, it is colored black; if the loop reaches the root, the blackness is simply discarded. After a node is deleted, `deleteFixup` adjusts the tree. In essence, it travels down through the tree, rotating nodes until the red-black tree conditions are met.

```
public void remove
    (
    Object item
    )
  {
    if (locks > 0)
      throw err_locked;

    // find node
    Node z = search(item);

    if (z == SENTINEL)
      throw err_not_found;

    // find node to splice out
    Node x, y;

    if ((z.prev == SENTINEL) || (z.next == SENTINEL))
      y = z;
    else
      y = successor(z);

    // find child to replace y
    if (y.prev == SENTINEL)
      x = y.prev;
    else
      x = y.next;

    // splice child to parent
    x.parent = y.parent;

    if (y.parent == SENTINEL)
      root = x;
    else
    {
      // splice
```

```
        if (y == y.parent.prev)
          y.parent.prev = x;
        else
          y.parent.next = x;
      }

      // save y if necessary
      if (y != z)
        z.content = y.content;

      // adjust tree for red-black rules
      if (!((RBData)(y.content)).red)
        deleteFixup(x);
    }
```

remove is almost — but not quite — identical to the Binary-
Tree::remove function. The assignment of y's parent as x's parent is
automatic; if x points to SENTINEL, its parent pointer now points to
y's parent. If y is black, a call to deleteFixup adjusts the tree based
on x. At that call, x is the node that was y's sole child before y was
spliced out of the tree — or x is the SENTINEL if y had no children. In
any case, x's parent pointer will reference the parent of y, allowing
deleteFixup to treat x in a generic fashion.

Onward

In a later chapter, I'll expand on our discussion of binary trees,
looking at data structures the efficiently in indexing large quantities
of data stored in files. But right now, I'm going to examine another
useful tool, the finite state machine — which is, essentially, a program within a program. Any application can be defined in terms of a
given set of states and an associated set of rules for changing states
based on inputs. In the next chapter, I'll show you how to implement
these finite state machines in Java.

7

Finite State Machines and Evolving Software

An introduction to finite state machines (FSMs) is a part of most college courses in algorithm development. The concept of a FSM is simple: the machine contains a specific number of distinct internal states, of which one represents the currently active state. A finite set of input symbols is mapped to a finite set of output symbols by each state; an input symbol is given to the FSM, which returns an output symbol before making a possible transition to a new state.

FSM Design

Figure 7-1 shows a 3-state machine with an input alphabet of { 0, 1 } and an output set of {A , B, C }.

Figure 7-1

A Finite
State Machine

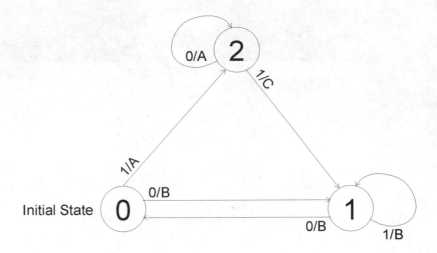

The following table shows how a sequence of input values produces an output string and state changes within the machine.

Table 7-1

Running the FSM

Current State	Input Symbol	Output Symbol	Next State
0 (initial)	1	A	2
2	0	A	2
2	1	C	1
1	1	B	1
1	0	B	0
0	0	B	1
1	0	B	0
0	1	A	2

The FSM in Figure 7-1 mapped the input string 11010001 to the output string AACBBBBA. While diagramming a FSM shows how it works graphically, a program can implement FSM as a simple two-dimensional look-up table with a number of rows equal to the number of states, and a number of columns equal to the size of the input alphabet. The following table shows the example finite state machine as a 3-by-2 table, with each element containing an output symbol and new state in the form O/S.

Table 7-2

The FSM as Table

	Input 0	Input 1
State 0	B/1	A/2
State 1	B/0	B/1
State 2	A/2	C/1

Finite state machines are computationally complete, meaning that a finite state machine can be constructed to accomplish any programmatic task. You can think of a FSM as a program or algorithm, and you'll find them at use in database search routines, string comparison algorithms, and robotic control systems.

Exceptions

Before taking a look at finite state machines themselves, I'll introduce a class for handling their exceptions. These include attempts at creating invalid machines and errors in changing state.

```
package coyote.tools;

public class FSMException
  extends RuntimeException
{
  public FSMException()
  {
    super();
  }

  public FSMException(String s)
  {
    super(s);
  }
}
```

Transitions

A "transition" object defines the output symbol and new state for a given input symbol. The FSMTransition class defines a simple structure to encapsulate transition data.

```
package coyote.tools;

public class FSMTransition
{
  //——————————-
  // fields
  //——————————-
  public int newState;
  public int output;

  //——————————-
  // constructors
  //——————————-
  public FSMTransition()
  {
    newState = 0;
    output   = 0;
  }

  public FSMTransition
    (
    int ns,
    int out
    )
  {
    newState = ns;
    output   = out;
  }
}
```

The FiniteStateMachine class contains an array of FSMTransition objects that define how the machine responds to various input symbols. Output symbols are generic Objects, allowing you to use any type of data as the output of a finite state machine.

The FSM Class

Finite state machines, for all their inherent complexity, are quite simple in implementation. The entire FiniteStateMachine class is just a bit more than 100 lines in length, including comments and whitespace! Here is the complete class:

```
package coyote.tools;

public class FiniteStateMachine
{
  //——————————-
  // fields
  //——————————-
  protected FSMTransition [][] tranTable; //
      transition table

  protected int initState; // starting state
  protected int state; // current state
  protected int maxOutput; // maximum output state


  //——————————-
  // exceptions
  //——————————-
  protected FSMException err_null_list =
    new FSMException("null input symbol set");

  protected FSMException err_inv_start =
    new FSMException("invalid starting state");

  protected FSMException err_bad_output_range =
    new FSMException("invalid output symbol range");

  protected FSMException err_bad_input =
    new FSMException("invalid input symbol");

  protected FSMException err_bad_output =
    new FSMException("invalid output symbol");

  protected FSMException err_bad_transition =
    new FSMException("invalid state transition");


  //——————————-
  // constructors
  //——————————-
  public FiniteStateMachine
    (
    FSMTransition [][] tran,
```

```
      int start,
      int maxOut
      )
{
  // verify parameters
  if (tran == null)
    throw err_null_list;

  if ((start < 0) || (start >= tran[0].length))
    throw err_inv_start;

  if (maxOut < 1)
    throw err_bad_output_range;

  // verify tranTable state changes
  for (int s = 0; s < tran.length; ++s)
  {
    for (int i = 0; i < tran[s].length; ++i)
    {
      if ((tran[s][i].newState < 0)
      ||  (tran[s][i].newState >= tran.length))
        throw err_bad_transition;

      if ((tran[s][i].output < 0)
      ||  (tran[s][i].output > maxOut))
        throw err_bad_output;
    }
  }

  // duplicate transition table
  tranTable = (FSMTransition [][])tran.clone();

  // set starting states
  initState = start;
  state  = start;
  maxOutput = maxOut;
}

public FiniteStateMachine
  (
  FiniteStateMachine fsm
```

```
    )
{
  // duplicate transition table
  tranTable =
      (FSMTransition [][])fsm.tranTable.clone();


  // set starting states
  initState = fsm.initState;
  state  = fsm.state;
  maxOutput = fsm.maxOutput;
}


//————————-
// properties
//————————-
public final FSMTransition getTransition
  (
  int state,
  int input
  )
{
  return tranTable[state][input];
}


public int getState()
{
  return state;
}


//————————-
// methods
//————————-
public int nextState
  (
  int input
  )
{
  // verify input
  if (input >= tranTable[state].length)
    throw err_bad_input;
```

```
    // save a reference to the output symbol
    int result = tranTable[state][input].output;

    // change the current state
    state = tranTable[state][input].newState;

    // return output symbol
    return result;
  }

  public void reset()
  {
    state = initState;
  }

  public String dumpStructure()
  {
    StringBuffer buf = new StringBuffer();

    buf.append("init: " + initState + "\n");

    for (int s = 0; s < tranTable.length; ++s)
    {
      for (int i = 0; i < tranTable[s].length; ++i)
      {
        buf.append
          ("s: "   + s +
           " i: " + i +
           " o: " + tranTable[s][i].output +
           " n: " + tranTable[s][i].newState +
           "\n"
          );
      }
    }

    return buf.toString();
  }
}
```

The constructor parameters include an array of transitions and the index of the initial state within that array. To ensure that state transitions fall within the bound of the transition array, the constructor verifies its parameters. Note that input/output symbols are identified by an integer value; if you wish to use a non-numeric or floating-point input symbol, define a correspondence between object symbols and integer values, possibly using an indexed array.

Running the machine involves calling `nextState` with an input symbol value; this method returns the `int` output associated with that input, and then the machine changes to the new state indicated in `tranTable`. The method exception is thrown if the input symbol is out-of-bounds; this is not absolutely necessary — since the Java runtime would throw its own exception for an invalid index — but I wanted to be able to trap an invalid input symbol as an explicit problem with finite state machines. This allows me to develop exception handlers specific to the operation of `FiniteStateMachine` objects.

The `reset` method returns the machine to its initial (start-up) state. The `getTransition` and `getState` methods provide information about the internal structure of a `FiniteStateMachine` object. I defined the `dumpStructure` method to create a `String` containing a simple description of a machine's states, symbols, and transitions.

Finite State Machines in Action

To implement the machine in Figure 7-1, I created an applet method that built an equivalent `FiniteStateMachine` object:

```
private void testFSM
  (
  TextArea output
  )
{
  output.append("\n——————————-\n" +
        "Testing Finite State Machines\n" +
        "——————————-\n");

  // create finite state machine
  final FSMTransition [][] tdata =
```

```
{
  // input 0          input 1
  //───────────   ───────────
  { new FSMTransition(1,1), new FSMTransition(2,0) },
  { new FSMTransition(0,1), new FSMTransition(1,1) },
  { new FSMTransition(2,0), new FSMTransition(1,2) }
};


FiniteStateMachine fsm =
    new FiniteStateMachine(tdata,0,2);


// perform transitions
int [] data = { 0,1,1,1,0,1,0,1,0,1 };


output.append("init state: " + fsm.getState()
    + "\n");


for (int i = 0; i < data.length; ++i)
{
  output.append("in: " + data[i] +
      ", out: " + ('A' + fsm.nextState(data[i])) +
        ", st: "  + fsm.getState() + "\n");
}


// try to use a false input symbol
try
{
  // ERROR: only two states!
  fsm.nextState(42);


  // this line should NEVER be executed
  output.append("BAD! Erroneous input
      NOT caught!\n");
}
catch (FSMException ex)
```

```
      {
        // what we want to see
        output.append("Good! Erroneous input
           caught!\n");
      }


      // try to create a bogus fsm
      final FSMTransition [][] tbad =
      {
        // input 0          input 1
        //——————————       ——————————
        { new FSMTransition(1,1),
            new FSMTransition(2,0) },
        { new FSMTransition(0,1),
            new FSMTransition(9,1) }, // error!
        { new FSMTransition(2,0),
            new FSMTransition(1,2) }
      };


      try
      {
        // this should fail
        FiniteStateMachine fsmBad =
            new FiniteStateMachine(tbad,0,2);


        // this line should NEVER be executed
        output.append("BAD! Didn't catch bad transition
           table!\n");
      }
      catch (FSMException ex)
      {
        // what we want to see
        output.append("Good! Caught bad transition
           table!\n");
      }
   }
```

The `init` method runs the FSM through a few states, showing the results in a list. Figure 7-2 shows the output of this applet.

Figure 7-2

Output of FSM
Test Applet

```
init state: 0
in: 0, out: B, st: 1
in: 1, out: B, st: 1
in: 1, out: B, st: 1
in: 1, out: B, st: 1
in: 0, out: B, st: 0
in: 1, out: A, st: 2
in: 0, out: A, st: 2
in: 1, out: C, st: 1
in: 0, out: B, st: 0
in: 1, out: A, st: 2
Good! Erroneous input caught!
Good! Caught bad transition table!
```

In real-world applications, finite state machines provide the ability to write programs within programs. The famous Xmodem communications protocol is most often implemented as a finite state machine; algorithms for regular-expression matching will compile an input expression into a FSM that describes a searching process. Almost any program, if it has been well-defined, can be implemented as a finite state machine. This is one good reason for developing clear and complete specifications for an application prior to writing any code. Often, a good spec can be directly translated into a finite state machine, making the act of programming a matter of defining an appropriate set of transitions.

One useful technique is to define a set of polymorphic "function" `Objects`, each defining an operation that can then be assigned as an output state of an FSM. You then define the process of your application as a series of state changes, with the output `int` values indexing into an array of "function" objects.

Evolving Software

A finite state machine is a computer program defined in a very simple way; this makes finite state machines easy to modify "on the fly." But why would you want to alter a machine once it is defined?

Consider, for a moment, that software can evolve. I'm not talking about the usual update-and-release cycle that produces new versions of human-designed software; my interest is in software that discovers solutions to problems via the principles of natural selection.

Computer programs tend to be static: they begin at point A and go to point B, mindlessly following a specific path. As the basis of most software, deterministic algorithms have proven their efficacy. Yet something is missing from software, something fundamental: *adaptability*. Simply put, the vast majority of applications are fixed entities that cannot adjust to situations unforeseen by their programmers. Furthermore, some problems (which I'll introduce later in this chapter) cannot be easily solved by deterministic programs.

If you're looking for a paradigm of adaptability, look no further than biology. Living things, based on a set of simple underlying chemical principles, have shown remarkable flexibility and adaptability throughout billions of years of changing environments. Implementing biological concepts creates software that evolves solutions. In some cases, a biological algorithm might find solutions that its programmer never envisioned — and that concept allows software to go beyond its human creator's vision.

In the mid-nineteenth century, Charles Darwin reasoned that immutable species would become increasingly incompatible with their restless environment. The resemblance of offspring to their parents suggested to him that traits pass from one generation to the next; he also noticed slight differences between siblings, which provide a species with a pool of unique individuals who compete for food and mates. From those observations, Darwin concluded that, as the environment changed, organisms best suited to the new conditions would bear offspring reflecting their successful traits. Darwin named this process "natural selection," and he believed that it was the central mechanism by which species evolved.

Modern science recognizes evolution as the mechanism that creates biological organization. While evolutionary theory has been refined in the century since Charles Darwin's death, the core concepts remain intact. We can see evolution operating today and we can see evidence of evolution in the fossil record of past species; we know that organisms change to survive in an ever-changing world.

While the survival of individuals determines the characteristics of the next generation, it is the reproductive success of a population as a whole that determines the evolution of a species. Natural selection is limited by the characteristics of a population; while it is often called *survival of the fittest*, natural selection really operates through the survival of the best available organisms. An organism's "fitness" is relative to a changing ecosystem, other species, and other members of its population. What is "best" today may not be "best" tomorrow.

Offspring inherit characteristics through genes received from one or more parents. Simple organisms such as fungi and bacteria reproduce asexually by duplicating themselves. A single-celled amoeba, for instance, creates offspring by splitting into two new organisms that contain identical DNA. Thus, asexual reproduction produces new organisms that differ little from each other or their progenitor. Most complex organisms reproduce sexually by combining genes from two parents in their offspring. By mixing and matching DNA from two organisms, sexual reproduction increases the variation within a species. The possibilities are almost endless; for example, a human couple can produce more than seven trillion different blueprints for a person.

Natural selection changes the frequencies of genes in a population, but it doesn't produce new genes. The first life forms began as self-replicating chemicals that bound to each other in mutual cooperation. The first complete organisms resembled an amoeba, and an amoeba clearly does not contain the genes required to evolve it into a human being. New characteristics must somehow arise; otherwise, the simple original life forms would never have evolved into the millions of species on Earth today. A *mutation* is a random change in an organism's genes. It is highly unlikely that a random genetic change will improve a complex organism that is well-adapted to its environment; most manifest mutations disappear from the population through natural selection. Fortunately, the vast majority of mutations have no effect. Studies of human DNA have found long sequences of "junk genes" that serve no explicit purpose; mutations in junk genes are likely to be meaningless. And sometimes, cells can repair damaged DNA, eliminating many mutations before they are passed along to new cells or offspring.

Natural selection mixes and sifts gene pools, acting on variations produced by reproduction and mutation. Sometimes a gene pool evolves in a straight line, carrying a species from one form to another, as in the earlier example of the peppered moth. In other cases, forces act to divide a gene pool, and natural selection works on the now-separate populations to produce new species. If a species encounters several open niches, it may quickly diversify in a process known as *adaptive radiation*. When the dinosaurs vanished 65 million years ago, they left unoccupied niches that were exploited by mammals. Through adaptive radiation, a few shrew-like species blossomed into thousands of types ranging from bears to people to whales.

Evolving Machines

In 1990, a computer scientist named W. Atmar invented a formula for calculating the number of possible finite state machines (N) that can be constructed given a number of states (n) and sizes of input (a) and output alphabets (b): $N = (n^a b^a)n$. More than half a million FSMs can be created using the states and symbols shown in Figure 7-1. Expanding the number of states and symbols dramatically increases the variety of possible machines; allowing five states with input and output alphabets of 3 symbols, for example, will allow the generation of nearly 438 *quadrillion* FSMs! This is the level of complexity we're seeking in an evolutionary algorithm. DNA may encode a simple set of proteins, but the combinations of those proteins produce the near-infinite variety of life we see around us. Diversity is the key to success in the natural world; FSMs offer us that level of diversity in software, and evolutionary algorithms allow us to explore and manipulate the incredible assortment of possible FSMs.

Programmers construct most finite state machines to accomplish a specific task; in the case of evolutionary programming, however, we're interested in constructing FSMs based on natural selection. In the mid-1960s, Larry Fogel of the University of California suggested techniques for doing just that. Fogel defined intelligence as the ability to predict and react to one's environment; his goal was to find a mechanism for evolving machine intelligence. Fogel's finite state machines evolve in much the same way as artificial chromosomes evolve in a genetic algorithm. A set of FSMs is tested against an environment that consists of a series of input symbols;

the evolutionary algorithm calculates a fitness value for each FSM
based on its performance. The fitness values define relative reproductive chances for the FSM population; offspring are generated by
copying a parent FSM and possibly mutating it. Possible mutations
include the change of an output symbol, alteration of a state transition, the assignment of a new initial state, the addition of a new
state, or the deletion of an existing state. The new population then
replaces its parents, and the cycle begins again.

In essence, an evolutionary algorithm is generating a program or
algorithm by testing FSMs against a problem. This is an incredibly
powerful concept in that it focuses on mechanism rather than data;
where a genetic algorithm alters anonymous strings representing
information, an *evolutionary algorithm* manipulates a *process*.

Using the principles outlined above, I subclassed `FiniteStateMa-
chine` to create the `MutableMachine` class. A `MutableMachine` offers
all the capabilities of a `FiniteStateMachine`, with the additional
ability of mutation. Reproduction will be handled by duplicating a
parent machine via the copy constructor.

```
package coyote.tools;

import coyote.stochastic.*;

public class MutableMachine
  extends FiniteStateMachine
{
  //————————————
  // constants
  //————————————
  public static final int OUTSYMBOL  = 0;
  public static final int TRANSITION = 1;
  public static final int ADDSTATE   = 2;
  public static final int DELSTATE   = 3;
  public static final int INITSTATE  = 4;
  public static final int NOCHANGE   = 5;


  //————————————
  // fields
  //————————————
```

```
        private static Stochastic rand =
            new StochasticLevel3();

        private int minStates;
        private int maxStates;


        //———————————-
        // exceptions
        //———————————-
        private static final FSMException err_bad_bounds =
          new FSMException("bad state boundaries");


        //———————————-
        // constructors
        //———————————-
        public MutableMachine
          (
          FSMTransition [][] tran,
          int    start,
          int    maxOut,
          int    minSt,
          int    maxSt
          )
        {
          super(tran,start,maxOut);

          if ((minSt < 0.0) || (maxSt <= minStates))
            throw err_bad_bounds;

          minStates = minSt;
          maxStates = maxSt;
        }

        public MutableMachine
          (
          MutableMachine mfsm
          )
        {
          super(mfsm);

          minStates = mfsm.minStates;
```

```
          maxStates = mfsm.maxStates;
}

//——————————-
// methods
//——————————-
public int mutate()
{
  // define variables
  FSMTransition [][] newTable;

  // select operation
  int c = rand.nextValue(5);

  final int nStates = tranTable.length;
  final int nInputs = tranTable[0].length;

  // perform operation
  switch (c)
  {
  case OUTSYMBOL:
    // change output symbol
    int o;

    do
    {
      o = rand.nextValue(maxOutput + 1);
    }
    while (o !=
      tranTable[rand.nextValue(nStates)]
          [rand.nextValue(nInputs)].output);

    tranTable[rand.nextValue(nStates)]
        [rand.nextValue(nInputs)].output = o;
    break;

  case TRANSITION:
    // change state transition
    int t;

    do
```

```
        {
          t = rand.nextValue(nStates);
        }
        while (t != tranTable
                  [rand.nextValue(nStates)]
                  [rand.nextValue(nInputs)].newState);

        tranTable[rand.nextValue(nStates)]
              [rand.nextValue(nInputs)].newState = t;
        break;

    case ADDSTATE:
        if (nStates >= maxStates)
          return NOCHANGE;

        // allocate a new table
        newTable = new FSMTransition [nStates + 1]
            [nInputs];

        // copy old states
        for (int s = 0; s < nStates; ++s)
        {
          for (int i = 0; i < nInputs; ++i)
                        {
            newTable[s][i] = new FSMTransition
              (
              tranTable[s][i].newState,
              tranTable[s][i].output
              );
          }
        }

        // fill new state with random transition data
        for (int i = 0; i < nInputs; ++i)
        {
          newTable[nStates][i] = new FSMTransition
            (
            rand.nextValue(nStates   + 1),
            rand.nextValue(maxOutput + 1)
            );
        }
```

```
    // change some old states to point to new state
    int i = rand.nextValue(nStates / 2) + 1;

    for (int n = 0; n < i; ++n)
      newTable[rand.nextValue(nStates)]
          [rand.nextValue(nInputs)].newState
              = nStates;

    // replace old table with new one
    tranTable = newTable;

    break;

  case DELSTATE:
    if (nStates <= minStates)
      return NOCHANGE;

    // can't delete to nothing!
    if (nStates == 1)
      break;

    // create new transition table
    newTable = new FSMTransition [nStates - 1]
        [nInputs];

    // select state to be deleted
    int del = rand.nextValue(nStates);

    // copy old states
    int s1 = 0;

    for (int s = 0; s < nStates; ++s)
    {
      if (s == del)
      {
        ++s;

        if (s == nStates)
          break;
      }
```

```
            for (int in = 0; in < nInputs; ++in)
            {
              // change any "new" states that are now
                 out-of-bounds
              if (tranTable[s][in].newState ==
                 (nStates - 1))
              {
                newTable[s1][in] = new FSMTransition
                  (
                  rand.nextValue(nStates - 1),
                  tranTable[s][in].output
                  );
              }
              else
              {
                newTable[s1][in] = new FSMTransition
                  (
                  tranTable[s][in].newState,
                  tranTable[s][in].output
                  );
              }
            }

            ++s1;
          }


          // change initial state, if need be
          if (initState == nStates)
            initState = rand.nextValue(nStates - 1);

          // use new table, delete the old one
          tranTable = newTable;

          break;

        case INITSTATE:
          if (nStates <= 1)
            return NOCHANGE;

          int newInit;
```

```
        // find new init state that isn't the current one
        do  {
          newInit = rand.nextValue(nStates);
          }
        while (newInit == initState);

        // set new init state
        initState = newInit;

        break;
      }

    reset();

    return c;
    }
  }
```

MutableMachine adds two constructor arguments to those defined by FiniteStateMachine: the minimum and maximum number of states allowed for this machine. The new mutate method selects one of the five mutation types, and returns an int code to identify the type of mutation performed. MutableMachine defines several public constants identifying the mutations.

Robot Ants

Assume, for a moment, that you are a robot ant, your movements defined by a finite state machine and your task to follow a trail of food. You can see the square directly in front of you, reacting to what is there by moving straight ahead or by turning 90 degrees left or right before moving. The edges of your universe are barriers you cannot cross — and you can only spend so much time following the path. How best should your finite state machine be defined to maximize your search path?

I formulated the problem above as an evolutionary programming problem defining an ant's search strategy as a finite state machine with an input "view" set of { 0 (food), 1 (empty), 2 (cliff) } and an output "move" set of { 0 (ahead), 1 (turn left), 2 (turn right) }.

Each ant begins its search at the top center of an 11-by-40 matrix, in which a zero square represents an empty space and a one element marks food. When an ant enters a "food" square, it eats the food, gaining a fitness point and converting the square to empty. The ant may face in one of four cardinal directions, and each move is determined by feeding the "view" an ant has into its finite machine to obtain a move symbol.

I've defined the robotic ant parameters as follows:

- *Population Size*: The number of robotic ants in the population to be tested.

- *Maximum Generations*: The number of generations to be run in this simulation.

- *Maximum States*: The initial population comprises 3-state machines; this parameter sets the maximum number of states allowed through mutation.

- *Maximum Moves*: The maximum number of moves an ant may make if it does not encounter the end of the search grid.

- *Mutation Rate*: The probability that a mutation will change any given offspring. This is set to 50%.

The "food grid" is an 11-by-40 array containing ones and zeros, with a one representing a food particle and a zero an empty space. The top of the grid is considered "north" in these experiences, and each ant begins its journey facing south in the middle of the first row. Figure 7-3 shows the grid, with gray squares representing the location of food.

Figure 7-3
The "Food Grid"

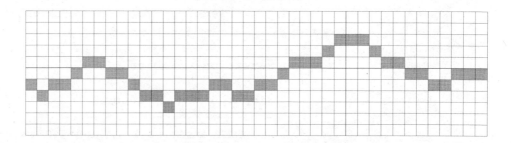

I randomly generate the initial population. Nothing about these first ants is planned or designed; they're simply a set of random machines from which solutions will evolve. Fitness testing begins by resetting a robotic ant FSM and initializing its fitness and the grid. For each move, the ant first scores a fitness point if it is sitting atop a piece of food; the food (if any) is then removed by replacing the one with a zero in grid.

After the ant "eats," I calculate the indexes that reference the grid cell directly in front it. Note that an ant has a facing that determines its direction of travel and view. A position beyond the edge of the grid is considered to be an impassable cliff; otherwise, the view is either "empty" or "food." I feed this view to the ant's FSM, which returns the ant's next move of ahead, left turn, or right turn. I then change the ant's position (and possibly its heading) before handling the next move. If the ant reaches the southernmost row in the grid, it automatically stops.

After fitness testing, I sort the population by fitness to find and display the best ant. Automatic elitist selection guarantees that the best ant will be represented in the new generation, by copying the most-fit ant from the parent population into the first element of the new population. Reproduction involves selecting a parent and applying mutations.

Here's how the final test code looks:

```
private void testEvolvingFSM
    (
    TextArea output
    )
  {
    output.append("\n————————————-\n" +
            "Testing Evolving Machines\n" +
            "————————————-\n");

    FSMTransition tranData[][] =
    {
      // input 0          input 1
      //——————————      ——————————
      { new FSMTransition(1,1), new FSMTransition(2,0) },
```

```
        { new FSMTransition(0,1), new FSMTransition(1,1) },
        { new FSMTransition(2,0), new FSMTransition(1,2) }
    };

    String [] muteType =
    {
      "Output Symbol",
      "Transition",
      "Add State",
      "Delete State",
      "Initial State",
      "None"
    };

    // check out mutable FSMs
    MutableMachine mMach = new MutableMachine
        (tranData,0,2,2,10);

    // show original machine
    output.append("Original machine:\n" +
        mMach.dumpStructure());

    MutableMachine child = new MutableMachine(mMach);

    // mutate
    for (int i = 0; i < 12; ++i)
    {
      output.append
        (
        "\n———— Mutation: " +
        muteType[child.mutate()] +
        "\n" +
        child.dumpStructure() +
        "\n"
        );
    }
}

private void testAnts
    (
    TextArea output
```

```
      )
   {
      output.append("\n————————————-\n" +
              "Robotic Ants\n" +
              "————————————-\n");

      final int POP_SIZE =  50;
      final int MAX_GEN  = 100;
      final int MIN_MACH =   3;
      final int MAX_MACH =  10;
      final int MAX_MOVE = 100;
      final int GRID_LEN =  40;
      final int GRID_WID =  11;

      final int VIEW_FOOD  = 0;
      final int VIEW_EMPTY = 1;
      final int VIEW_CLIFF = 2;

      final String [] MOVE_SET =
        {
        "A",// ahead
        "L",// left
        "R"  // right
        };

      final String [] VIEW_SET =
        {
        "F",// sees food
        "E",// sees empty square
        "C"  // sees a cliff
        };

      final int [][] MASTER_GRID =
      {
        {0,0,0,0,0,1,0,0,0,0,0},
        {0,0,0,0,0,1,0,0,0,0,0},
        {0,0,0,0,0,1,0,0,0,0,0},
        {0,0,0,0,0,0,1,0,0,0,0},
        {0,0,0,0,0,0,1,0,0,0,0},
        {0,0,0,0,0,1,0,0,0,0,0},
        {0,0,0,0,0,1,0,0,0,0,0},
```

```
    {0,0,0,0,1,0,0,0,0,0,0},
    {0,0,0,0,1,0,0,0,0,0,0},
    {0,0,0,1,0,0,0,0,0,0,0},
    {0,0,1,0,0,0,0,0,0,0,0},
    {0,0,1,0,0,0,0,0,0,0,0},
    {0,0,1,0,0,0,0,0,0,0,0},
    {0,0,0,1,0,0,0,0,0,0,0},
    {0,0,0,0,1,0,0,0,0,0,0},
    {0,0,0,0,1,0,0,0,0,0,0},
    {0,0,0,0,1,0,0,0,0,0,0},
    {0,0,0,0,0,1,0,0,0,0,0},
    {0,0,0,0,0,0,1,0,0,0,0},
    {0,0,0,0,0,0,1,0,0,0,0},
    {0,0,0,0,0,0,0,1,0,0,0},
    {0,0,0,0,0,0,0,1,0,0,0},
    {0,0,0,0,0,0,1,0,0,0,0},
    {0,0,0,0,0,0,1,0,0,0,0},
    {0,0,0,0,0,0,0,1,0,0,0},
    {0,0,0,0,0,0,0,1,0,0,0},
    {0,0,0,0,0,0,0,1,0,0,0},
    {0,0,0,0,0,0,0,0,1,0,0},
    {0,0,0,0,0,0,0,1,0,0,0},
    {0,0,0,0,0,0,0,1,0,0,0},
    {0,0,0,0,0,0,1,0,0,0,0},
    {0,0,0,0,0,1,0,0,0,0,0},
    {0,0,0,0,0,1,0,0,0,0,0},
    {0,0,0,0,1,0,0,0,0,0,0},
    {0,0,0,0,1,0,0,0,0,0,0},
    {0,0,0,0,0,1,0,0,0,0,0},
    {0,0,0,0,0,0,1,0,0,0,0},
    {0,0,0,0,0,0,1,0,0,0,0},
    {0,0,0,0,0,0,0,1,0,0,0},
    {0,0,0,0,0,0,1,0,0,0,0}
};


final int [][] OFFSET =
  {
  {  0, -1 },
  {  1,  0 },
  {  0,  1 },
```

```
      {   -1, 0 }
      };


final int [] LTURN = { 3, 0, 1, 2 };
final int [] RTURN = { 1, 2, 3, 0 };


Stochastic rand = new StochasticLevel3();


// create empty transition table
FSMTransition [][] tran = new FSMTransition
    [3][3];


// create population
MutableMachine [] pop = new MutableMachine
    [POP_SIZE];


// initialize machines
int n, s, i;

for (n = 0; n < POP_SIZE; ++n)
{
  for (s = 0; s < 3; ++s)
  {
    for (i = 0; i < 3; ++i)
    {
      tran[s][i] = new FSMTransition
              (
              rand.nextValue(3),
              rand.nextValue(3)
              );
    }
  }


  pop[n] = new MutableMachine
    (
    tran,
    rand.nextValue(3),
    3,
```

```
                MIN_MACH,
                MAX_MACH
                );
        }


        // create fitness tracking array
        int [] fit = new int [POP_SIZE];


        // test loop
        for (int g = 0; ; ++g)
        {
          // track total fitness
          int totFit  =  0;
          int bestFit = -1;
          int bestIdx =  0;


          for (n = 0; n < POP_SIZE; ++n)
          {
            // reset the machine
            pop[n].reset();
            fit[n] = 0;


            // initialize temporary search grid
            int [][] grid = (int [][])MASTER_GRID.clone();


            // start at top line, center, moving down
            int x = 5;
            int y = 0;
            int d = 2;


            // move and eat
            for (int m = 0; m < MAX_MOVE; ++m)
            {
              if (grid[y][x] != 0)
              {
                // increase fitness
                fit[n] += 1;
```

```
  // 'eat' food
  grid[y][x] = 0;
}

// look ahead
int view;
int viewX = x + OFFSET[d][0];
int viewY = y + OFFSET[d][1];

// done if at end of grid
if (viewY == GRID_LEN)
{
  // give fitness bonus for getting done
  fit[n] += (MAX_MOVE - m);
  break;
}

// what does the ant see?
if ((viewX < 0) || (viewX >=
    GRID_WID) || (viewY < 0))
  view = VIEW_CLIFF;
else
{
  if (grid[viewY][viewX] != 0)
    view = VIEW_FOOD;
  else
    view = VIEW_EMPTY;
}

// change ant state and get move
int move = pop[n].nextState(view);

// apply move
switch (move)
{
case 0: // move ahead
  // no turn, do nothing here
  break;
case 1: // left turn
  d = LTURN[d];
  viewX = x + OFFSET[d][0];
```

```
            viewY = y + OFFSET[d][1];
            break;
          case 2: // right turn
            d = RTURN[d];
            viewX = x + OFFSET[d][0];
            viewY = y + OFFSET[d][1];
            break;
        }

        if ((viewX >= 0) && (viewY >= 0) && (viewX
            < GRID_WID) && (viewY < GRID_LEN))
        {
          x = viewX;
          y = viewY;
        }
      }

      // track best ant
      if (fit[n] > bestFit)
      {
        bestFit = fit[n];
        bestIdx = n;
      }

      // maintain fitness total
      totFit += fit[n];
    }

    // display best machine fitness
    output.append("gen: " + g +
          ", best fitness = " +
          bestFit + "\n");

    // increment generation
    ++g;

    if (g == MAX_GEN)
    {
      output.append
        (
        "\nThe best machine was:\n" +
```

```
          pop[bestIdx].dumpStructure()
          );

      break;
  }


  // create a new population
  MutableMachine [] newPop =
      new MutableMachine [POP_SIZE];

  // elitist selection
  newPop[0] = pop[bestIdx];

  // produce new members by cloning and mutating
  for (int j = 1; j < POP_SIZE; ++j)
  {
    // pick a parent ant
    int f = rand.nextValue(totFit);
    int sel = 0;

    while (f > fit[sel])
    {
      f -= fit[sel];
      ++sel;
    }

    // clone by copy constructor
    newPop[j] = new MutableMachine(pop[sel]);

    // mutate
    if (rand.nextFloat() < 0.50)
      newPop[j].mutate();
  }

  // replace old population with new
  pop = newPop;
  }
  }
  }
```

The best finite state machine that has evolved in my tests is shown schematically in Figure 7-4. This ant scores 35 out of a possible 40 points. I've replaced the numeric input and output symbols with letters representing the initials of the moves and views.

Figure 7-4

A 35-point
Robotic Ant

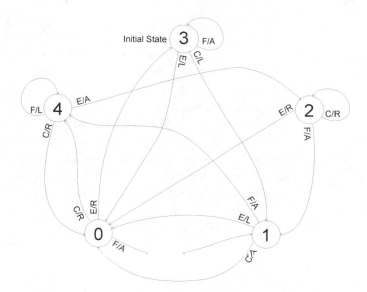

The important question is: has the simulation evolved an "intelligent" ant with useful strategies, or is the finite state machine's success merely the result of luck? To find out, I manually mapped the movements of the 35-point ant, producing the grid shown in Figure 7-5.

Figure 7-5

Mapping the 35-Point
Ant's Movement

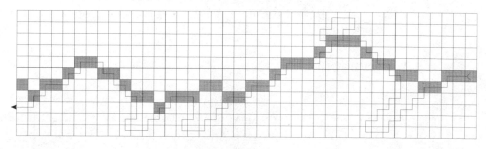

In 94 moves the ant finds 35 of forty pieces of food. What struck me as most interesting was the "backtracking" algorithm evolved by this FSM ant. Upon losing contact with the food trail, the ant moves diagonally toward the edge of the grid, until it encounters the edge. Once at the cliff, the ant turns around and backtracks northeast without walking over its previous path! The FSM's westward backtracking subroutine in the FSM might have been a fortuitous accident — but, remarkably, the ant also evolved a looping mechanism that travels to the east. In other simulation runs, I've seen similar behaviors appear in the most successful ants, indicating that certain patterns of movement are, indeed, being chosen through natural selection.

Certainly this ant is not as intelligent as a real ant, and it is only evolved to follow the fixed, specific trail given in my program. Still, the ants do appear to get better at finding food in a shorter number of moves. Extending the simulation could involve penalties for re-examining squares and bonuses for reaching the end of the grid in the fewest moves. I've also experimented with evolving ants via a set of grids, as opposed to the single grid implemented above. To evolve the most effective ants, it would be best to provide them with a varied environment. It might also be interesting to have ants compete, simultaneously, on a larger grid for a shared food supply.

Stochastic Algorithms

Evolutionary computing is only one of many different applications that require the generation of thousands, millions or even billions of "random numbers." Unfortunately, the built-in `rand` function is entirely inadequate in circumstances where thousands — or even millions — of random values need to be generated. A run of the algorithm from Chapter 2 may use a hundred thousand or more random values.

Random Numbers

A random number is just that: a number whose value cannot be predicted in advance of its existence. While the human mind has been known to be unpredictable, it isn't very good at generating a completely unrelated set of numbers. Try creating a list of twenty random integers selected from the range one through one hundred, inclusive. Are those numbers *really* random? And wouldn't it be tedious if you had to generate a thousand or a million random numbers?

Computers are supposed to be good at reducing tedious numeric operations. Unfortunately, computers perform calculations via algorithms, and truly random numbers cannot be generated by an algorithm. By definition, an algorithm is a specific sequence of operations that produces a predictable output for a given set of parameters. In the case of random numbers, the last thing we want is something predictable! The best we can do with a computer is create an algorithm that *appears* to generate a random sequence of numbers. The numbers aren't really random — a human with a sharp mind or a calculator could predict the numbers in the sequence by following the algorithm. But the sequence of numbers is very difficult to follow, and a human looking at the values will not be able to see any algorithmic pattern to them. For practical applications, pseudo-random numbers suffice.

Algorithms

In general, a pseudo-random number generator is initialized with a *seed* value that begins the sequence. A set of mathematical operations is performed on the seed, generating a value that is reported as a pseudo-random number. That return value is then used as the next seed value. Researchers have devoted copious time to inventing and analyzing pseudo-random number generators. The goal of this research has been to produce the most unpredictable sequence of values. Designing a good random number generator involves solving two problems:

- Increasing the size of the repetition cycle. As the algorithm is applied, the seed will eventually return to its starting value, and the values will begin to repeat themselves. An algorithm that repeats after generating a million numbers is more useful than a generator that repeats itself every hundred numbers.

- Avoiding predictability. A random number generator that always returns values with the same last digit is worthless. An algorithm that only generates odd numbers is equally useless.

While there are many fancy and complicated algorithms that generate pseudo-random numbers, one of the most commonly-used algorithms is also one of the simplest. First introduced by D. Lehmer in 1951, the *linear congruential* method involves only two mathematical operations. This is the algorithm followed by Java's `Random` class — it works well if your random numbers don't need to be very unpredictable and the repetition of those values is not important to your work. Statistically, even the best linear congruential generators suffer from convergence in their numeric sequences.

I began by creating a common base class, `Stochastic`, for a series of subclasses implementing different algorithms. `Stochastic` provides several "wrapper" methods to translate the output of the abstract `nextValue()` method into `double`, `float`, or ranged values.

```java
package coyote.stochastic;

public abstract class Stochastic
{
    //-------------------
    // fields
    //-------------------
    protected int seed = 0;


    //-------------------
    // constants
    //-------------------
    protected static final float  FLT_MAX =
        1.0F - 1.192092896e-07F;
    protected static final float  FLT_AM  =
        1.0F / 2147483563.0F;
    protected static final double DBL_MAX =
        1.0D - 1.192092896e-07F;
    protected static final double DBL_AM  =
        1.0D / 2147483563.0D;


    //-------------------
    // exceptions
    //-------------------
    private static final StochasticException err_hilo =
        new StochasticException("invalid lo-hi range");
```

```
//——————————-
// constructors
//——————————-
public Stochastic()
{
  // set seed to current time in milliseconds
  seed = (int)System.currentTimeMillis();
}

// constructor with seed value
public Stochastic
  (
  int seed
  )
{
  seed = seed;
}


//——————————-
// methods
//——————————-
// get next value in sequence
public abstract int nextValue();

// get next uniform deviate as a float
final public float nextFloat()
{
  // get next value
  nextValue();

  // convert
  float temp = FLT_AM * seed;

  if (temp > FLT_MAX)
    return FLT_MAX;
  else
    return temp;
}

// get next uniform deviate as a double
final public double nextDouble()
```

```
{
  // get next value
  nextValue();

  // convert
  double temp = DBL_AM * seed;

  if (temp > DBL_MAX)
    return DBL_MAX;
  else
    return temp;
}

// get next value between hi and low extrema
final public int nextValue
  (
  int lo,
  int hi
  )
{
  // verify parameters
  if (lo >= hi)
    throw err_hilo;

  // return ranged value
  return (int)((long)lo + ((long)hi - (long)lo)
      * nextFloat());
}

// get next value between hi and low extrema
final public int nextValue
  (
  int hi
  )
{
  // return ranged value
  return (int)((float)hi * nextFloat());
}

// get next uniform deviate as an float within a range
final public float nextFloat
```

```
      (
      float lo,
      float hi
      )
    {
      // verify parameters
      if (lo >= hi)
        throw err_hilo;

      // return ranged value
      return lo + (hi - lo) * nextFloat();
    }

    // get next uniform deviate as an double within a range
    final public double nextDouble
      (
      double lo,
      double hi
      )
    {
      // verify parameters
      if (lo >= hi)
        throw err_hilo;

      // return ranged value
      return lo + (hi - lo) * nextDouble();
    }
  }
```

In 1988, S.K. Park and L.W. Miller studied a variety of random number generators before suggesting what they termed to be the "minimum standard." They studied several random number generators, and they selected a multiplicative congruential algorithm as the best. Essentially, the algorithm updates the seed with the formula:

$$S_{new} = (a * S) \bmod m$$

The two factors a and m must be picked with great care; Park and Miller decided that $a = 16807$ and $m = 2,147,483,647$ were the best possible choices. Their algorithm is a solid performer, providing a good tool for many applications. I've implemented their algorithm in the `StochasticLevel1` class.

```
package coyote.stochastic;

public class StochasticLevel1
  extends Stochastic
{
  //——————————-
  // constants
  //——————————-
  private static final int A   = 16807;
  private static final int M   = 2147483647;
  private static final int Q   = 127773;
  private static final int R   = 2836;
  private static final int MASK = 123459876;


  //——————————-
  // constructors
  //——————————-
  public StochasticLevel1()
  {
    super();
  }

  public StochasticLevel1
    (
    int seed
    )
  {
    super(seed);
  }

  //——————————-
  // methods
  //——————————-
  public int nextValue()
  {
    seed ^= MASK; // prevent zero seed

    int k = seed / Q;
    seed = A * (seed - k * Q) - R * k;

    if (seed < 0)
```

```
          seed += M;

      return seed;
   }
}
```

In a later issue of *Communications of the ACM,* Paul L'Ecuyer suggests a variety of algorithms for the production of reliable, long-period random deviates. By combining two generators based on the Minimal Standard, L'Ecuyer creates a routine that avoids the pitfalls of simpler algorithms. In a nutshell, L'Ecuyer's algorithm uses an approximate factorization, shuffling the result to remove correlation in low-order bits. The class `StochasticLevel3` implements L'Ecuyer's algorithm.

```java
package coyote.stochastic;

public class StochasticLevel3
   extends Stochastic
{
   //———————————-
   // constants
   //———————————-
   private static final int M1 =  2147483563;
   private static final int A1 =       40014;
   private static final int Q1 =       53668;
   private static final int R1 =       12211;

   private static final int M2 =  2147483399;
   private static final int A2 =       40692;
   private static final int Q2 =       52774;
   private static final int R2 =        3791;

   private static final int TBL_LEN = 32;
   private static final int DIV =
       1 + (M1  - 1) / TBL_LEN;

   //———————————-
   // fields
   //———————————-
   private int dummy   = 123456789;
```

```
      private int hold    = 0;
      private int [] val = new int [TBL_LEN];


      //———————————-
      // constructors
      //———————————-
      public StochasticLevel3()
      {
        super();

        if (seed > 0)
          seed *= -1;
      }


      public StochasticLevel3
        (
        int seed
        )
      {
        super(seed);

        if (seed > 0)
          seed *= -1;
      }


      //———————————-
      // methods
      //———————————-
      public int nextValue()
      {
        int j, k;

        if (seed <= 0L)
        {
          // initailize tables
          if (-seed < 1)
            seed = 1;
          else
            seed = -seed;

          dummy = seed;
```

```
        // load shuffle table
        for (j = TBL_LEN + 7; j >= 0; —j)
        {
          k = seed / Q1;
          seed = A1 * (seed - k * Q1) - k * R1;

          if (seed < 0)
            seed += M1;

          if (j < TBL_LEN)
            val[j] = seed;
        }

        hold = val[0];
      }

    k = seed / Q1;

    seed = A1 * (seed - k * Q1) - k * R1;

    if (seed < 0)
      seed += M1;

    k = dummy / Q2;

    dummy = A2 * (dummy - k * Q2) - k * R2;

    if (dummy < 0)
      dummy += M2;

    j = hold / DIV;
    hold = val[j] - dummy;

    val[j] = seed;

    if (hold < 1)
      hold += M1 - 1;

    return seed;
  }
}
```

Running a thousand generations for a population of a hundred chromosomes may require millions of random values. Combining two generators, as L'Ecuyer suggests, with a judicious selection of factors, gives us a "repeat" period of approximately 2.3×10^{18}, which should be more than effective in genetic algorithms of any practical scope.

Onward

Many scientific and engineering applications require programs to manipulate two-dimensional matrices. In the next chapter, I'll demonstrate methods that implement a variety of matrix operations for matrix math and linear algebra, extending Java's mathematical abilities.

8

Matrices and Linear Algebra

A *matrix* is a two-dimensional array that can be perceived as a rectangle containing rows and columns of numeric values. A 3 by 4 matrix, for example, has 12 elements arranged in three rows and four columns.

Java Arrays & Matrices

This is a 2-row by 3-column (2 by 3) matrix of integers:

$$A = \begin{pmatrix} 0 & 1 & 2 \\ 3 & 0 & 6 \end{pmatrix}$$

A *square matrix* has the same number of rows and columns.

Java defines two-dimensional matrices as an array of arrays; for example, to create the example above in Java, you would write:

```
double [][] A = new double [2][3];

A[0][0] = 0;
A[0][1] = 1;
A[0][2] = 2;
A[1][0] = 3;
A[1][1] = 0;
A[1][2] = 6;
```

Or, you could instantiate A using a constant like this:

```
double [][] A =
{
  { 0, 1, 2 },
  { 3, 0, 6 }
};
```

Java's two-dimensional array support provides range checking and constant initialization; I saw no need to create a wrapper "matrix" class. Instead, I've implemented a class named `Matrix` that defines a set of static methods for manipulating two-dimensional arrays. `Matrix` functions in much the same way as `java.lang.Math`, delivering utility methods for general application to an existing primitive type.

For the purpose of brevity, I'll be demonstrating methods based on arrays of `double` values; you can easily convert the code to using `float` values if your applications so require.

Exceptions

The `Matrix` methods may throw exceptions of type `Matrix-Exception`.

```
package coyote.math;

public class MatrixException
```

```
      extends RuntimeException
{
  public MatrixException()
  {
    super();
  }

  public MatrixException(String s)
  {
    super(s);
  }
}
```

The Matrix class begins by defining two standard exception objects.

```
public class Matrix
{
  //-------------------------
  // exceptions
  //-------------------------
  protected static MatrixException err_incompat =
    new MatrixException("incompatible matrices");

  protected static MatrixException err_singular =
    new MatrixException("singular matrix");
```

Basic Operations

A *vector* is a one-dimensional array. You can view a matrix as comprising a set of row vectors or column vectors. I defined a pair of methods to extract vectors from matrices.

```
  public static double [] makeRowVector
    (
    double [][] matrix,
    int row
    )
  {
    double [] rvec = new double [matrix.length];
```

```
    for (int c = 0; c < matrix[0].length; ++c)
      rvec[c] = matrix[row][c];

    return rvec;
  }

public static double [] makeColVector
    (
    double [][] matrix,
    int col
    )
  {
    double [] cvec = new double [matrix[0].length];

    for (int r = 0; r < matrix.length; ++r)
      cvec[r] = matrix[r][col];

    return cvec;
  }
```

One of the most basic matrix operations, the *transpose*, is created by exchanging rows as columns. The transpose of matrix *A*, for example, is:

$$A^T = \begin{pmatrix} 0 & 2 \\ 3 & 0 \\ 3 & 0 \end{pmatrix}$$

The `transpose` method returns a new matrix containing the transpose of the argument.

```
public static double [][] transpose
    (
    double [][] matrix
    )
  {
    double [][] result =
        new double [matrix[0].length][matrix.length];

    for (int r = 0; r < matrix.length; ++r)
```

```
    {
      for (int c = 0; c < matrix[0].length; ++c)
      {
        result[c][r] = matrix[r][c];
      }
    }

    return result;
  }
```

Matrix Characteristics

A matrix can exhibit a variety of properties based on the organization of its elements. For example, if the transpose of a matrix is identical to the original matrix, the matrix is said to be *symmetric*. In a *zero matrix*, every element is zero.

In a *diagonal matrix*, all elements are zero except those where the row index equals the column index. If all non-zero values in a diagonal matrix are one (1), it is called an *identity matrix*.

$$D = \begin{pmatrix} 1 & 0 & 0 & 0 \\ 0 & 1 & 0 & 0 \\ 0 & 0 & 1 & 0 \\ 0 & 0 & 0 & 1 \end{pmatrix}$$

The `Matrix` class declares several methods that determine if a matrix has a given characteristic.

```
public static boolean isZero
  (
  double [][] matrix
  )
{
  for (int r = 0; r < matrix.length; ++r)
  {
    for (int c = 0; c < matrix[0].length; ++c)
    {
```

```
        if (matrix[r][c] != 0.0)
          return false;
    }
  }

  return true;
}

public static boolean isDiagonal
  (
  double [][] matrix
  )
{
  for (int r = 0; r < matrix.length; ++r)
  {
    for (int c = 0; c < matrix[0].length; ++c)
    {
      if (r == c)
      {
        if (matrix[r][c] == 0.0)
          return false;
      }
      else
      {
        if (matrix[r][c] != 0.0)
          return false;
      }
    }
  }

  return true;
}

public static boolean isIdentity
  (
  double [][] matrix
  )
{
  for (int r = 0; r < matrix.length; ++r)
  {
    for (int c = 0; c < matrix[0].length; ++c)
```

```
    {
      if (r == c)
      {
        if (matrix[r][c] != 1.0)
          return false;
      }
      else
      {
        if (matrix[r][c] != 0.0)
          return false;
      }
    }
  }

  return true;
}

public static boolean isTridiagonal
  (
  double [][] matrix
  )
{
  for (int r = 0; r < matrix.length; ++r)
  {
    for (int c = 0; c < matrix[0].length; ++c)
    {
      if (r != c)
      {
        if (r > c)
        {
          if ((r - c) > 1)
          {
            if (matrix[r][c] != 0.0)
              return false;
          }
        }
        else
        {
          if ((c - r) > 1)
          {
            if (matrix[r][c] != 0.0)
```

```
                          return false;
                  }
              }
          }
      }
  }

  return true;
}

public static boolean isUpperTriangular
  (
  double [][] matrix
  )
{
  for (int r = 0; r < matrix.length; ++r)
  {
    for (int c = 0; c < matrix[0].length; ++c)
    {
      if (r > c)
      {
        if (matrix[r][c] != 0.0)
          return false;
      }
    }
  }

  return true;
}

public static boolean isLowerTriangular
  (
  double [][] matrix
  )
{
  for (int r = 0; r < matrix.length; ++r)
  {
    for (int c = 0; c < matrix[0].length; ++c)
    {
      if (r < c)
      {
```

```
          if (matrix[r][c] != 0.0)
            return false;
      }
    }
  }


  return true;
}

public static boolean isPermutation
  (
  double [][] matrix
  )
{
  if (matrix[0].length != matrix.length)
    return false;

  int [] ctags = new int [matrix[0].length];
  int [] rtags = new int [matrix.length];

  for (int r = 0; r < matrix.length; ++r)
  {
    for (int c = 0; c < matrix[0].length; ++c)
    {
      if (matrix[r][c] != 0.0)
      {
        if ((matrix[r][c] > 1.0)
        ||  (rtags[r] == 1)
        ||  (ctags[c] == 1))
          return false;

        rtags[r] = 1;
        ctags[c] = 1;
      }
    }
  }


  return true;
}

public static boolean isSingular
```

```
(
double [][] matrix
)
{
if (matrix[0].length != matrix.length)
  return false;

double [] csum = new double[matrix[0].length];
double [] rsum = new double[matrix.length];

for (int r = 0; r < matrix.length; ++r)
{
  for (int c = 0; c < matrix[0].length; ++c)
  {
    csum[c] += matrix[r][c];
    rsum[r] += matrix[r][c];
  }
}

for (int i = 0; i < matrix.length; ++i)
{
  if ((csum[i] == 0.0) || (rsum[i] == 0.0))
    return true;
}

return false;
}
```

If a matrix is *tridiagonal* it follows this pattern, where n represents any value:

$$T = \begin{pmatrix} n & n & 0 & 0 & 0 & 0 \\ n & n & n & 0 & 0 & 0 \\ 0 & n & n & n & 0 & 0 \\ 0 & 0 & n & n & n & 0 \\ 0 & 0 & 0 & n & n & n \\ 0 & 0 & 0 & 0 & n & n \end{pmatrix}$$

An *upper triangular* matrix is such that the elements are zero when their row index is greater than their column index:

$$U = \begin{pmatrix} n & n & n & n \\ 0 & n & n & n \\ 0 & 0 & n & n \\ 0 & 0 & 0 & n \end{pmatrix}$$

The counterpart is a *lower triangular* matrix:

$$L = \begin{pmatrix} n & 0 & 0 & 0 \\ n & n & 0 & 0 \\ n & n & n & 0 \\ n & n & n & n \end{pmatrix}$$

Elements in a *permutation* matrix are zero, with the exception that there is a single one (1) in each row or column:

$$P = \begin{pmatrix} 1 & 0 & 0 & 0 \\ 0 & 0 & 0 & 1 \\ 0 & 1 & 0 & 0 \\ 0 & 0 & 1 & 0 \end{pmatrix}$$

Multiplying a vector against a compatible permutation matrix will reorder, but not change the value of, its elements.

A *symmetric* matrix is one that equals its transpose. This is a symmetric matrix:

$$S = \begin{pmatrix} 1 & 4 & 5 \\ 4 & 6 & 2 \\ 5 & 2 & 3 \end{pmatrix}$$

Basic Operations

Two matrices can only be added if they have exactly the same number of rows and columns. The result of adding two matrices is a new matrix of the same dimensions; each element in the result equals the sum of the corresponding elements in the source matrices. For example:

$$\begin{pmatrix} 7 & 7 & 4 \\ 4 & 4 & 8 \end{pmatrix} = \begin{pmatrix} 0 & 1 & 2 \\ 3 & 4 & 5 \end{pmatrix} + \begin{pmatrix} 7 & 6 & 2 \\ 1 & 0 & 3 \end{pmatrix}$$

The same principle holds true for subtraction, multiplication, and division of two same-size matrices. In `Matrix`, I've implemented `add`, `sub`, `mul`, and `div` methods to perform basic operations on two matrices.

```
public static double [][] add
  (
  double [][] matrix1,
  double [][] matrix2
  )
{
  if ((matrix1.length != matrix2.length)
  || (matrix1[0].length != matrix2[0].length))
    throw err_incompat;

  double [][] result =
      new double [matrix1.length][matrix1[0].length];

  for (int r = 0; r < matrix1.length; ++r)
  {
    for (int c = 0; c < matrix1[0].length; ++c)
    {
      result[r][c] = matrix1[r][c] + matrix2[r][c];
    }
  }

  return result;
}
```

```
public static double [][] sub
  (
  double [][] matrix1,
  double [][] matrix2
  )
{
  if ((matrix1.length != matrix2.length)
  || (matrix1[0].length != matrix2[0].length))
    throw err_incompat;

  double [][] result =
      new double [matrix1.length][matrix1[0].length];

  for (int r = 0; r < matrix1.length; ++r)
  {
    for (int c = 0; c < matrix1[0].length; ++c)
    {
      result[r][c] = matrix1[r][c] - matrix2[r][c];
    }
  }

  return result;
}

public static double [][] mul
  (
  double [][] matrix1,
  double [][] matrix2
  )
{
  if ((matrix1.length != matrix2.length)
  || (matrix1[0].length != matrix2[0].length))
    throw err_incompat;

  double [][] result =
      new double [matrix1.length][matrix1[0].length];

  for (int r = 0; r < matrix1.length; ++r)
  {
    for (int c = 0; c < matrix1[0].length; ++c)
    {
```

```
            result[r][c] = matrix1[r][c] * matrix2[r][c];
        }
    }

    return result;
}

public static double [][] div
    (
    double [][] matrix1,
    double [][] matrix2
    )
{
    if ((matrix1.length != matrix2.length)
    || (matrix1[0].length != matrix2[0].length))
        throw err_incompat;

    double [][] result =
        new double [matrix1.length][matrix1[0].length];

    for (int r = 0; r < matrix1.length; ++r)
    {
        for (int c = 0; c < matrix1[0].length; ++c)
        {
            result[r][c] = matrix1[r][c] / matrix2[r][c];
        }
    }

    return result;
}
```

Scalar operations apply a single operation to every member of a matrix. Here is an example of a scalar multiply:

$$2 \cdot \begin{pmatrix} 1 & 2 \\ 3 & 4 \end{pmatrix} = \begin{pmatrix} 2 & 4 \\ 6 & 8 \end{pmatrix}$$

Additional versions of `add`, `sub`, `mul`, and `div` implement the scalar operations in `Matrix`.

```java
public static double [][] add
  (
  double [][] matrix,
  double x
  )
{
  double [][] result =
      new double [matrix.length][matrix[0].length];

  for (int r = 0; r < matrix.length; ++r)
  {
    for (int c = 0; c < matrix[0].length; ++c)
    {
      result[r][c] = matrix[r][c] + x;
    }
  }

  return result;
}

public static double [][] sub
  (
  double [][] matrix,
  double x
  )
{
  double [][] result =
      new double [matrix.length][matrix[0].length];

  for (int r = 0; r < matrix.length; ++r)
  {
    for (int c = 0; c < matrix[0].length; ++c)
    {
      result[r][c] = matrix[r][c] - x;
    }
  }

  return result;
}
```

```
public static double [][] mul
  (
  double [][] matrix,
  double x
  )
{
  double [][] result =
      new double [matrix.length][matrix[0].length];

  for (int r = 0; r < matrix.length; ++r)
  {
    for (int c = 0; c < matrix[0].length; ++c)
    {
      result[r][c] = matrix[r][c] * x;
    }
  }

  return result;
}

public static double [][] div
  (
  double [][] matrix,
  double x
  )
{
  double [][] result =
      new double [matrix.length][matrix[0].length];

  for (int r = 0; r < matrix.length; ++r)
  {
    for (int c = 0; c < matrix[0].length; ++c)
    {
      result[r][c] = matrix[r][c] / x;
    }
  }

  return result;
}
```

Matrix Multiplication

Matrix multiplication requires two compatible matrices, in the sense that the number of columns in matrix A must be equal to the number of rows in column B. If A is an m by n matrix, and B is a n by p matrix, then the result by multiplication, matrix C, will be an m by p matrix. Each element of C is calculated according to the following formula:

$$C_{ik} = \sum_{j=1}^{n} A_{ij} B_{jk}$$

for $i = 1$ to m and $k = 1$ to p. For example:

$$\begin{pmatrix} 1 & 0 & 2 \\ 1 & 3 & 2 \end{pmatrix} \bullet \begin{pmatrix} 1 & 4 \\ 2 & 5 \\ 3 & 6 \end{pmatrix} = \begin{pmatrix} 7 & 16 \\ 13 & 31 \end{pmatrix}$$

In general, the rules of algebra apply to matrix multiplication. For example, multiplying any matrix times a zero matrix results in a zero matrix. Multiplication is associative and distributive over addition; however, the multiplication is not communitive.

```
public static double [][] mulMatrix
  (
  double [][] matrix1,
  double [][] matrix2
  )
{
  if (matrix1[0].length != matrix2.length)
    throw err_incompat;

  double [][] result =
      new double [matrix1.length][matrix2[0].length];

  for (int i = 0; i < matrix1.length; ++i)
  {
    for (int j = 0; j < matrix2[0].length; ++j)
```

```
        {
          result[i][j] = 0.0;

          for (int k = 0; k < matrix1[0].length; ++k)
            result[i][j] += matrix1[i][k] *
                matrix2[k][j];
        }
      }

    return result;
  }
```

An *inner product* is the summation of the products of corresponding elements in a row and column vector, as defined by this formula:

$$Inner(x,y) = \sum_{i=1}^{n} x_i y_i$$

My code for calculating the inner product is:

```
public static double [] innerProduct
  (
  double [][] matrix,
  double []   vector
  )
{
  if (vector.length != matrix[0].length)
    throw err_incompat;

  double [] result = new double [matrix.length];

  for (int i = 0; i < matrix.length; ++i)
  {
    for (int n = 0; n < vector.length; ++n)
    {
      result[i] += matrix[i][n] * vector[n];
    }
  }

  return result;
}
```

The *outer product* of two matrices works like matrix addition, where two like-dimensioned matrices generate a matrix of the same size whose elements are the result of multiplying corresponding source elements.

```
public static double [][] outerProduct
  (
  double [] vector1,
  double [] vector2
  )
{
  if (vector1.length != vector2.length)
    throw err_incompat;

  double [][] result =
      new double [vector1.length][vector1.length];

  for (int i = 0; i < vector1.length; ++i)
  {
    for (int j = 0; j < vector2.length; ++j)
    {
      result[i][j] = vector1[i] * vector2[j];
    }
  }

  return result;
}
```

I define two broad classes of scalar comparison operations to compare the elements of one matrix with another of the same dimensions. Here's an example of a matrix comparison:

$$\begin{pmatrix} 1 & 0 \\ 2 & 1 \\ 4 & 3 \end{pmatrix} > \begin{pmatrix} 0 & 1 \\ 3 & 0 \\ 4 & 1 \end{pmatrix} = \begin{pmatrix} 1 & 0 \\ 0 & 1 \\ 0 & 1 \end{pmatrix}$$

The result of such a comparison is a matrix of `boolean` values, each set according to the corresponding relationships of elements in the target matrices.

```
public static boolean equal
  (
  double [][] matrix1,
  double [][] matrix2
  )
{
  if ((matrix1.length != matrix2.length)
  ||  (matrix1[0].length != matrix2[0].length))
    throw err_incompat;

  for (int r = 0; r < matrix1.length; ++r)
  {
    for (int c = 0; c < matrix1[0].length; ++c)
    {
      if (matrix1[r][c] != matrix2[r][c])
        return false;
    }
  }

  return true;
}

public static boolean [][] compEqual
  (
  double [][] matrix1,
  double [][] matrix2
  )
{
  if ((matrix1.length != matrix2.length)
  ||  (matrix1[0].length != matrix2[0].length))
    throw err_incompat;

  boolean [][] result =
    new boolean [matrix1.length][matrix1[0].length];

  for (int r = 0; r < matrix1.length; ++r)
  {
    for (int c = 0; c < matrix1[0].length; ++c)
    {
      result[r][c] = matrix1[r][c] == matrix2[r][c];
    }
  }
```

```
      return result;
}


public static boolean [][] compNotEqual
  (
  double [][] matrix1,
  double [][] matrix2
  )
{
  if ((matrix1.length != matrix2.length)
  || (matrix1[0].length != matrix2[0].length))
    throw err_incompat;


  boolean [][] result =
    new boolean [matrix1.length][matrix1[0].length];


  for (int r = 0; r < matrix1.length; ++r)
  {
    for (int c = 0, c < matrix1[0].length; ++c)
    {
      result[r][c] = matrix1[r][c] != matrix2[r][c];
    }
  }


  return result;
}


public static boolean [][] compLess
  (
  double [][] matrix1,
  double [][] matrix2
  )
{
  if ((matrix1.length != matrix2.length)
  || (matrix1[0].length != matrix2[0].length))
    throw err_incompat;


  boolean [][] result =
    new boolean [matrix1.length][matrix1[0].length];
```

```
      for (int r = 0; r < matrix1.length; ++r)
      {
        for (int c = 0; c < matrix1[0].length; ++c)
        {
          result[r][c] = matrix1[r][c] < matrix2[r][c];
        }
      }

      return result;
    }

    public static boolean [][] compGreater
      (
      double [][] matrix1,
      double [][] matrix2
      )
    {
      if ((matrix1.length != matrix2.length)
      || (matrix1[0].length != matrix2[0].length))
        throw err_incompat;

      boolean [][] result =
        new boolean [matrix1.length][matrix1[0].length];

      for (int r = 0; r < matrix1.length; ++r)
      {
        for (int c = 0; c < matrix1[0].length; ++c)
        {
          result[r][c] = matrix1[r][c] > matrix2[r][c];
        }
      }

      return result;
    }
```

Minors

A *minor* is formed by removing a specific row and column from a matrix; its most prominent use is in recursively calculating the determinant of a *Matrix*. For example, for this matrix:

$$A = \begin{pmatrix} 2 & 1 & 4 & 7 \\ 3 & 0 & 9 & 7 \\ 8 & 0 & 1 & 3 \\ 1 & 2 & 6 & 5 \end{pmatrix}$$

The minor created by removing row 1, column 2 is:

$$A_{[12]} = \begin{pmatrix} 3 & 9 & 7 \\ 8 & 1 & 3 \\ 1 & 6 & 5 \end{pmatrix}$$

The `createMinor` method returns a minor created by removing a row and column from a target matrix:

```
public static double [][] createMinor
  (
  double [][] matrix,
  int rdel,
  int cdel
  )
{
  if ((matrix.length !=
      matrix[0].length) || (matrix.length < 2))
    throw err_incompat;

  double [][] result =
    new double [matrix.length - 1]
        [matrix[0].length - 1];

  int rdest = 0;

  for (int r = 0; r < matrix.length; ++r)
    {
    if (r != rdel)
      {
      int cdest = 0;
```

```
      for (int c = 0; c < matrix[0].length; ++c)
        {
        if (c != cdel)
          {
          result[rdest][cdest] = matrix[r][c];
          ++cdest;
          }

        ++cdest;
        }
      }
    else
      ++rdest;

    ++rdest;
    }

  return result;
}
```

You can calculate the *determinant* of an *n*-by-*n* matrix from its minors, following this formula:

$$\det(A) = \begin{cases} a_{11} & n = 1 \\ a_{11}\det(A_{[11]}) - a_{12}\det(A_{[12]}) + \cdots + (-1)^{n+1}a_{1n}\det(A_{[1n]}) & n > 1 \end{cases}$$

In matrix, the `det` computes the determinant of a square matrix using a recursive "helper" method:

```
public static double det
  (
  double [][] matrix
  )
{
  if (matrix.length != matrix[0].length)
    throw err_incompat;

  if (matrix.length == 1)
    return matrix[0][0];

  if (isSingular(matrix))
    return 0.0;
```

```
    return detRecursive(matrix);
}

// recursive function for determinant
protected static double detRecursive
  (
  double [][] matrix
  )
{
  if (matrix.length == 2)
    return (matrix[0][0] * matrix[1][1])
        - (matrix[0][1] * matrix[1][0]);

  double result = 0.0;

  for (int n = 0; n < matrix.length; ++n)
  {
    if ((n & 1) == 1)
      result -= matrix[n][0]
            * detRecursive(createMinor(matrix,0,n));
    else
      result += matrix[n][0]
            * detRecursive(createMinor(matrix,0,n));
  }

  return result;
}
```

Linear Equations and Gaussian Elimination

Scientific calculations often involve the search for solutions to systems of linear equations. Such solutions can be found from a square matrix in which the number of unknown values is equal to the number of equations. For example, the simultaneous equations

$$
\begin{aligned}
x_1 + 3x_2 - 4x_3 &= 8 \\
x_1 + x_2 - 2x_3 &= 2 \\
-x_1 - 2x_2 + 5x_3 &= -1
\end{aligned}
$$

can be conveniently rewritten as the matrix-vector equation:

$$\begin{pmatrix} 1 & 3 & -4 \\ 1 & 1 & -2 \\ -1 & 2 & 5 \end{pmatrix} \bullet \begin{pmatrix} x_1 \\ x_2 \\ x_3 \end{pmatrix} = \begin{pmatrix} 8 \\ 2 \\ -1 \end{pmatrix}$$

One method of solving linear equations is to use a 150 year old technique known as *Gaussian elimination*. Based on the properties of matrices, certain manipulations can be performed without altering the solution. The order of the equations does not affect the outcome, and we can multiply the equations by a constant with impunity. Also, any equation can be replaced by summing it with another equation. For example, the second equation can be replaced by its difference with the first equation:

$$\begin{pmatrix} 1 & 3 & -4 \\ 0 & 2 & -2 \\ -1 & 2 & 5 \end{pmatrix} \bullet \begin{pmatrix} x_1 \\ x_2 \\ x_3 \end{pmatrix} = \begin{pmatrix} 8 \\ 6 \\ -1 \end{pmatrix}$$

That eliminates x_1 from the second equation. The same technique can be used to eliminate x_1 from the third equation, by summing the first and third equations:

$$\begin{pmatrix} 1 & 3 & -4 \\ 0 & 2 & -2 \\ 0 & 1 & 1 \end{pmatrix} \bullet \begin{pmatrix} x_1 \\ x_2 \\ x_3 \end{pmatrix} = \begin{pmatrix} 8 \\ 6 \\ 7 \end{pmatrix}$$

This operation can be performed over and over again, until the original system of equations has been transformed into a triangular matrix that can easily be solved:

$$\begin{pmatrix} 1 & 3 & -4 \\ 0 & 2 & -2 \\ 0 & 0 & -4 \end{pmatrix} \bullet \begin{pmatrix} x_1 \\ x_2 \\ x_3 \end{pmatrix} = \begin{pmatrix} 8 \\ 6 \\ -8 \end{pmatrix}$$

Obviously, the third equation has been reduced to where we can calculate x_3 as 2. If we substitute x_3 into the second equation, it is simple to compute x_2 as 5. Substituting both x_3 and x_2 into the first equation solves for the third unknown, x_1, which equals 1.

Forward substitution is the first phase of reducing the equations; after reducing the coefficient matrix to a triangular form, we employ back *substitution* to calculate the values of each unknown in x.

To make the procedure simpler, I designed my Gaussian elimination function to work with an $n \times n+1$ matrix, where the $n+1$st column holds the solution vector b.

To avoid the chance of division by zero, `linSolve` includes code to exchange rows. If called for a singular matrix, division by zero cannot be avoided, and `linSolve` throws an exception.

```java
public static double [] linSolve
  (
  double [][] matrix
  )
{
  if (((matrix[0].length - matrix.length) != 1)
  ||  (isSingular(matrix)))
    throw err_incompat;

  int i, j, k, max;
  double temp;

  // forward elimination
  for (i = 0; i < matrix.length; ++i)
  {
    max = i;

    for (j = i + 1; j < matrix.length; ++j)
    {
      if (Math.abs(matrix[j][i]) >
          Math.abs(matrix[max][i]))
        max = j;
    }
```

```
        for (k = i; k < matrix[0].length; ++k)
        {
          temp = matrix[i][k];
          matrix[i][k] = matrix[max][k];
          matrix[max][k] = temp;
        }

        for (j = i + 1; j < matrix.length; ++j)
        {
          for (k = matrix.length; k >= i; --k)
          {
            matrix[j][k] -= matrix[i][k]
                      * matrix[j][i]
                      / matrix[i][i];

            if (k == 0) break;
          }
        }
      }

      // backward substitution
      double [] result =
          new double [matrix.length]; // results

      for (j = matrix.length - 1; ; --j)
      {
        temp = 0.0;

        for (k = j + 1; k < matrix.length; ++k)
          temp += matrix[j][k] * result[k];

        result[j] = (matrix[j][matrix.length]
            - temp) / matrix[j][j];

        if (j == 0) break;
      }

      return result;
    }
```

`linSolve` destroys the original matrix in its calculation; I could have created a copy of the input matrix (`this`), but for large matrices, creating the copy would use considerable memory. If you want to preserve the original matrix, simply create an explicit copy for use internally by `linSolve`.

LUP Decomposition

Gaussian elimination is a common tool for solving equations, but it isn't the only technique available. LUP decomposition, for instance, offers some interesting capabilities.

Begin by decomposing matrix A into a pair of matrices L and U, such that:

$$L \bullet U = A$$

The process of creating L and U is called *decomposition*. L is a lower-triangular matrix, and U is upper-triangular. According to matrix math, a linear equation can be rewritten as:

$$A \bullet x = (L \bullet U) \bullet x = L \bullet (U \bullet x) = b$$

In turn, *forward substitution* can solve:

$$L \bullet y = b$$

allowing backward substitution to find a solution to:

$$U \bullet x = y$$

At first, it might not seem that L and U can provide a superior solution to Gaussian elimination. However, once we have L and U, we can solve the set of equations for any b. Also, the decomposition into L and U allows for a simple calculation of a matrix's inverse. And, in most cases, decomposition is faster than Gaussian elimination.

Where does the P come from in LUP? While solving for the two triangular components, rows may (and probably will) be swapped — and a permutation matrix P is maintained to track these exchanges.

It's possible to create a single composite matrix of L and U. Known as *Crout's algorithm*, this technique copies the combined triangular matrices into the source matrix. This is accomplished by the following formulas:

```
for (j = 0; j < n; ++j)
  {
  for (i = 0; i < j; ++i)
```

$$\beta_{ij} = a_{ij} - \sum_{k=0}^{i-1} a_{ik}\beta_{kj}$$

```
  for (i = j; i < n; ++n)
```

$$a_{ij} = \frac{1}{\beta_{\ddot{\mu}}}\left(a_{ij} - \sum_{k=0}^{j-1} a_{ik}\beta_{kj}\right)$$

```
  }
```

The above results in a combine LU-matrix that looks like this:

$$\begin{pmatrix} \beta_{00} & \beta_{01} & \beta_{02} & \beta_{03} \\ a_{10} & \beta_{11} & \beta_{12} & \beta_{13} \\ a_{20} & a_{21} & \beta_{22} & \beta_{23} \\ a_{30} & a_{31} & a_{32} & \beta_{33} \end{pmatrix}$$

Swapping rows to avoid division by zero creates a permutation of the matrix above; furthermore, the algorithm makes the best selection for the fraction $\frac{1}{\beta_{ji}}$ by exchanging rows so as to make an optimal (largest) choice for β_{ji}.

```
// LUP decomposition
public static int [] lupDecompose
  (
```

```
    double [][] matrix
    )
{
  // make sure its square
  if ((matrix.length != matrix[0].length) ||
      (matrix.length < 2))
    throw err_incompat;

  int i, j, k, k2 = 0, t;
  double p, temp;

  int [] perm = new int [matrix.length];

  // initialize permutation
  for (i = 0; i < matrix.length; ++i)
    perm[i] = i;

  // LU decomposition
  for (k = 0; k < (matrix.length - 1); ++k)
  {
    p = 0.0;

    for (i = k; i < matrix.length; ++i)
    {
      temp = Math.abs(matrix[i][k]);

      if (temp > p)
      {
        p  = temp;
        k2 = i;
      }
    }

    if (p == 0.0)
      throw err_singular;

    // exchange
    t    = perm[k];
    perm[k]  = perm[k2];
    perm[k2] = t;
```

```
      for (i = 0; i < matrix.length; ++i)
      {
        temp        = matrix[k][i];
        matrix[k][i]  = matrix[k2][i];
        matrix[k2][i] = temp;
      }

      for (i = k + 1; i < matrix.length; ++i)
      {
        matrix[i][k] /= matrix[k][k];

        for (j = k + 1; j < matrix.length; ++j)
          matrix[i][j] -= matrix[i][k] * matrix[k][j];
      }
    }

    // return values
    return perm;
  }


  // LUP decomposition (call w/ result of LUPDecomp)
  public static double [] lupSolve
    (
    double [][] matrix,
    double []    vector,
    int []     perm
    )
  {
    if ((matrix.length != vector.length)
    || (matrix.length != perm.length))
      throw err_incompat;

    int i, j, j2;
    double sum, u;
    double [] y = new double [matrix.length];
    double [] x = new double [matrix.length];

    for (i = 0; i < matrix.length; ++i)
    {
      sum = 0.0;
      j2  = 0;
```

```
        for (j = 1; j <= i; ++j)
        {
          sum += matrix[i][j2] * y[j2];
          ++j2;
        }

        y[i] = vector[perm[i]] - sum;
      }

      i = matrix.length - 1;

      while (true)
      {
        sum = 0.0;
        u   = matrix[i][i];

        for (j = i + 1; j < matrix.length; ++j)
          sum += matrix[i][j] * x[j];

        x[i] = (y[i] - sum) / u;

        if (i == 0) break;

        --i;
      }

      return x;
    }
```

The `lupDecompose` function returns the permutation matrix representing the row exchanges performed, and replaces the original matrix with its LU decomposition.

To solve for a given solution matrix b, call `lupSolve` with a matrix processed by `lupDecompose`. `lupSolve` performs forward substitution to calculate y from L and b; then the routine uses back substitution to compute x from U and y. Don't change the permutation or decomposition matrix returned by `lupDecompose`, since that will result in bogus output from `lupSolve`.

Inversion

Once a matrix is decomposed, its inverse can be calculated by using a
permutation matrix to systematically compute an inverse for each row.

```java
// LUP inversion (call w/ result of LUPDecomp)
public static double [][] lupInvert
  (
  double [][] matrix,
  int []    perm
  )
{
  int i, j;

  double [] p = new double [matrix.length];

  double [][] result =
      new double [matrix.length][matrix.length];

  for (j = 0; j < matrix.length; ++j)
  {
    for (i = 0; i < matrix.length; ++i)
      p[i] = 0.0;

    p[j] = 1.0;

    p = lupSolve(matrix,p,perm);

    for (i = 0; i < matrix.length; ++i)
      result[i][j] = p[i];
  }

  return result;
}
```

Onward

Any significant application will store and retrieve data from external
files. Java provides several facilities for serializing objects and connecting to databases, and I'll be looking into these topics in the next
set of chapters. I'll also introduce several tools for developing your own
database applications, and for customizing Java's database support.

Chapter 9

Serialization

The ability to save, transfer, and restore the state of objects is essential to most significant applications. Whether it's a program saving objects between runs or a network application transferring objects from one process to another, it is essential that the objects be identifiable and reconstructable from some external format. In Java, this is accomplished via *serialization*: the translation of objects to and from an abstract representation.

Notes

For this chapter, I'm assuming that you have a basic knowledge of the java.io *package and the use of streams. This is a basic overview of serialization, providing enough information so that you understand the material in subsequent chapters. With Java version 1.2 (not available at the time of this writing), Sun will introduce a few new concepts, none of which appear to affect the discussion herein.*

Concepts

Serialization is also known in computer science as *persistence*, which is perhaps a more understandable term. Our goal is to make an object persist outside the context of its original application instance, by converting the object to a form that is compatible with extra program storage — a file on disk, for example. The stored data must contain all the information required to reconstruct the original object. For primitive types, this process is trivial; an integer value can easily be stored and retrieved as a sequence of bytes. For class-defined objects, however, we need some way to maintain the identity of its components and their relationship to a class definition.

"Persistence" can be a misleading term. For example, serialization is part of the Remote Method Invocation (RMI) package introduced with Java 1.1. An object transferred via serialization from one process to another is not persistent, since it isn't being stored for later retrieval. In an interprocess context, serialization provides a tool for transmitting objects from one execution unit to another, providing some assurance that the object reaches its destination in a form that can be translated back into a copy of the original object. Serialization implements a form of type-safe interprocess communication, as well as the ability to save and restore objects from disk files and other forms of extraprogram storage.

On the most basic level, serialization requires the preservation of the parts of an object that make it unique. We never need to store method code with a persistent object, since methods are a part of the compiled class file. When it comes to fields, the problem becomes a bit murkier. At first glance, it might seem that we can avoid storing final and static fields, since the former have a constant value and the latter belong to all objects defined by the class. But a final field might be a constant assigned in a constructor, and static fields may change between versions of a class. Understanding how an object works is essential to serializing it.

Another item must be stored in conjunction with an object: its class. On disk or traveling down a communication line, a serialized object is merely a sequence of bits; the application which "deserializes" the object must know the associated class in order to unload the encoded data correctly and associate it with an appropriate set of methods. That, in turn, requires the encoded object to contain some sort of mark or code identifying its class. With those considerations in mind, Sun introduced a general-purpose system for serializing objects with Java 1.1.

Notes

All serialization classes belong to the `java.io` *package.*

Object Identity

The `ObjectStreamClass` provides a descriptor for a serialized object. This descriptor contains both the fully-qualified name and a serial number for a class. `ObjectStreamClass` is a `Serializable` object itself, so it can be stored to a stream as the identity of an associated serialized object. The class is defined as:

```
public class ObjectStreamClass
  implements Serializable
{
  // return an ObjectStreamClass object for a given
     class
  public static ObjectStreamClass lookup(Class cl);

  // return fully-qualified name of this class
  public String getName();

  // return serial version ID of this class
  public long getSerialVersionUID();

  // return class object from VM
  public Class forClass();

  // return a String for this descriptor
  public String toString();
}
```

Java assigns every serializable class a 64-bit serial version unique identifier (SUID). A class can either define a member named `serialVersionUID` containing this value, or allow the system to calculate the SUID. The SUID is computed from the class definition with the National Institute of Standards and Technology (NIST) Secure Hash Algorithm (SHA-1). Essentially, the process involves combining the class name, its modifiers, interface names, and information about fields (other than private static and private transient ones) and methods into a value that is then processed by the SHA-1 algorithm to produce an array of five 32-bit quantities. The SUID is the first two of these values combined into a 64-bit `long`.

You don't need to perform this calculation yourself: the `Object-StreamClass` will compute the number if you do not specify a `serialVersionUID` field containing a value. With its Java SDK, Sun provides a handy utility, `serialver`, for calculating and inserting a `serialVersionUID` value into your classes. Bringing up `serialver` with the `-show` option under Microsoft Windows 95 produces a display like that shown in Figure 9-1.

Figure 9-1

The `serialver` Application

Serial Version Inspector

Full Class Name: | Show
Serial Version: |

Enter the name of your class in the text field, and click the **Show** button. The computer SUID will be displayed as a line of text that you can cut and paste into your class. Since `serialVersionNumber` is a `private static` field, adding it to your class will not change the SUID. In Figure 9-2, I show what happens when I ask `serialver` to calculate the SUID for the Complex class introduced back in Chapter 3.

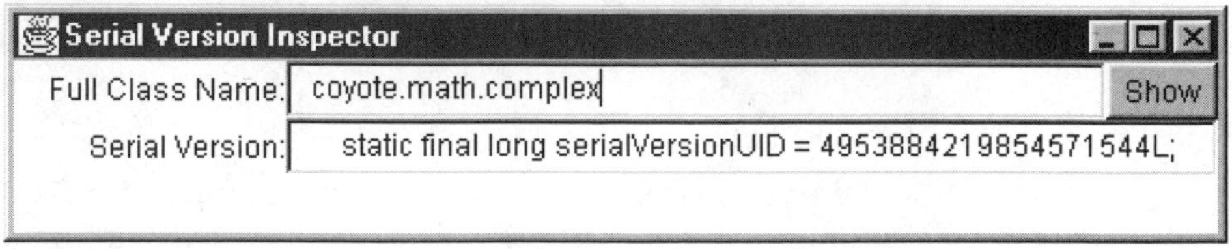

Figure 9-2

Computing the SUID for Complex

Serial Version Inspector

Full Class Name: coyote.math.complex | Show
Serial Version: static final long serialVersionUID = 4953884219854571544L;

In order to use `serialver` in this example, I had to change `Complex` to implement the `Serializable` class. I then cut the text in `serialver`'s "Serial Version" text field and inserted it into the `Complex` class text.

The SUID will always be identical for an identical definition of a class; it will not change unless you modify the class in some way, for example, by changing an identifier or adding a field. Different versions of a class will have different SUIDs; later in the chapter, I'll look at how serialization manages versioning.

Object Streams

The standard Java data streams, such as `FileInputStream` and `FileOutputStream`, operate on arrays of bytes. This shouldn't be surprising; be it from a disk file or a communications link, a data stream is essentially a sequence of bits organized into bytes. Such primitive data sequences lack an intrinsic meaning, taking on structure only when processed within our applications. Since objects have structure, the bytes associated with a stream must be translated into meaningful fields. To implement serialization, Java's designers devised the concept of an *object stream*, which translates an object to and from a sequence of bytes.

ObjectOutput

The `ObjectOutput` interface defines the contract for an object that writes an object to an output byte stream. Its definition is:

```
public interface ObjectOutput
  extends DataOutput
{
  public void writeObject(Object obj) throws
      IOException;

  public void write(int b) throws IOException;
  public void write(byte b[]) throws IOException;
  public void write(byte b[], int off, int len)
      throws IOException;
```

```
public void flush() throws IOException;
public void close() throws IOException;
}
```

The `writeObject` method writes an object to the destination as a series of bytes; the actual translation process is handled by the implementing class. Three `write` methods allow raw byte arrays to be stored; `flush` explicitly writes any information stored in output buffers; `close` closes the output stream.

ObjectOutputStream

The `java.io` package provides a single `ObjectOutput` implementation with the `ObjectOutputStream` class. `ObjectOutputStream` extends `OutputStream` and implements `ObjectOutput`; its definition is:

```
public class ObjectOutputStream
  extends OutputStream
  implements ObjectOutput, ObjectStreamConstants

{
  // constructor
  public ObjectOutputStream(OutputStream out) throws
      IOException;

  // write an object
  public final void writeObject(Object obj) throws
      IOException;

  // write non-static, non-transient fields (used
      by subclass)
  public final void defaultWriteObject() throws
      IOException;

  // implemented by subclasses to store additional
      class information
```

```
protected void annotateClass(Class cl) throws
    IOException;

// allow subclass to replace an object being
    serialized with another
protected Object replaceObject(Object obj) throws
    IOException;

// set whether or not objects can be replaced
protected final boolean enableReplaceObject
    (boolean enable)
    throws SecurityException;

// write single bytes or arrays of bytes
public void write(int data) throws IOException;
public void write(byte b[]) throws IOException;
public void write(byte b[], int off, int len)
    throws IOException;

// flush and close methods
public void flush() throws IOException;
public void close() throws IOException;

// primitive serialization methods
public void writeBoolean(boolean data) throws
    IOException;
public void writeByte(int data) throws IOException ;
public void writeShort(int data) throws IOException;
public void writeChar(int data) throws IOException;
public void writeInt(int data) throws IOException;
public void writeLong(long data) throws IOException;
public void writeFloat(float data) throws
    IOException;
public void writeDouble(double data) throws
    IOException;
public void writeBytes(String data) throws
    IOException;
public void writeChars(String data) throws
    IOException;
public void writeUTF(String data) throws
    IOException;
}
```

In creating an `ObjectOutputStream`, an instance of an `Output-Stream` provides the actual destination for serialized objects. Examples of `OutputStream`s include `FilterOutputStream`s, `ByteArray-OutputStream`s and `FileOutputStream`s. In essence, the `ObjectOutputStream` is a shell over another output stream that provides object-writing capabilities; thus, an `ObjectOutputStream` can store objects in any type of `OutputStream`, be it a file or an array of `bytes` in memory.

Special facilities of an `ObjectInputStream`, such as annotation and object replacement, will be described later in this chapter.

ObjectInput

The `ObjectInput` interface defines the contract for an object that reads an object from an input byte stream. Its definition is:

```
public interface ObjectInput
   extends DataInput
{
   public Object readObject() throws
       ClassNotFoundException, IOException;

   public int read() throws IOException;
   public int read(byte b[]) throws IOException;
   public int read(byte b[], int off, int len) throws
       IOException;

   public long skip(long n) throws IOException;

   public void close() throws IOException;
}
```

The `readObject` method reads an object from the destination, as defined by the implementing class. Three `read` methods allow raw byte arrays to be retrieved; `skip` causes the input stream to ignore a specified number of sequential input bytes; `close` closes the input stream.

ObjectInputStreams

The `java.io` package provides a single `ObjectInput` implementation with the `ObjectInputStream` class. `ObjectInputStream` extends `InputStream` and implements `ObjectInput`; its definition is:

```
public class ObjectInputStream
  extends InputStream
  implements ObjectInput, ObjectStreamConstants
{
  // constructor
  public ObjectInputStream(InputStream in)
    throws IOException, StreamCorruptedException;

  // read an object
  public final Object readObject()
    throws OptionalDataException,
      ClassNotFoundException, IOException;

  // read non-static, non-transient fields
  public final void defaultReadObject()
    throws IOException, ClassNotFoundException,
      NotActiveException;

  // object and class validation
  public synchronized void registerValidation
    (ObjectInputValidation obj,
     int prio)
    throws NotActiveException, InvalidObjectException

  protected Class resolveClass(ObjectStreamClass v)
    throws IOException, ClassNotFoundException;

  protected Object resolveObject(Object obj)
    throws IOException;

  protected final boolean enableResolveObject
      (boolean enable)
    throws SecurityException;
```

```
// read the stream header and magic number
protected void readStreamHeader()
   throws IOException, StreamCorruptedException;

// read a single byte
public int read() throws IOException;
public void readFully(byte[] data) throws
     IOException;

// read an array of bytes
public int read(byte[] data, int offset, int length)
       throws IOException;

public void readFully(byte[] data, int offset,
     int size)
   throws IOException;

// close output stream
public void close() throws IOException;

// read primitives
public boolean readBoolean() throws IOException;
public byte readByte() throws IOException ;
public int readUnsignedByte() throws IOException;
public short readShort() throws IOException;
public int readUnsignedShort() throws IOException;
public char readChar() throws IOException;
public int readInt() throws IOException;
public long readLong() throws IOException;
public float readFloat() throws IOException;
public double readDouble() throws IOException;

// skip a sequence of bytes
public int skipBytes(int len) throws IOException;

// read a line of textc
public String readLine() throws IOException;
public String readUTF() throws IOException;
}
```

In creating an `ObjectInputStream`, an instance of an `Input-Stream` provides the actual destination for serialized objects. Examples of `OutputStream`s include `FilterInputStream`s, `ByteArray-InputStream`s and `FileInputStream`s. In essence, the `ObjectInputStream` is a shell over another output stream that provides object-writing capabilities; thus, an `ObjectInputStream` can store objects in any type of `OutputStream`, be it a file or an in-memory array of `bytes`.

Special facilities of an `ObjectInputStream`, such as validation and object resolution, are described later in this chapter.

Notes

Serialization automatically provides input and output facilities for primitive types such as int *and* float. *Java defines explicit byte sizes for all primitive types; for example, a four-byte* int *will be stored in four bytes. Only the size of a* boolean *type is undefined; for the purpose of serialization, a* boolean *value will persist as a single byte containing 1 for* true *and 0 for* false.

Serialization Interfaces

Java defines a serializable object as belonging to a class that implements either the `Serializable` or `Externalizable` interfaces. The former invokes an automated mechanism for storing and retrieving persistent objects, whereas the latter requires a class to be solely responsible for the persistent format of its elements. As often happens, a serializable object may contain other objects as fields or superclasses; such elements must also support `Serializable` or `Externalizable`, to allow the complete context of the enclosing object to be maintained in persistent storage.

Serializable

`Serializable` is an empty interface; it defines nothing other than the characteristic of being `Serializable`. By default, serialization stores all the non-transient and non-static fields of a class, in order of declaration, via the `OutputObject` method `default-WriteObject`. A `Serializable` class can also define `writeObject` and `readObject` methods, allowing it to manipulate the information stored or to append additional data. These methods *must* have signatures identical to the following:

```
private void writeObject(ObjectOutputStream stream)
    throws IOException;

private void readObject(ObjectInputStream stream)
    throws IOException, ClassNotFoundException;
```

By defining `writeObject` and `readObject`, a class declares that its objects will provide additional control to the serialization of their state information. Essentially, the class stores or retrieves its fields directly from the stream argument of these methods. If a class does not define these two methods, objects will be serialized via the `defaultWrite-Object` method of the target `ObjectOutputStream`. I'll look into this process in detail when describing object output later in this chapter.

Transient Fields

The `transient` keyword denotes a field with a value that can change at any time, possibly outside the context of the current execution unit. For example, a transient field may represent a system characteristic or information received via asynchronous communication. Generally, a compiler generates less efficient bytecode when working with transient fields, since it must reload the field's value every time it is used instead of optimizing code based on past values.

For serialization, `transient` takes on an additional meaning, identifying a field that is not automatically serialized. You could still serialize a transient field directly in the `writeObject` and `readObject` methods, and this may be desirable if the transient field requires special output processing. Keep in mind, though, that a `transient` qualifier will likely produce slower and larger code for any computations involving a field so designated.

Externalizable

The `Externalizable` interface identifies a class of objects that completely control the serialization of their state. Unlike `Serializable`, `Externalizable` declares a pair of methods that must be implemented:

```
public interface Externalizable
  extends Serializable
{
  void writeExternal(ObjectOutput out)
    throws IOException;

  void readExternal(ObjectInput in)
    throws IOException, ClassNotFoundException;
}
```

An `ObjectOutputStream` will only store a class descriptor identifying an `Externalizable` object; all other persistent data must be handled manually by the `writeExternal` and `readExternal` method. An output object stream will not maintain any fields, superclasses, or other information; the maintenance of such information is the responsibility of the `Externalizable` object. In Chapter 12, you'll see an example of an `Externalizable` object that serializes a BTree "page."

Object Output

The `writeObject` method performs special handling for certain classes of objects being serialized:

1. If the object reference is `null`, a `null` is output to the stream and `writeObject` returns.

2. The `ObjectOutputStream` maintains an internal list of all objects that have been serialized to the stream. If an attempt is made to serialize an object already stored to the stream, the `ObjectOutputStream` instead stores a "handle" or reference to the first serialization of the object. In this way, serialization prevents the same object from being serialized more than once. Use the `ObjectOutputStream` method reset to clear the list of serialized objects.

3. If the object is a `Class`, the corresponding `ObjectStream-Class` is serialized and `writeObject` returns.

4. If the object is an `ObjectStreamClass`, a descriptor for the class will be written, including the name, SUID, and list of fields by

name and type. A call is made to the `annotateClass` method (which is empty unless overloaded by a subclass) to add any additional information about the class, before `writeObject` returns.

5. If the object is a `String`, it is written in Universal Transfer Format (UTF). A limitation in the current Java definition prevents serialization of any `String` longer than 65,535 characters.

6. If the object is an array, `writeObject` calls itself recursively to write a single `ObjectStreamClass` object identifying the type of elements being stored. Next, the length of the array is written, followed by the elements of the array, the latter written by recursive calls to `writeObject`.

7. If the object replacement is enabled via `enableReplaceObject`, `writeObject` calls `replaceObject` to obtain a substitute object. Both `enableReplaceObject` and `replaceObject` are `protected` methods implemented internally by a subclass; by default, object replacement is set to `false` and `replaceObject` returns its `Object` argument without change. Now `writeObject` goes back through this list, checking to see if the replacement object is one of the special categories mentioned above.

Assuming that none of the special cases have caused `writeObject` to return, the method proceeds to serialize the object. First, an `ObjectStreamClass` object is written to describe the object. For objects that do not implement either `Externalizable` or `Serializable`, `writeObject` will throw a `NotSerializableException`.

If the object is `Externalizable`, its `writeExternal` method is called to serialize the object. As mentioned above, `writeExternal` has all the responsibility for storing the persistent state of the object; if `writeExternal` places nothing in the stream, nothing about the object (other than its class descriptor) will be stored.

If the object is `Serializable`, the `defaultWriteObject` method is called to serialize its components — unless the object's class defines a `writeObject` method. The `defaultWriteObject` method serializes the non-`transient`, non-`static` methods in a class; it recursively calls `ObjectOutputStream.writeObject` to serialize object fields or superclass objects. The superclass hierarchy is serialized recursively, with the highest level superclass being stored first. Object references in fields will also be serialized recursively; this allows dynamic data structures like binary trees and linked lists to be serialized naturally, with each node or link stored.

However, if the `Serializable` object's class does define `writeObject`, that method is called with a reference to the output stream. Often, `writeObject` will begin by calling `ObjectOutputStream.defaultWriteObject` to serialize the object's fields, then `writeObject` will add additional state information for the object. This technique is often useful when an object needs to provide information about itself that isn't reflected in its serializable fields.

Notes

`defaultWriteObject` can only be called from an object's `writeObject` method; calling `defaultWriteObject` from any other method will result in a `NotActiveException` being thrown.

You may implement `writeObject` to store fields qualified as `transient`; the `transient` keyword can denote a value that may change outside the control of an object. In some cases, you may want to save this `transient` value — for instance, when your object is maintaining a history of dynamic information.

Object Input

For the most part, an `ObjectInputStream` acts as a reflection of the `ObjectOutputStream`, reversing the process for retrieving an object. The input stream begins by obtaining an `ObjectStreamClass` object from the stream; this identifies the class associated with the associated persistent data. Essentially, the `ObjectInputStream` reconstructs the object by reading its superclass information, fields, and subobjects in the same order as they were written. Corresponding to `ObjectOutputStream`'s `defaultWriteObject` method is the `defaultReadObject` method. Using these default serializations, objects will be recreated in their original state.

In recovering a serialized object, the `ObjectInputStream` begins by creating a new object by calling the no-argument constructor to create an empty object. This will initialize all fields of the new object to their default (usually zero) value. For an `Externalizable` object, your class' `readExternal` method will be responsible for extracting and interpreting the state of an object.

If you implement a `writeObject` method for your `Serializable` class, you must also define a corresponding `readObject` method. Care must be taken to ensure the compatibility of `writeObject` and `readObject`: what is stored by the former must be retrieved by the latter.

If the `enableResolveObject` method has enabled the replacement of input objects, the `resolveObject` method is called to allow a subclass of `ObjectInputStream` to replace the newly-restored object with another. This is the counterpart to object replacement implemented by subclasses of `ObjectOutputStream`. By default, `ObjectInputStream` does not replace an object; its implementation of `resolveObject` simply returns a reference to the original object.

Versioning

Everything I've discussed so far is based on the assumption that the classes of objects remain constant across the serialization process; essentially, the class of a persistent object will be the same when it is read as when it was written. The real world, however, involves classes that evolve over time. An object in persistent storage cannot be aware of changes in its class definition; it may be retrieved into a class that has added or deleted fields. Serialization handles this situation via the versioning of serializable objects.

Serialization defines changes in classes as *compatible* or *incompatible*. A compatible change does not affect the contract between an object and its callers. Versioning only works with classes that implement `Serializable`; since the serialization mechanism has no control over the persistent representation of `Externalizable` classes, such classes cannot support versioning.

Among the goals of versioning are:

- Allow newer versions of a class to read objects stored by an older version, and vice-versa.

- Provide default handling of versioning, so that classes are not forced to implement version-specific serialization support.

- New versions must satisfy the contract for older versions, although they may extend or modify the implementation of that contract. This means that a newer version cannot remove any public fields or methods supported by older versions. The responsibility for compatibility resides solely with new versions of a class.

- The SUID of a newer version defines the older version with which it is compatible. Thus, in the initial version of a class, the SUID is computed using the NIST SHA-1 algorithm; all compatible subsequent versions will define a `serialVersionUID` member equal to the SUID of the compatible ancestral class.

If a serializable class implements `readObject` and `writeObject`, these methods must call the `defaultReadObject` and `defaultWriteObject` methods, respectively, to ensure that required data is written for objects. Incompatible changes in a newer version include:

- Deleting a field.

- Reordering fields.

- Changing the type of a primitive field.

- Changing `readObject` or `writeObject` (if defined) such that they do not maintain the same information as in previous versions.

- Changing a class from `Serializable` to `Externalizable` or vice versa.

Compatible changes to a class include:

- Adding fields — If an object defined by an older class is retrieved, new fields will be initialized to their default (usually zero) value.

- Adding classes — Superclass objects added by the new class or its fields will be initialized using their no-argument constructor.

- Removing classes — Superclass objects removed by the new class or its fields will be ignored.

- Changing a non-static field to `static`.

- Changing a non-transient field to `transient`.

- Adding `readObject` and `writeObject` methods. If the version reading the stream has these methods, then `readObject` is expected to call `defaultReadObject` before reading any optional data; `writeObject` is expected to call `default-WriteObject` before writing any optional data.

- Removing `readObject` and `writeObject` methods. Any optional data stored by previous versions will be ignored and discarded.

- Changing access to a field. The access modifiers `public`, `private`, and `protected` have no affect on serialization.

- Changing a `static` field to non-static.

- Changing a `transient` field to non-transient.

Onward

Serialization is a powerful tool, but it has one limiting facet: it only works with sequential storage. For sophisticated database algorithms, it is often necessary to locate information via random access. In the next two chapters, I explore techniques for applying serialization to random access files and BTree indexes.

10

Data Compression

Most of the data we generate is redundant. A text document consists of the same three dozen characters or so, yet we're using a full eight bits (representing 256 possible values) to represent each character when five bits (representing 32 possible values) might do. Graphic information often contains series of identical bytes representing areas filled with the same color.

Data compression tries to solve this problem by changing the representation of data. For example, run-length encoding replaces a string of identical characters by one copy of the character and a count. Run-length encoding works well for consistent data, such as bitmap graphic images, but it isn't effective with less homogenous information, such as documents or database files. A useful compression algorithm will convert an input object into a smaller form that can later be expanded into a copy of the original. No algorithm can perform this feat in every case; there will always be some piece of data that simply can't be compressed. In a few rare cases, a compression algorithm may actually make data larger. The best algorithms minimize the chance of encountering an extreme case.

One of the most popular of these algorithms was developed D.A. Huffman in 1952. Huffman encoding uses a simple idea: create a set of codes for which the shortest code represents the most common piece of data. Codes created by the Huffman algorithm require a file to be analyzed, counting bytes to determine their frequency. From the frequencies, the Huffman algorithm builds a table of codes used to compress the information. Including the table of codes with the compressed data allows the original file to be reconstructed. To be most effective, Huffman encoding uses a variable length code; no code is a prefix of any other, which makes decompression easier by allowing the extraction of the file bit-by-bit. The shortest codes are assigned to the most common characters, with infrequent characters receiving longer codes. To create the codes, the Huffman algorithm creates a special binary tree — known as a *trie* (pronounced *try*) — based on the byte frequencies of the original data.

A trie is a binary tree that only has data in its leaf nodes. Each internal trie node has two branches, designated 1 and 0, which correspond to the "greater than" and "less than" links in binary tree nodes. With the frequency counts in hand, the Huffman algorithm constructs a trie based on the frequencies of bytes. The compression process begins by counting the bytes in the original data, storing these values in a frequency table. For example, the frequency counts for "A SIMPLE STRING TO BE ENCODED USING A MINIMAL NUMBER OF BITS" would look like this (omitting letters with zero occurrence):

Letter	Frequency
A	3
B	3
C	1
D	2
E	5
F	1
G	2
I	6

Letter	Frequency
L	2
M	4
N	5
O	3
P	1
R	2
S	4
T	3
U	2
space	11

The trie is constructed by sorting the values into order via the heap technique presented in Chapter 5. Trie construction is done from the bottom up (working from the least common values to the most common). Once you've counted characters and constructed a trie, encoding a file is a simple matter of following the tree from root to the character being encoded. For example, whenever you store a letter 'A', you'll use the binary code 0110 by beginning at the root and following the left, right, right, and left branches in the tree.

To convert Huffman-encoded data to its original form, use the bits input to follow the tree to the compressed character. Let's look at decoding this sequence of encoded input bytes, 110110100110100 using the above trie. The first bit takes us to the right; then we move right, left, right, and right again, reaching the terminal node containing 'T'. Having found a character, we begin again at the root with a zero bit, moving to the right, then left, and right twice to find the letter 'O'. The remaining bits take our algorithm to the 'P' character, thus completing our word 'TOP.' The trie ensures that the same sequence of bits always leads to the same character, and that no two characters have the same encoding.

Compression using the Huffman algorithm is very effective on text files. For example, the test string "A SIMPLE STRING TO BE ENCODED USING A MINIMAL NUMBER OF BITS" can be shrunk from its original 480 bits (at 8 bits per character) to only 261 bits — a savings of more than 45 percent. Of course, when storing the compressed information for later expansion — in a file, perhaps — you'll need to include a copy of the encoding table from which you can construct a decompression trie.

Object-Oriented Compression

I developed my Java compression tool with the idea of applying it to objects. The Huffman algorithm is designed for compressing arrays of 8-bit bytes; objects, however, are usually complex structures, not simple arrays. Fortunately, Java serialization comes to the rescue, since it allows us to convert and serialize an object into an array of bytes via `ObjectOutputStream` and a `ByteArrayOutputStream`. To store an object in compressed form:

1. Create a `ByteArrayOutputStream` as the destination for the serialized object.

2. Create an `ObjectOutputStream` from the `ByteArrayOutput-Stream`.

3. Write the serializable object to the `ObjectOutputStream`.

4. Compress the byte array from the `ByteArrayObject`.

Reading compressed objects is the reverse of the above sequence:

1. Decompress the Huffman-encoded data into the original array of bytes.

2. Create a `ByteArrayInputStream` from the decoded array.

3. Create an `ObjectInputStream` from the `ByteArrayInput-Stream`.

4. Read the reconstituted object from the `ObjectInputStream`.

Encoded Data

An encoded object is held by a byte array associated with tables and other data required for decoding the information. Essentially, the Huffman algorithm becomes a pair of static methods, one creating `HuffmanEncoded` objects containing compressed data, and the other method reproducing an object from a `HuffmanEncoded` parameter. `HuffmanEncoded` objects are themselves serializable, allowing a compressed object to be stored in a stream.

Headers

The header for encoded data contains the original length of the data, the length of the encoded data, and a pointer to a dynamically-allocated memory buffer containing the compressed information. Two arrays hold the codes generated from the trie and the lengths of those codes. This implementation allows codes of up to 32 bits in length.

```java
package coyote.tools;

import java.io.*;

//
//
// HuffmanHeader
//
//
public class HuffmanHeader
  implements Serializable
{
  static final long serialVersionUID =
      2324944752979350437L;

  //-------------------------
  // fields
  //-------------------------
  boolean  oneValue;       // one value flag
  int    lenOrig;       // # of bytes in orig data
```

```
int    lenData;        // # of encoded bytes
int    [] code = new int    [256]; // character codes
short [] cLen = new short [256]; // character code
    lengths
}
```

I've defined `HuffmanHdr` as a simple structure, its members only
accessible from within the **coyote.tools** package.

Compressed Data

My routines hold encoded information in a byte array.

```
package coyote.tools;

import java.io.*;

//
//
// HuffmanEncoded
//
//
public class HuffmanEncoded
  implements Serializable
{
  static final long serialVersionUID =
      73798330641254621103L;

  //-------------------------
  // fields
  //-------------------------

  // buffer containing compressed data
  byte [] compData;

  // encoding table and other data
  HuffmanHeader hdr = new HuffmanHeader();
```

```
//------------------------
// property methods
//------------------------

// get pointer to buffer
public byte [] GetData()
{
  return compData;
}

// get header
public HuffmanHeader GetHeader()
{
  return hdr;
}
}
```

Each `HuffmanEncoded` object contains a header and a pointer to an associated block of memory, `compData`, that is `hdr.lenData` bytes long. The default constructor creates an empty `HuffmanEncoded` object.

The Huffman Class

The `Huffman` class is the "meat" of my compression library; it defines `public static` methods that create `HuffmanEncoded`objects from input data, and makes objects when asked to decode compressed information. In essence, `Huffman` encapsulates a set of processes implementing the compression algorithm.

Compression

The complete `Huffman` class is defined as:

```
package coyote.tools;

import java.io.*;
```

```
//
//
// Huffman
//
//
public class Huffman
{
  //------------------------
  // methods
  //------------------------
  public static HuffmanEncoded Encode
    (
    Object obj
    )
    throws IOException
  {
    // serialize object
    if ((obj instanceof Serializable) ||
        (obj instanceof Externalizable))
    {

      // create an output byte array
      ByteArrayOutputStream raw =
          new ByteArrayOutputStream();

      // create an object Output stream
      ObjectOutputStream out =
          new ObjectOutputStream(raw);

      // write object to output stream
      out.writeObject(obj);
      out.flush();

      // encode bytes
      return Compress(raw.toByteArray());
    }
    else
      throw new HuffmanException
          ("can't encode non-serializable object");
  }
```

```
public static Object Decode
  (
  HuffmanEncoded enc
  )
  throws IOException, ClassNotFoundException
{
  // decode compressed data
  byte [] decoded = Decompress(enc);


  // create byte input stream from decoded bytes
  ByteArrayInputStream raw =
      new ByteArrayInputStream(decoded);


  // create an object input stream
  ObjectInputStream in = new ObjectInputStream(raw);


  // return the object
  return in.readObject();
}
//------------------------
// internal utility methods
//------------------------
private static void HeapAdjust
  (
  int [] freq,
  int [] heap,
  int n,
  int k
  )
{
  // this function compares the values in the array
  // 'freq' to order the elements of 'heap' according
  // in an inverse heap.
  int j;


  int v = heap[k - 1];
  while (k <= (n / 2))
  {
    j = k + k;
```

```
      if ((j < n) && (freq[heap[j - 1]] >
          freq[heap[j]]))
        ++j;

      if (freq[v] < freq[heap[j - 1]])
        break;

    heap[k - 1] = heap[j - 1];
    k = j;
  }

heap[k - 1] = v;
  }


// Huffman compression function
private static HuffmanEncoded Compress
  (
  byte [] info
  )
{
  // get length of info
  int bytes = info.length;

  // allocate data space
  byte [] edata = new byte [bytes + 1];

  // allocate frequency table
  int [] freq = new int [512];

  // allocate heap
  int [] heap = new int [256];

  // allocate link array
  int [] link = new int [512];

  // create work area
  HuffmanEncoded encoded = new HuffmanEncoded();

  int   [] code = encoded.hdr.code;
  short [] clen = encoded.hdr.cLen;
```

```
// count frequencies
int i;

byte a = -1;

for (i = 0; i < bytes; ++i)
  ++freq[info[i] < 0 ? 256 + info[i] : info[i]];

// create indirect heap based on frequencies

int n = 0;

for (i = 0; i < 256; ++i)
{
  if (freq[i] != 0)
  {
    heap[n] = i;
    ++n;
  }
}

for (i = n; i > 0; --i)
  HeapAdjust(freq,heap,n,i);

// generate a trie from heap
int temp;

// at this point, n contains the number of
//   characters
// that occur in the info array
while (n > 1)
{
  // take first item from top of heap
  --n;
  temp= heap[0];
  heap[0] = heap[n];

  // adjust the heap to maintain properties
  HeapAdjust(freq,heap,n,1);
```

```
    // in upper half of freq array, store sums of
    // the two smallest frequencies from the heap
    freq[256 + n] = freq[heap[0]] + freq[temp];
    link[temp]    =   256 + n; // parent
    link[heap[0]]  = -256 - n; // left child
    heap[0]        =   256 + n; // right child

    // adjust the heap again
    HeapAdjust(freq,heap,n,1);
}


link[256 + n] = 0;

// generate codes
int j, k, x, maxx = 0, maxi = 0;
int l;

for (k = 0; k < 256; ++k)
{
  if (freq[k] == 0) // character does not occur
  {
    code[k] = 0;
    clen[k] = 0;
  }
  else
  {
    i = 0;   // length of current code
    j = 1;   // bit being set in code
    x = 0;   // code being built
    l = link[k]; // link in trie

    while (l != 0) // while not at end of trie
    {
      if (l < 0) // left link (negative)
      {
        x +=  j; // insert 1 into code
        l  = -l; // reverse sign
      }

      l  = link[l]; // move to next link
      j <<= 1;  // next bit to be set
```

```
        ++i;      // increment code length
    }


    code[k] = x; // save code
    clen[k] = (short)i; // save code len


    // keep track of biggest key
    if (x > maxx)
      maxx = x;


    // keep track of longest key
    if (i > maxi)
      maxi = i;
  }
}


// make sure longest codes fit in unsigned
    long-bits
if (maxi > 32)
  throw new HuffmanException("code size overflow");


// encode data
int  mask;  // mask for extracting bits
int  nout = 0;    // number of bytes output
byte bout = 0;    // byte of encoded data
int  bit  = -1;   // count of bits stored in bout


// watch for one-value file!
if (maxx == 0)
{
  edata[0] = (byte)info[0];
  nout = 1;
  encoded.hdr.oneValue = true;
}
else
{
  for (j = 0; j < bytes; ++j)
  {
    int ibyte = info[j] < 0 ? 256 + info[j] :
        info[j];
```

```
// start copying at first bit of code
mask = 1 << (clen[ibyte] - 1);


// copy code bits
for (i = 0; i < clen[ibyte]; ++i)
{
  if (bit == 7)
  {
    // store full output byte
    edata[nout] = bout;
    ++nout;

    // check for overflow
    if (nout == bytes)
      throw new HuffmanException
          ("compression overflow");

    bit  = 0;
    bout = 0;
  }
  else
  {
    // move to next bit
    ++bit;
    bout <<= 1;
  }

  if ((code[ibyte] & mask) != 0)
    bout |= 1;

  mask >>>= 1;
  }
}


// output any incomplete bytes
bout <<= (7 - bit);
edata[nout] = bout;
++nout;
}
```

```
        // store all information
        encoded.hdr.lenOrig = bytes;
        encoded.hdr.lenData = nout;

        encoded.compData = edata;

        // return result
        return encoded;
    }

// decompress encoded data
private static byte [] Decompress
    (
    HuffmanEncoded data
    )
{
    int  i, j, n, mask, k, t;
    byte c;

    // allocate output array
    byte [] dec = new byte [data.hdr.lenOrig];

    // handle decompression of one-value file
    if (data.hdr.oneValue)
    {
        for (i = 0; i < dec.length; ++i)
            dec[i] = data.compData[0];
        return dec;
    }

    // allocate heap
    int [] heap = new int [256];

    // allocate output character buffer
    byte [] outc = new byte [256];

    // initialize work areas
    int    [] code = data.hdr.code;
    short [] clen = data.hdr.cLen;

    // create decode table as trie heap
    for (j = 0; j < 256; ++j)
```

```
{
  outc[j] = (byte)j;

  // if code exists for this byte
  if ((code[j] | clen[j]) != 0)
  {
    // begin at first code bit
    k = 0;
    mask = 1 << (clen[j] - 1);

    // find proper node, using bits in code as
        path.
    for (i = 0; i < clen[j]; ++i)
    {
      k = k * 2 + 1; // right link

      if ((code[j] & mask) != 0)
        ++k; // go left

      mask >>>= 1; // next bit
    }

    heap[j] = k; // store link in heap
  }
}

// sort outc based on heap
for (i = 1; i < 256; ++i)
{
  t = heap[i];
  c = outc[i];
  j = i;

  while ((j != 0) && (heap[j - 1] > t))
  {
    heap[j] = heap[j - 1];
    outc[j] = outc[j - 1];
    --j;
  }
  heap[j] = t;
  outc[j] = c;
}
```

```
// find first character in table
for (j = 0; heap[j] == 0; ++j) ;

// decode data
k = 0; // link in trie
i = j;
mask = 0x80;
n = 0;
int cptr = 0;
int dptr = 0;

while (n < data.hdr.lenOrig)
{
  k = k * 2 + 1; // right link

  if ((data.compData[cptr] & mask) != 0)
    ++k; // left link if bit on

  // search heap until link >= k
  while (heap[i] < k)
    ++i;

  // code matches, character found
  if (k == heap[i])
  {
    dec[dptr] = outc[i];
    ++dptr;
    ++n;
    k = 0;
    i = j;
  }

  // move to next bit
  if (mask > 1)
    mask >>>= 1;
  else
  { // code extends into next byte
    mask = 0x80;
    ++cptr;
  }
}
```

```
        // return decoded data
        return dec;
    }
}
```

The `Encode` method implements the sequence described above for compressing an object. It takes its `Object` argument and converts it into an array of bytes via an `ObjectOutputStream` and a `ByteArrayOutputStream`. That array is then fed to the `Compress` method, which returns a `HuffmanEncodedObject`.

`Compress` is the engine that constructs the trie, creates the codes, and encodes the data. It begins by allocating work space and creating a frequency count; it then creates an indirect heap based on these frequencies. The heap itself is a set of index links that show the organization of the heap, and it is built via the `HeapAdjust` utility method.

Notes

Chapter 5 explains the heap algorithm, which I customized in the case of `Huffman.`

From the heap, `Compress` creates a sequence of codes in the `code` array, with the length of each code stored in the corresponding elements of the `clen` array. I accomplish this by defining a set of linked lists in the `link` array, based on the trie structure built from frequency information. Once the trie is built, the program generates codes by following its nodes from character to root. `Compress` proceeds to encode the information by copying encoded bits into the `compData` member of the `HuffmanEncoded` object being produced. The information on codes and sizes is stored in the `header` record.

To decode compressed information, call the `Decode` method. The algorithm begins by expanding a `HuffmanEncoded` object into its original form via the `Decompress` method. `Decompress` constructs a trie from the code information stored in the compressed data's header. Once the `code`, `clen`, and `heap` arrays have been allocated and loaded, `Decompress` reads the `compData` information a bit at a time, following the heap-based trie to encoded characters. The function also keeps track of how many characters have been input and how many output. This ensures that it decodes as many characters as were encoded.

Exceptions

The `Huffman` classes throw exceptions of type `HuffmanException`.

```
package coyote.tools;

//
//
// HuffmanException
//
//
public class HuffmanException
  extends RuntimeException
{
  public HuffmanException()
  {
    super();
  }

  public HuffmanException(String s)
  {
    super(s);
  }
}
```

For example, an attempt to compress a non-serializable object will generate a `HuffmanException`.

Elaborations

I originally designed the `Huffman` class for use in one of my applications where a considerable amount of data was being stored to and read from a disk file. A dynamic implementation of this algorithm would reduce its memory requirements and allow for the construction of the compression code trie "on the fly" as data is read from a specific source.

So how does the `Huffman` algorithm work in practice? The following code segment shows the Huffman class in action, compressing and decompressing the poem *Jabberwocky* written by Lewis Carroll for *Through the Looking Glass*.

```java
import java.applet.*;
import java.awt.*;

import coyote.tools.*;

public class Chapter10 extends Applet
{

  public String getAppletInfo()
  {
    return "Java Algorithms and Components:
        Chapter Ten" +
          "Copyright 1997 Scott Robert Ladd" +
          "All rights reserved";
  }

  private static final String Jabberwocky =
    "JABBERWOCKY\n" +
    "\n" +
    "'Twas brillig, and the slithy toves\n" +
    "  Did gyre and gimble in the wabe;\n" +
    "All mimsy were the borogoves,\n" +
    "  And the mome raths outgrabe.\n" +
    "\n" +
    "`Beware the Jabberwock, my son!\n" +
    "  The jaws that bite, the claws that catch!\n" +
    "Beware the Jujub bird, and shun\n" +
    "  The frumious Bandersnatch!'\n" +
    "\n" +
    "He took his vorpal sword in hand:\n" +
    "  Long time the manxome foe he sought--\n" +
    "So rested he by the Tumtum tree,\n" +
    "  And stood awhile in thought.\n" +
    "\n" +
    "And as in uffish thought he stood,\n" +
    "  The Jabberwock, with eyes of flame,\n" +
```

```
          "Came whiffling through the tulgey wood,\n" +
          "  And burbled as it came!\n" +
          "\n" +
          "One, two!  One, two!  And through and through\n" +
          "  The vorpal blade went snicker-snack!\n" +
          "He left it dead, and with its head\n" +
          "  He went galumphing back.\n" +
          "\n" +
          "`And has thou slain the Jabberwock?\n" +
          "  Come to my arms, my beamish boy!\n" +
          "O frabjous day!  Calloh!  Callay!'\n" +
          "  He chortled in his joy.\n" +
          "\n" +
          "'Twas brillig, and the slithy toves\n" +
          "  Did gyre and gimble in the wabe;\n" +
          "All mimsy were the borogoves,\n" +
          "  And the mome raths outgrabe.\n";

   public void init()
   {
      // define applet area
      setSize(480,320);
      setLayout(new BorderLayout(0,0));
      setBackground(Color.lightGray);


      // create output list
      TextArea before = new TextArea();
      add(before,BorderLayout.NORTH);


      TextArea after = new TextArea();
      add(after,BorderLayout.SOUTH);


      // add the text
      before.append(Jabberwocky);


      try
      {
         // compress text using huffman
         HuffmanEncoded enc = Huffman.Encode(Jabberwocky);
```

```
        // now decompress
        String j = (String)Huffman.Decode(enc);

        // display decompressed text
        after.append(j);
    }
    catch (Exception ex)
    {
      after.append(ex.getClass().getName() + ": " +
          ex.getMessage());
    }
  }


}
```

The program above produces an applet display like that shown in Figure 10-1.

Figure 10-1

Before and After Compression

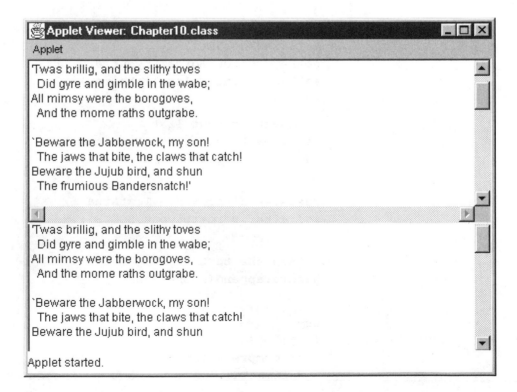

The previous Huffman compression routines show that Java serialization is more than just a system for saving objects in sequential files. Consider implementing data compression as part of object replacement and substitution; objects could automatically replace and restore themselves from compressed form, saving considerable data space in either transmissions or external files.

Onward

Now let's take a look at developing a set of classes for serializing object — including `HuffmanEncoded` ones — into random access files for database algorithms.

11

Serializing Objects in Random Access Files

For some applications, it isn't desirable to serialize objects to a sequential file, or to store them in some external database system via JDBC. You may want to explicitly control the indexing of your objects; the application you're working on may have unique requirements, or may be used in an environment where an SQL-compatible database is not available. In such cases, you'll need to implement some form of database directly in your Java application, creating tools for storing and retrieving objects using a custom design.

Random Access Objects

To implement any sort of sophisticated database, you need to access objects by associating their location in a file with some key value. Java serialization is an excellent tool for managing objects in sequential files, but there isn't any support for storing `Objects` in random-access files. The `RandomAccessFile` class provides tools for moving around within a file, but it isn't derived from `OutputStream` and subsequently does not implement the interfaces `ObjectInput` and `ObjectOutput`. This would seem to be a serious limitation, but it isn't. You can serialize objects to a `RandomAccessFile` by using a `ByteArrayOutputStream` as an intermediary between the random access file and an `ObjectOutputStream` (see Figure 11-1).

Figure 11-1
Storing an Object in a
RandomAccessFile

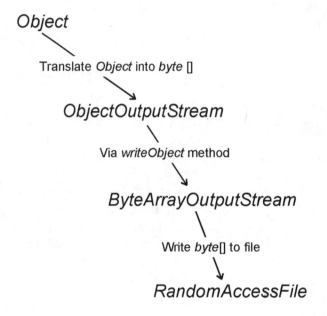

Object

Translate *Object* into *byte* []

ObjectOutputStream

Via *writeObject* method

ByteArrayOutputStream

Write *byte*[] to file

RandomAccessFile

To store an `Object` to a `RandomAccessFile`, a program creates a `ByteArrayOutputStream` object and uses it in constructing an `ObjectOutputStream`. The object is written into the `ObjectOutputStream` and stored in the `ByteArrayOutputStream`. The process is complete when the `RandomAccessFile` writes the `ByteArrayOutputStream`'s contents. In essence, the `ByteArrayOutputStream` acts as a translator between the high-level definition of an object (as understood by `ObjectOutputStream`) and the binary data requirements of a `RandomAccessFile`. Using a similar process, a `ByteArrayInputStream` allows an object to be created from an array of bytes read from a `RandomAccessFile`.

Information is written sequentially to `ObjectOutputStream`, and read sequentially from `ObjectInputStreams`. Once data is stored, it cannot be retrieved, changed, or deleted. The data can only be retrieved in the same order it was written. New data is simply appended to the end of a file. For a database application, we need the ability to read and write objects at specific locations within a file. `RandomAccessFile` provides methods for positioning the read/write pointer inside a file, letting us manipulate records as our indexing algorithm requires. Most applications need the ability to delete and change records, too.

Before building a class to implement `RandomAccessFiles` for serialized objects, we need to define a file structure. For the purposes of this discussion, I'll use the term *record* to refer to a distinct piece of data stored at a specific location in a file. When I refer to a *database* file, I mean one in which objects are stored in distinct records, and where the file maintains an internal structure that facilitates locating object data.

Random Access File Concepts

A *file pointer* value references a position or location within a random access file, the *current file pointer* points to the locations where I/O operations will be performed. Each record is located at a specific file pointer. Files that allow records to be read and written in any position is, of course, a *random access file*, as exemplified by the `RandomAccessFile` class.

An *index* is a data structure that associates a key value with a file pointer. The file pointer for a record is found by looking up the record's key in the index. When writing a record, we need to know where it is stored within the file; that position value, along with a key, is stored in an index so that the key can be used to find the record again. Chapter 12 looks at an indexed-sequential indexing system for object databases; for now, we'll just assume that we need to know the file pointer whenever an object is serialized.

It's often useful to implement a database file such that it manages fixed-length or variable length records. This is a bit more complicated than a file containing fixed-length records, where every record has the same length and moving through the file is merely a matter of incrementing the current file pointer by the fixed record size. To handle variable-length records, the file will need to record the size of each record.

Variable length records complicate the deletion of records from a file. One technique would be to remove the deleted record from the file, shifting other records to eliminate the now empty space. Such a design is incredibly inefficient: deleting the second record in a thousand-record file would mean moving 998 other records! Moving the records would also require regeneration of any index that references the file pointers for those records. It makes more sense to reuse deleted record space as opposed to physically removing the record, by marking empty records as available for reuse. When new records are written to the file, a program can check to see if any deleted record is large enough to hold the new record; if so, the new record is written into the same place as a deleted record. Otherwise, the new record is appended to the end of the file. No records move, so indexes for "live" records don't need to change.

To accomplish this, I designed my file to maintain a linked list called a *deleted list*. The first information in the file is a pointer to the first deleted record in the list. Each deleted record contains a file pointer to the next deleted record in the list; the last record in the list has a value to indicate that no more deleted records exist. When a record is deleted, the file stores the deleted file pointer as the "head" of the list, storing the old head in the newly-removed record. Inserting a new record involves a traverse of the deleted list, looking for an empty record large enough to contain the new information. If the deleted list is empty, or the new record is too large to fit into any open slots, the new object is appended to the file.

Reusing deleted record space has a drawback: it leaves dead space in the file. Deleted records use space in the file until a new record is written into their location. Since we are using variable-length records, new records may be shorter than the deleted records they overwrite, leaving various sized "holes" in the file. Periodically, it makes sense to *compact* the file, removing the wasted space and eliminating deleted records. This can be accomplished by simply rewriting the file, record by record, using exact record lengths and ignoring deleted records. When a file is compacted, every record could change positions within the file. For an indexed file, where a table stores keys and file pointers, a new index will need to be built or an existing index updated to reflect the new record positions.

An Object Database Class

An advantage of object-oriented programming is the ability to hide the complexities of an implementation. To serialize objects to a `RandomAccessFile`, I created a class that encapsulates the details above. My `ObjectDatabaseFile` looks like this with the more complex method implementations removed:

```
package coyote.io;

import java.io.*;

public class ObjectDatabaseFile
{
  //-------------------------
  // constants
  //-------------------------
  private static final long DEL_LIST_END = -1;

  private static final byte IS_DELETED = 0;
  private static final byte IS_ACTIVE  = 1;

  //-------------------------
  // fields
  //-------------------------
  private RandomAccessFile dataFile;

  private String fileName;

  private long firstDel;

  //-------------------------
  // constructors
  //-------------------------
  public ObjectDatabaseFile
    (
    String name
    )
    throws IOException;
```

```
public ObjectDatabaseFile
   (
   File file
   )
   throws IOException;

private void constructorHelper()
   throws IOException;


//------------------------
// implement object I/O
//------------------------


// write object to current position
public long writeObject
   (
   Object obj
   )
   throws IOException;


// read object from current record
public Object readObject()
   throws IOException, ClassNotFoundException;


// delete the current object record
public void delete()
   throws IOException;


// go to beginning of file
public void rewind()
   throws IOException;


// skip over an object record
public void skip()
   throws IOException;


// compact file by removing deleted records
public void compact
   (
```

```
      ObjectDatabaseCallback callback
      )
      throws IOException, Throwable;

   //---------------------------------------------
   // provide shells for RandomAccessFile methods
   //---------------------------------------------
   public final FileDescriptor getFD()
      throws IOException
   {
      return dataFile.getFD();
   }

   public long getFilePointer()
      throws IOException
   {
      return dataFile.getFilePointer();
   }

   public void seek(long pos)
      throws IOException
   {

      dataFile.seek(pos);
   }

   public long length()
      throws IOException
   {
      return dataFile.length();
   }

   public void close()
      throws IOException
   {

      dataFile.close();
   }
}
```

Why didn't I derive `ObjectDatabaseFile` from `RandomAccess-File`? Java limits the ability of subclasses to hide or control access to superclass methods; a subclass cannot declare a superclass as private or protected, for example, and an overriding method cannot restrict access to a method beyond the restrictions imposed by the superclass. I wanted my class to be specific to `Objects`, and to prevent the possible confusion of allowing calls to primitive I/O methods such as `writeInt`.

In an `ObjectDatabaseFile`, each record contains five elements, as shown in Figure 11-2:

Figure 11-2
ObjectDatabaseFile
Record Format

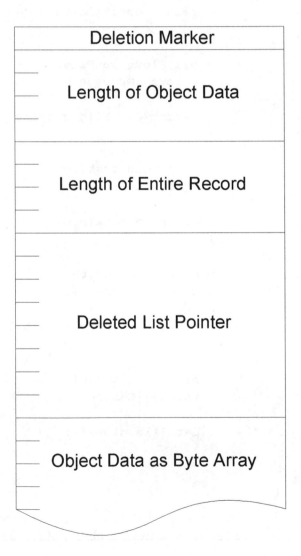

Each record has 17 bytes of header information. The first byte in each record is a marker byte, set to either of the constants IS_DELETED or IS_ACTIVE as appropriate to the record's status. The deleted list pointer only serves a purpose when the "deleted" byte is IS_DELETED, in which case, it contains the file pointer of the next deleted record in the list. The constant DEL_LIST_END marks the last item in the deleted list. The first eight bytes in the file contain a file pointer locating the first item in the deleted list.

Constructing an ObjectDatabaseFile requires either a File or String argument naming the file. Notice that the private RandomAccessFile is always opened in read-write mode. The private helper method constructorHelper completes the construction job for both constructors, either creating a "first deleted pointer" for a new file or reading the existing pointer into the field firstDel.

```
public ObjectDatabaseFile
  (
  String name
  )
  throws IOException
{
  fileName = new String(name);
  dataFile = new RandomAccessFile(name,"rw");
  constructorHelper();
}

public ObjectDatabaseFile
  (
  File file
  )
  throws IOException
{
  fileName = new String(file.getName());
  dataFile = new RandomAccessFile(file,"rw");
  constructorHelper();
}

private void constructorHelper()
  throws IOException
{
```

```
      // check for new file
      if (dataFile.length() == 0)
      {
        // write a new file header
        dataFile.writeLong(DEL_LIST_END);
        firstDel = DEL_LIST_END;
      }
      else
        firstDel = dataFile.readLong();
    }
```

The writeObject method writes an object to a file. The procedure begins by encoding the Object into a byte array using a ByteArrayOutputStream that is the target of an ObjectOutputStream. Now that writeObject knows the length of the serialized object, it searches the deleted list for the first empty record large enough to hold the new record; if such an empty record is found, writeObject stores the byte array there and updates that record's header and the deleted list. If the deleted list is empty, or if the new object is too large for any available slots, the new data is appended to the file as a new record. The file position of the new record is returned, so that indexing tools can associate the object with its key.

```
    // write object to current position
    public long writeObject
      (
      Object obj
      )
      throws IOException
    {
      // create a byte stream to hold the encoded object
      ByteArrayOutputStream bytes =
          new ByteArrayOutputStream();

      // create a stream to write the object
      ObjectOutputStream ostrm =
          new ObjectOutputStream(bytes);

      // write the object
      ostrm.writeObject(obj);
```

```
// ensure that the entire object is written
ostrm.flush();

// get the length of the output data
int  datalen = bytes.size(); // data length
int  reclen  = datalen;      // rec length
long pos;                    // beginning of rec header

// find someplace to put the record
if (firstDel == DEL_LIST_END) // append
{
  // find end of file
  pos = dataFile.length();

  // move to end of the file
  dataFile.seek(pos);
}
else // replace a deleted record
{
  // start with first deleted record
  long prev = DEL_LIST_END;

  pos = firstDel;

  while (true)
  {
    // move to the record
    dataFile.seek(pos);

    // read header info
    byte deleted = dataFile.readByte();
            dataFile.readInt();
    reclen  = dataFile.readInt();
    long next = dataFile.readLong();

    // check integrity
    if (deleted == IS_ACTIVE)
      throw new IOException("corrupt delete list");

    // is deleted record big enough for new data?
    if (reclen >= datalen)
```

```
        {
          // adjust chain by changing next to prev
          if (prev == DEL_LIST_END)
          {
            // change file header deletion mark
            firstDel = next;

            // write new deleted record # at beginning
                of file
            dataFile.seek(0);
            dataFile.writeLong(firstDel);
          }
          else // go back to previous record
          {
            // read and change prev header
            dataFile.seek(prev + 1 + 4 + 4);
            dataFile.writeLong(next);
          }

          dataFile.seek(pos);

          break;
        }

        // deleted record is too small; go to next
            (or end)
        prev = pos;

        // do we have any more deleted records in the
            chain?
        if (next == DEL_LIST_END)
        {
          // append to end of file
          pos = dataFile.length();
          dataFile.seek(pos);
          break;
        }
        else
          pos = next;
      }
    }
```

```
                 // make sure this record is marked as not deleted
                 dataFile.writeByte(IS_ACTIVE);

                 // write the length of the output
                 dataFile.writeInt(datalen);

                 // write the length of the record
                 dataFile.writeInt(reclen);

                 // write the "deleted" pointer
                 dataFile.writeLong(DEL_LIST_END);

                 // store the object to the actual file
                 dataFile.write(bytes.toByteArray());

                 // return length of output
                 return pos;
             }
```

Reading records is much simpler than writing them. readObject assumes that the current file pointer is positioned at the beginning of a record; if the record is marked as deleted, the procedure skips to the next record. Otherwise, it retrieves the header information and byte array from dataFile, and translates the serialized object via an ObjectInputStream and a ByteArrayInputStream.

```
          // read object from current record
          public Object readObject()
            throws IOException, ClassNotFoundException
          {
            while (true)
            {
              // check record status
              byte deleted = dataFile.readByte();

              // break from loop if this is an active record
              if (deleted == IS_ACTIVE)
                break;
```

```
      // skip length of object
      dataFile.skipBytes(4);
      // get the length of the object
      int n = dataFile.readInt();

      // seek to beginning of next record
      dataFile.skipBytes(n + 8);
   }

   // get the length of the object
   int datalen = dataFile.readInt();

   // get length of record
   int reclen = dataFile.readInt();

   // skip the "deleted" pointer
   dataFile.skipBytes(8);

   // retrieve the object data and store it
   byte [] data = new byte [datalen];
   dataFile.readFully(data);

   // position pointer to beginning of next record
   int diff = reclen - datalen;

   if (diff > 0)
      dataFile.skipBytes(diff);

   // create a byte stream to contain the input
      object
   ByteArrayInputStream bytes =
      new ByteArrayInputStream(data);

   // create a stream to translate the object
   ObjectInputStream istrm =
      new ObjectInputStream(bytes);

   // return the object
   return istrm.readObject();
}
```

Like `readObject`, the `delete` method assumes that the current file pointer is located at the beginning of a record. It marks a record as deleted by changing its marker byte to `IS_DELETED`, then adds the record's file pointer to the deleted list by storing the old `firstDel` pointer in the record's header and storing the position of the newly-deleted record at the beginning of the file. In other words, newly-deleted records are added to the beginning of the deleted list.

```
// delete the current object record
public void delete()
  throws IOException
{
  // assume beginning of record, get pointer
  long pos = dataFile.getFilePointer();

  // is this record already deleted?
  byte deleted = dataFile.readByte();

  if (deleted == IS_DELETED)
    return;

  // back up and write new marker
  dataFile.seek(pos);
  dataFile.writeByte(IS_DELETED);

  // skip length value
  dataFile.skipBytes(4 + 4);

  // write next-deleted marker from header
  dataFile.writeLong(firstDel);

  // now change file header
  firstDel = pos;
  dataFile.seek(0);
  dataFile.writeLong(firstDel);
}
```

The `rewind` method sets the current file pointer to the beginning of the first record in the file — basically, at the byte directly after the pointer to the first record in the deleted list.

```
// go to beginning of file
public void rewind()
  throws IOException
{
  dataFile.seek(8);
}
```

When reading an `ObjectDatabaseFile` sequentially, you may want to skip a record. The `skip` method moves through the file one record at a time without reading the stored `Objects`.

```
// skip over an object record
public void skip()
  throws IOException
{
  // skip over parts of record header
  dataFile.skipBytes(1 + 4);

  // read record length
  int reclen = dataFile.readInt();

  // skip to beginning of next record
  dataFile.skipBytes(8 + reclen);
}
```

Earlier, I explained how wasted space is the result of deleting and inserting variable length records. An active file, where deletions and insertions are common, will develop significant amounts of wasted space. The `compact` method generates a new file, named with the current system time; time-stamped temporary file names prevent multiple files from being created with the same name. Once the temporary file is open, the procedure writes `DEL_LIST_END` (since the new file has no deleted records) and sequentially writes the active records from the original file. When the copy is complete, the old file is closed and deleted; the new file is then renamed and opened as `dataFile`.

```
// compact file by removing deleted records
public void compact
  (
```

```
      ObjectDatabaseCallback callback
      )
      throws IOException, Throwable
{
  // generate temporary file name
  File tempName = new File("TMP" +
      System.currentTimeMillis());

  // create the temporary file
  RandomAccessFile newFile =
      new RandomAccessFile(tempName,"rw");

  // write file header
  newFile.writeLong(DEL_LIST_END);

  // read and write records
  while (true)
  {
    try
    {
      byte deleted = dataFile.readByte();
      int  dataLen = dataFile.readInt();
      int  recLen  = dataFile.readInt();

      if (deleted == IS_DELETED)
      {
        // skip to next record
        dataFile.skipBytes(8 + recLen);
      }
      else
      {
        // skip deleted marker
        dataFile.skipBytes(8);

        // create array for input data
        byte [] data = new byte [dataLen];

        // read raw data
        dataFile.readFully(data);
        // skip over any waste space
        int diff = recLen - dataLen;
```

```
              if (diff > 0)
                dataFile.skipBytes(diff);

              // remember where this record starts
              long pos = newFile.getFilePointer();

              // write new header to output file
              newFile.writeByte(IS_ACTIVE);
              newFile.writeInt(dataLen);
              newFile.writeInt(dataLen);
              newFile.writeLong(DEL_LIST_END);

              // write raw data
              newFile.write(data);

              // create a byte stream to contain the
                  input object
              ByteArrayInputStream bytes =
                      new ByteArrayInputStream(data);

              // create a stream to translate the object
              ObjectInputStream istrm =
                  new ObjectInputStream(bytes);

              // notify the callback method
              if (callback != null)
                callback.compactNotify(pos,
                    istrm.readObject());
            }
          }
          catch ( EOFException eof )
          {
            break;
          }
          catch ( Throwable ex)
          {
            throw ex;
          }
        }
        // close and delete the old file
        dataFile.close();
```

```
        File goAway = new File(fileName);

        goAway.delete();

        // rename the new file
        newFile.close();

        tempName.renameTo(new File(fileName));

        // now we use the new file
        dataFile = new RandomAccessFile(fileName,"rw");
        constructorHelper();
    }
```

If the records have been indexed, the indexing algorithm will need to know the new positions of the objects. The argument for `compact` is an object that implements the `ObjectDatabaseCallback` interface; the single method defined by this interface accepts an `Object` reference and a file pointer, which can be used to generate a new keyed index for the file.

```
public interface ObjectDatabaseCallback
{
  void compactNotify
    (
    long    pos,
    Object obj
    );
}
```

You'll see how this works in Chapter 12, where I implement a BTree-based file indexing system.

The final set of methods provide shells for methods declared by the RandomAccessFile class.

```
public final FileDescriptor getFD()
    throws IOException
  {
    return dataFile.getFD();
  }
```

```
        public long getFilePointer()
          throws IOException
        {
          return dataFile.getFilePointer();
        }

        public void seek(long pos)
          throws IOException
        {
          dataFile.seek(pos);
        }

        public long length()
          throws IOException
        {
          return dataFile.length();
        }

        public void close()
          throws IOException
        {
          dataFile.close();
        }
```

An Example

Working with an `ObjectDatabase` file is remarkable easy. For this example, I'll use an array of `String`s for records. Each `String` is the name of a letter in the Greek alphabet, providing me with a set of variable-length objects. The `String` class implements the `Serializable` interface.

```
        public void exercide
          (
          TextField output
          )
        {
          long rec10pos = 0;
          long rec12pos = 0;
```

```
try
{
  // create a file object and delete the old file
  File testFile = new File("Chapter09.dat");
  testFile.delete();

  // create an ObjectDatabaseFile
  ObjectDatabaseFile objFile =
      new ObjectDatabaseFile(testFile);

  // write objects to data file
  output.append("--> writing records:\n\n");

  for (int n = 0; n < stringRecs.length; ++n)
  {
    long pos = objFile.writeObject(stringRecs[n]);

    if (n == 10)
      rec10pos = pos;

    if (n == 12)
      rec12pos = pos;

    output.append("writing: " + stringRecs[n] +
        "\n");
  }

  // read items
  output.append("\n--> reading records:\n\n");

  objFile.rewind();

  for (int n = 0; n < stringRecs.length; ++n)
  {
    String s = (String)objFile.readObject();

    output.append("reading: " + s + "\n");
  }
```

The `exercise` method manipulates an `ObjectDatabaseFile` object, appending progress information to the `TextField` specified by the `output` argument. To begin, `exercise` writes the array of `Strings` to the file, and then reads them back again.

```
private String [] stringRecs =
{
  "alpha",
  "beta",
  "gamma",
  "delta",
  "epsilon",
  "zeta",
  "eta",
  "theta",
  "iota",
  "kappa",
  "lambda",
  "mu",
  "nu",
  "xi",
  "omicron",
  "pi",
  "rho",
  "sigma",
  "tau",
  "upsilon",
  "phi",
  "chi",
  "psi",
  "omega"
};
```

The result is a data file containing serialized Strings. Here's a hexadecimal dump of the file's contents:

```
00000000 FFFF FFFF FFFF FFFF 0100 0000 0C00 0000
         ...............
00000010 0CFF FFFF FFFF FFFF FFAC ED00 0574 0005
         .............t..
00000020 616C 7068 6101 0000 000B 0000 000B FFFF
         alpha..........
```

```
00000030 FFFF FFFF FFFF ACED 0005 7400 0462 6574
         .........t..bet
00000040 6101 0000 000C 0000 000C FFFF FFFF FFFF
         a..............
00000050 FFFF ACED 0005 7400 0567 616D 6D61 0100
         ......t..gamma..
00000060 0000 0C00 0000 0CFF FFFF FFFF FFFF FFAC
         ...............
00000070 ED00 0574 0005 6465 6C74 6101 0000 000E
         ...t..delta.....
00000080 0000 000E FFFF FFFF FFFF FFFF ACED 0005
         ...............
00000090 7400 0765 7073 696C 6F6E 0100 0000 0B00
         t..epsilon......
000000A0 0000 0BFF FFFF FFFF FFFF FFAC ED00 0574
         .............t
000000B0 0004 7A65 7461 0100 0000 0A00 0000 0AFF
         ..zeta.........
000000C0 FFFF FFFF FFFF FFAC ED00 0574 0003 6574
         ..........t..et
000000D0 6101 0000 000C 0000 000C FFFF FFFF FFFF
         a..............
000000E0 FFFF ACED 0005 7400 0574 6865 7461 0100
         ......t..theta..
000000F0 0000 0B00 0000 0BFF FFFF FFFF FFFF FFAC
         ...............
00000100 ED00 0574 0004 696F 7461 0100 0000 0C00
         ...t..iota......
00000110 0000 0CFF FFFF FFFF FFFF FFAC ED00 0574
         .............t
00000120 0005 6B61 7070 6101 0000 000D 0000 000D
         ..kappa.........
00000130 FFFF FFFF FFFF FFFF ACED 0005 7400 066C
         ............t..l
00000140 616D 6264 6101 0000 0009 0000 0009 FFFF
         ambda..........
00000150 FFFF FFFF FFFF ACED 0005 7400 026D 7501
         ..........t..mu.
00000160 0000 0009 0000 0009 FFFF FFFF FFFF FFFF
         ...............
```

```
00000170 ACED 0005 7400 026E 7501 0000 0009 0000
        ....t..nu.......
00000180 0009 FFFF FFFF FFFF FFFF ACED 0005 7400
        ..............t.
00000190 0278 6901 0000 000E 0000 000E FFFF FFFF
        .xi............
000001A0 FFFF FFFF ACED 0005 7400 076F 6D69 6372
        ........t..omicr
000001B0 6F6E 0100 0000 0900 0000 09FF FFFF FFFF
        on.............
000001C0 FFFF FFAC ED00 0574 0002 7069 0100 0000
        .......t..pi....
000001D0 0A00 0000 0AFF FFFF FFFF FFFF FFAC ED00
        ...............
000001E0 0574 0003 7268 6F01 0000 000C 0000 000C
        .t..rho.........
000001F0 FFFF FFFF FFFF FFFF ACED 0005 7400 0573
        ............t..s
00000200 6967 6D61 0100 0000 0A00 0000 0AFF FFFF
        igma...........
00000210 FFFF FFFF FFAC ED00 0574 0003 7461 7501
        .........t..tau.
00000220 0000 000E 0000 000E FFFF FFFF FFFF FFFF
        ...............
00000230 ACED 0005 7400 0775 7073 696C 6F6E 0100
        ....t..upsilon..
00000240 0000 0A00 0000 0AFF FFFF FFFF FFFF FFAC
        ...............
00000250 ED00 0574 0003 7068 6901 0000 000A 0000
        ...t..phi.......
00000260 000A FFFF FFFF FFFF FFFF ACED 0005 7400
        ..............t.
00000270 0363 6869 0100 0000 0A00 0000 0AFF FFFF
        .chi...........
00000280 FFFF FFFF FFAC ED00 0574 0003 7073 6901
        .........t..psi.
00000290 0000 000C 0000 000C FFFF FFFF FFFF FFFF
        ...............
000002A0 ACED 0005 7400 056F 6D65 6761
....t..omega
```

Now `exercise` deletes the record containing "lambda."

```
objFile.seek(rec10pos);
objFile.delete();
```

The procedure deletes another object, this one containing "nu:"

```
objFile.seek(rec12pos);
objFile.delete();
```

This changed a section of the data file to look like this:

```
00000000 0000 0000 0000 015F 0100 0000 0C00 0000
         ......._........
00000010 0CFF FFFF FFFF FFFF FFAC ED00 0574 0005
         .............t..
   .
   .
   .
00000120 0005 6B61 7070 6100 0000 000D 0000 000D
         ..kappa.........
00000130 FFFF FFFF FFFF FFFF ACED 0005 7400 066C
         ............t..l
00000140 616D 6264 6101 0000 0009 0000 0009 FFFF
         ambda..........
00000150 FFFF FFFF FFFF ACED 0005 7400 026D 7500
         ..........t..mu.
00000160 0000 0009 0000 0009 0000 0000 0000 0127
         ...............'
00000170 ACED 0005 7400 026E 7501 0000 0009 0000
         ....t..nu.......
   .
   .
   .
```

See how the deleted list works? The `firstDel` pointer at the beginning of the file points to the record that once held "nu;" that record, in turn, contains a pointer to the old "lambda" record, which is the end of the deleted list.

It's time to add some new objects to the file. First, I write the record "12345:"

```
objFile.writeObject("12345");
```

The new record replaced the old "lambda" record, being shorter in length. The deleted list is changed to reflect this:

```
00000000 0000 0000 0000 015F 0100 0000 0C00 0000
     ......._........
00000010 0CFF FFFF FFFF FFFF FFAC ED00 0574 0005
     .............t..
  .
  .
  .
00000120 0005 6B61 7070 6101 0000 000C 0000 000D
     ..kappa........
00000130 FFFF FFFF FFFF FFFF ACED 0005 7400 0531
     ............t..1
00000140 3233 3435 6101 0000 0009 0000 0009 FFFF
     2345a..........
00000150 FFFF FFFF FFFF ACED 0005 7400 026D 7500
     .........t..mu.
00000160 0000 0009 0000 0009 FFFF FFFF FFFF FFFF
     ..............
00000170 ACED 0005 7400 026E 7501 0000 0009 0000
     ....t..nu.......
  .
  .
  .
```

Now I write the String "longrecord" to the file.

```
objFile.writeObject("longrecord");
```

The only deleted record contained the much-shorter String "nu," so the new record ends up appended to the file:

```
00000000 0000 0000 0000 015F 0100 0000 0C00 0000
        ......._........
00000010 0CFF FFFF FFFF FFFF FFAC ED00 0574 0005
        .............t..
    .


    .


    .
00000120 0005 6B61 7070 6101 0000 000C 0000 000D
        ..kappa.........
00000130 FFFF FFFF FFFF FFFF ACED 0005 7400 0531
        ............t..1
00000140 3233 3435 6101 0000 0009 0000 0009 FFFF
        2345a...........
00000150 FFFF FFFF FFFF ACED 0005 7400 026D 7500
        ..........t..mu.
00000160 0000 0009 0000 0009 FFFF FFFF FFFF FFFF
        ................
00000170 ACED 0005 7400 026E 7501 0000 0009 0000
        .....t..nu.......
    .


    .


    .
000002A0 ACED 0005 7400 056F 6D65 6761 0100 0000
        ....t..omega....
000002B0 1100 0000 09FF FFFF FFFF FFFF FFAC ED00
        ................
000002C0 0574 000A 6C6F 6E67 7265 636F 7264
        .t..longrecord
```

Onward

By employing Java's built-in support for serialized objects, the ObjectDatabaseFile becomes versatile, able to hold any type of object. In fact, nothing prevents an ObjectDatabaseFile from containing Objects of different classes; any class that implements Serializable is a potential record. As you'll see in the next chapter, this makes ObjectDatabaseFile a powerful tool for implementing custom databases.

12

BTree Indexed Databases

Binary trees are very useful in many contexts, but they fail to provide an effective solution to indexing files. Binary trees can easily become unbalanced, and even a balanced binary tree will be too "high" for practical use on large files. Balancing techniques and paged binary files improve the situation, but only slightly. What we need is a tree structure that stores many keys in a few records, and which automatically maintains its balance. That type of tree is known as a *BTree*.

Properties of BTrees

BTrees were invented and introduced by R. Bayer and E. McCreight in a 1972 paper named "Organization and Maintenance of Larger Order Indexes." Within a very few years, BTrees were synonymous with file handling; nearly every major database system, from ISAM to dBASE, uses BTrees. A binary tree's problems stem from the way in which it is constructed. We begin with a root and build downward from there; if the root key is a bad one, such that most subsequent keys are greater or less than the root, the tree will become unbalanced. Various algorithms can then come into play to rebalance the tree — in other words, fixing the problem after it has occurred.

Pages and Keys

Bayer and McCreight solved the binary tree's problems by looking at the problem from a new perspective. They decided to build a tree structure from the bottom up, letting the root emerge as keys are added. To reduce the number of nodes in the tree, they decided to store more than one key per node. Bayer and McCreight apparently named their creation a BTree because it sounded appropriate.

Figure 12-1

A BTree Page

Figure 12-1 shows a BTree node, known as a *page*. Each page contains a set of keys and a set of pointers (also called *links*) to other pages. The keys are stored in an ordered sequential list. There is always one more pointer than there are keys, and the maximum number of pointers in a page is known as the BTree's *order*. Figure 12-1 shows a BTree page of order 6. The pointer to the left of a key points to a subtree that contains all lesser keys. The key to the right points to a subtree containing all greater keys.

Figure 12-2 shows a BTree of order 5, in which the single-letter keys "CAKRMGOTDHXSLJZNPY" have been inserted.

Figure 12-2

An Order-5 BTree
Containing 17 Keys

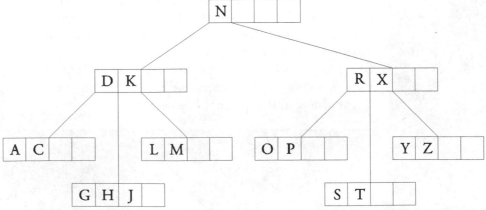

BTrees follow these rules:

- A BTree consists of pages that contain *order* links and *order − 1* keys.

- The keys are stored in sequential lists.

- Every page has a maximum of *order* descendants.

- All leaf pages are the same number of links away from the root.

- With the exception of the root and leaf pages, every page has at least *order / 2* links (rounded up for odd orders).

- The root has at least one key (and thus two links), unless it is also a leaf page.

- A leaf page has at least *order / 2 − 1* keys (rounded for odd orders).

- New keys are only added to leaf pages.

Searching

The construction of this tree will be described later; however, first let's look at searching a BTree for a given key. To describe searching, I'll use these terms: the *search key* is the key being sought, and the *page key* is a key in a page. The algorithm compares the search key against page keys until a match is found or the end of the tree is reached. Searching a page consists of sequentially comparing page keys with the search key. The algorithm's actions depend on the relationship of the search key and page key:

- If a match is found, the search has been successful.

- If the page key is less than the search key, we move to the next key in the page. If the algorithm has reached the last key in the page, it follows the rightmost link to a page that contains greater keys.

- If the page key is greater than the search key, we can move to a new page by following the link to a page containing keys less than the page key.

- In cases 2 and 3, the algorithm may find that the link it wishes to follow does not connect to another page, indicating that the search is in a leaf page. When this happens, the algorithm has failed to find the search key, since there are no more pages to search.

To search the entire tree, begin by examining the first key in the root page. The search routine can be called recursively when the algorithm moves to a new page.

Figure 12-3 shows the process followed in looking for some keys in the BTree from Figure 12-2. Here are the steps involved in looking for the key S:

1. We begin at the root page. S is greater than the first root key, N. N is the only key in the root page, so we follow the link to the pages which contain keys greater than N.

2. The next page contains the keys R and X. S is between R and X, so we follow the middle link to the next page.

3. The first key in the page matches S — and we're done!

Figure 12-3

Searching for S

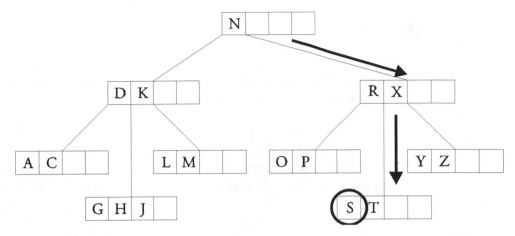

Figure 12-4 shows how looking for *B* leads us down a different path:

1. *B* is less than the root key *N*, so we move to the page that contains keys less than *N*.

2. *B* is less than *D*, so we move to a new page.

3. *B* is between *A* and *C* — but this is a leaf page, so we can't go any farther. *B* was not found.

Figure 12-4

Searching for *B*

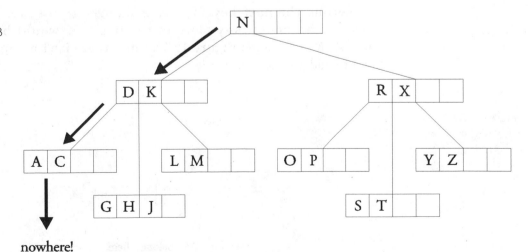

Insertion

To demonstrate key insertion, I'll use an order 5 BTree. Each page can contain up to five links and four keys.

Inserting the first key into a BTree is simple: it becomes the only key in a new root page. Note that the root page begins existence as a leaf page. Figure 12-5 shows a new root containing a single key, *C*.

Figure 12-5
A New Root Page,
with One Key

a new root containing one key

The root page is full after inserting the three keys *AKR*. Figure 12-6 shows the full root page.

Figure 12-6
A Full Root Page

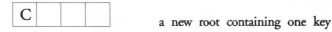

the root after inserting the keys A, K, and R

Inserting the next key, *M*, forces changes in the tree structure. Were there enough key slots in the page, *M* would be inserted between *K* and *R* (see Figure 12-7). Since there isn't an open slot, we need to add pages to the tree.

Figure 12-7
Identifying the Components
when a Page Splits

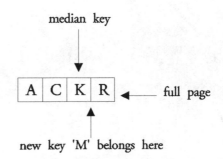

For the purpose of making the algorithm simpler, let's assume that we can "squeeze" M in between K and R. We then *split* the page by creating a new page and distributing the keys between it and the original page. The keys A and C will remain in the original page, and the keys M and R move into the new page. The median (middle) key K is then *promoted* to separate the original page and its new sibling. Since the original page was the root, K becomes the sole key in a new root, increasing the height of the tree by one level. Figure 12-8 shows the result of this process.

Figure 12-8

Splitting and Promotion

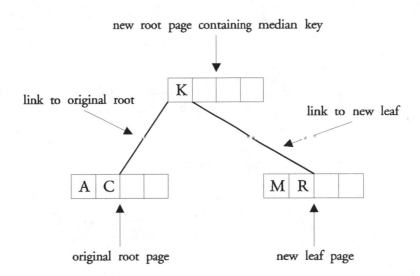

After adding the keys *GODT*, the both leaf pages are full. Figure 12-9 shows the tree just before the key H is inserted.

Figure 12-9

Adding a Few More Keys

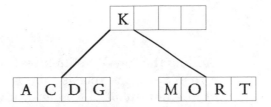

When a non-root page is split, it promotes its median key into its parent. Thus, the page containing *ACDG* splits, creating two pages with the keys *AC* and *GH*, respectively. The median key *D* is promoted into the parent page (which is also the root). Figure 12-10 shows the result of this split and promotion.

Figure 12-10
Splitting and Promoting a
Key into a Parent Page

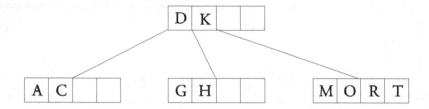

When a key is promoted, it will cause a full parent page to split and promote, too. This chain reaction broadens the base of the tree by splitting and pushes the root up by promotion. Figure 12-11 shows that after adding the keys *XSLJZNP* to the tree, the root page has become full through promotions.

Figure 12-11
A Full Root Page

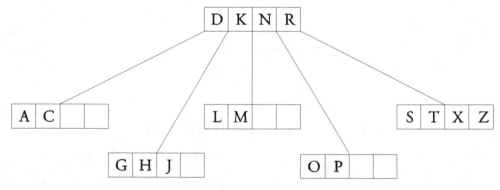

Adding the key *Y* splits a leaf node and promotes the key *X* into the root. Since the root is full, it too splits. A new root is generated, and the height of the tree is uniformly increased by one level (Figure 12-2).

Figure 12-12

The Tree After
Inserting Z

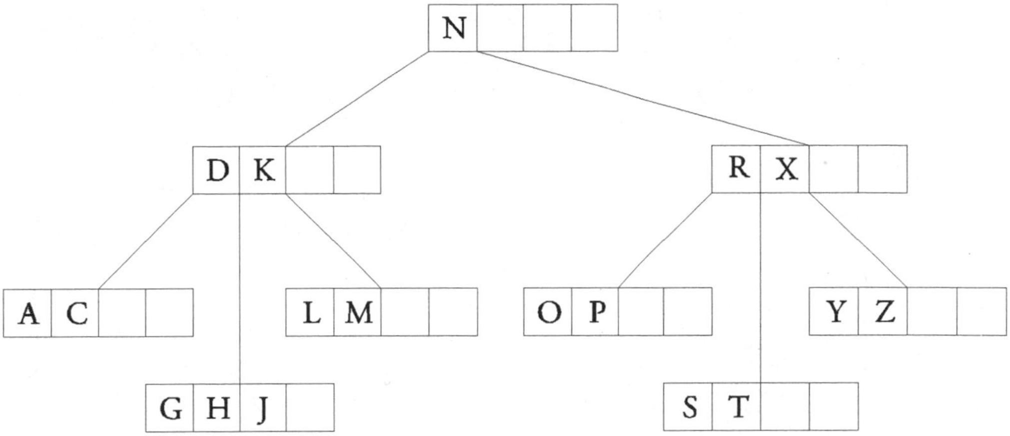

This algorithm guarantees that insertions do not cause the tree to become unbalanced, and that the internal nodes always have at least *order / 2* keys. In the tree above, 18 keys were stored in 9 pages. Assuming that each page is stored as a record in a file, no more than three records must be read from the file to find any key.

Deletion

When I embarked upon creating my own BTree class library, I encountered a significant problem: a general lack of documentation on the *deletion* of keys! Most references explain insertion and searching in depth — but when it comes to deletion, they give vague excuses about complexity. The implementation of BTree key deletion is often given as a reader exercise.

Deleting a key isn't very difficult, once you realize that it involves three major actions that are implemented for a variety of tree configurations. When deleting a key, one must maintain the rules of a BTree as set forth above. This involves the following process:

1.   Search the tree for the key to be deleted. We'll presume that the key is found.

2. If the key is in the root or an internal page, replace the key with its immediate successor (the first key in the right-hand page), deleting the successor from the leaf. If the key is found in a leaf page, simply remove it.

3. A page has now shrunk by one key entry. This may reduce the number of keys in the page below *order* / *2*. If so, we must reorganize the tree.

4. If the leaf page has a sibling with more than *order* / *2* keys, we simply redistribute keys among the sibling, its parent, and the leaf page.

5. If the page's siblings have only *order* / *2* keys, then we concatenate the page and a sibling. The key in the parent page that separates the deletion page and its sibling is demoted into the combined page. If demoting a key from the parent reduces the parent below *order* / *2* keys, we process the parent page beginning at Step 4. This recursive process continues until we reach a parent node that has more than *order* / *2* keys, or we can redistribute rather than concatenate.

It is possible that the concatenations and demotions will remove the only key from a single-key node, thus reducing the height of the tree by one level. In essence, deleting a key from the tree involves the reverse of an insertion. Where insertion splits nodes and promotes keys, deletion concatenates nodes and demotes keys. Where insertions can increase the height of the tree by splitting the root page, deletion can reduce the height of the tree by concatenating two sibling pages and demoting the only key out of the root page.

Implementation Issues

A compromise must be struck between the size of a tree's pages and its height. The larger the order, the shorter the tree — which reduces the number of pages that must be read to find a key. However, larger pages require longer sequential searches for keys in each page. A tree with order 500, for example, will store a million keys in three levels, while a tree with order 10 will require six levels of pages. In general, since reading data from disk is vastly slower than sequentially searching a list of keys in memory, the page size should be made as large as possible.

When using a BTree as an index, each key must be associated with a pointer to a data record. In my implementation, I decided to implement a BTree-indexed file using two physical disk files. One file contains the BTree pages, and the other contains the data records. After I write a record to the data file, I pass its key and file pointer to the routine that inserts the information into the BTree.

Until now, the file types described in this book have stored variable-length records. A list of deleted records is kept, and when a new record is written to the file, the empty records are scanned to see if any of them are large enough to contain the new record. When a variable-length record is changed it may become larger, and it may not be written into the same position it originally occupied. This scheme works well for data records, since they often vary a great deal in length.

A file that contains BTree pages has different requirements. Since pages have links to other pages, it makes algorithms simpler to implement if pages are treated as fixed-length records stored in a fixed location. This requires a file that contains fixed-length record, and which stores a modified record in the same location it was read from. Since pages are sometimes deleted from the tree when keys are deleted, the page file will need to keep a list of deleted records for use by newly-generated pages.

Exceptions

The `BTreeException` class identifies exceptions thrown by the package of BTree objects.

```
public class BTreeException
  extends IOException
{
  public BTreeException()
  {
    super();
  }
```

```
    public BTreeException(String s)
    {
      super(s);
    }
}
```

Several exceptions can be thrown by related classes; I
defined these exceptions in the BTreeSharedExceptions interface,
which is then implemented by other classes that throw these
exceptions.

```
interface BTreeSharedExceptions
{
  BTreeException err_inv_order =
    new BTreeException("invalid BTree order");

  BTreeException err_inv_keylen =
    new BTreeException("invalid BTree key length");

  BTreeException err_inv_page =
    new BTreeException("invalid BTree page");

  BTreeException err_corrupt_page =
    new BTreeException("corrupt BTree page");
}
```

I also created another interface, BTreeSharedConstants, that
defines a single value identifying a "null" (empty) file pointer:

```
interface BTreeSharedConstants
{
  long NULL_PTR = -1;
}
```

I've found it very useful to encapsulate package-wide constants in
interfaces.

BTree Page Classes

When I began implementing the page file class, I ran into another problem: assuming that the pages were fixed in length meant that the keys themselves had to have a fixed length, too. This isn't a problem when using elementary data types, such as `longs` or `floats`, but it did mean that I couldn't use a variable-length type such as a `char` array or `String`. Since most databases will be indexed via a text key, I needed to store fixed-length `String` key by converting the array of `String` objects to and from a fixed-length array of characters. This ensures that all pages of the same order a key length will produce records of the same length.

Page Class

Every page requires a header containing information about the order and structure of the information. The header is a simple structure object: one in which the fields are all public and for which no methods have been defined. This is just a structured piece of data; encapsulating the fields behind property methods would only have made code more complex and harder to read, when direct access to the fields is simpler. This is not a data type, per se, but rather a collection of related fields.

In the header, `order` is the order of the tree, `keyLen` is the maximum length of the keys it contains, `numKeys` is the number of keys currently stored in a `Page`, `maxKeys` is the maximum number of keys, and `minKeys` is the minimum number of keys allowed in an internal `Page`. The file pointer of a `Page`'s parent is stored in its `parentPtr` member, and `filePtr` contains the location in the `PageDatabaseFile` where a `Page` is stored.

The `Page` structure defines a single page in a BTree. I defined its fields as `public` to simplify manipulation of its contents.

```
public class Page
    implements Externalizable,
               BTreeSharedExceptions,
               BTreeSharedConstants
```

```
{
  // serialization constant
  static final long serialVersionUID =
      5521257935120563452L;


  //——————————-
  // fields
  //——————————-
  public PageHeader header;
  public String []  key; // array of key values
  public long []ptr; // record pointers
  public long []lnk; // links to other pages


  //——————————-
  // constructors
  //——————————-
  public Page()
  {
    header = null;
    key = null;
    ptr = null;
    lnk = null;
  }


  public Page
    (
    int order,
    int keyLen
    )
    throws BTreeException
  {
    if (order < 3)
      throw err_inv_order;

    if (keyLen < 1)
      throw err_inv_keylen;

    // load header information
    header = new PageHeader();
```

```
      header.filePtr   = NULL_PTR;
      header.parentPtr = NULL_PTR;
      header.order = order;
      header.maxKeys   = order - 1;
      header.minKeys   = order / 2;
      header.numKeys   = 0;
      header.keyLen = keyLen;

      // allocate arrays
      key = new String [header.maxKeys];

      for (int n = 0; n < header.maxKeys; ++n)
        key[n] = new String();

      ptr = new long    [header.maxKeys];
      lnk = new long    [header.order];

      // fill arrays with empty values
      for (int n = 0; n < header.order; ++n)
        lnk[n] = NULL_PTR;
    }


    //——————-
    // serialization
    //——————-
    public void writeExternal
      (
      ObjectOutput out
      )
      throws IOException
    {
      // write order and key length
      out.writeObject(header);

      // write pointers and links
      out.writeObject(ptr);
      out.writeObject(lnk);

      // create raw key data
      char [] rawKeys = new char [header.maxKeys
          * header.keyLen];
```

```java
        int pos = 0;


    for (int n = 0; n < header.maxKeys; ++n)
    {
      // copy characters from string to raw data
      int i = 0;


      while ((i < key[n].length()) &&
          (i < header.keyLen))
      {
        rawKeys[pos] = key[n].charAt(i);
        ++pos;
        ++i;
      }


      // fill any extra space with nulls
      while (i < header.keyLen)
      {
        rawKeys[pos] = '\0';
        ++pos;
        ++i;
      }
    }


    // write raw keys
    out.writeObject(rawKeys);
  }


public void readExternal
    (
    ObjectInput in
    )
    throws IOException, ClassNotFoundException
{
    // read back key information
    header = (PageHeader)in.readObject();
```

```
// read link arrays
ptr = (long [])in.readObject();
lnk = (long [])in.readObject();

// read raw key data
char [] rawKeys = (char [])in.readObject();

// get and check raw key length
int rawLen = header.maxKeys * header.keyLen;

if (rawKeys.length != rawLen)
  throw err_corrupt_page;

// allocate key arrays
key = new String [header.maxKeys];

// extract strings from their raw format
int n = 0;
int pos = 0;

for (n = 0; n < header.maxKeys; ++n)
{
  // create a buffer
  StringBuffer newKey = new StringBuffer();

  int i;

  // copy characters to buffer
  for (i = 0; (i < header.keyLen)
   && (rawKeys[pos + i] != '\0'); ++i)
    newKey.append(rawKeys[pos + i]);

  // create string from buffer
  key[n] = new String(newKey);

  // go to beginning of next key
  pos += header.keyLen;
}
}
}
```

The `key`, `ptr`, and `lnk` fields point to dynamically-allocated arrays of keys and `longs`. The constructor's parameters define the order and key size for a new `Page`. Other header values are calculated from the order. A new `Page` is always empty; it has no parent, no children, and does not contain any keys or links.

`Page` implements `Externalizable` for serialization support; implementing `Serializable` would have the output object stream automatically storing the variable length strings in the key array. Since I wanted fixed length records, I designed the `writeExternal` and `readExternal` methods to translate the key array to and from a fixed-length array of characters.

Page Files

A `PageDatabaseFile` is a file type specifically optimized for storing BTree Page objects; since I need to know where a page is written before I actually write it, `PageDatabaseFile` extends `ObjectDatabaseFile` to implement a method that locates the record into which a new page will be written.

```
public class PageDatabaseFile
  extends ObjectDatabaseFile
{
  //———————————-
  // constructors
  //———————————-
  public PageDatabaseFile
    (
    String name
    )
    throws IOException
  {
    super(name);
  }

  public PageDatabaseFile
    (
    File file
    )
```

```
        throws IOException
    {
        super(file);
    }


    //——————————-
    // methods
    //——————————-
    public long getNextOpen()
        throws IOException
    {
        if (firstDel == DEL_LIST_END)
            return dataFile.length();
        else
            return firstDel;
    }
}
```

The `PageFileHeader` stores the order of pages stored in the file, the maximum size of a key, a file pointer to the root page, and a file pointer to the first deleted record. All pages stored in a given `Page-File` will have the same order and page size, allowing a `PageFile` to treat `Pages` as fixed-length records.

```
public class PageFileHeader
    implements Serializable
{
    //——————————-
    // fields
    //——————————-
    public int  order;
    public int  keyLen;
    public long rootPtr;
}
```

The `BTreePageFile` class uses a `PageDatabaseFile` internally to store `Pages`. Each page will be located at a fixed location in the page file; pages are read and written by using pointers, either stored in a `lnk` array or in the page header's `filePtr`.

```
public class BTreePageFile
  implements BTreeSharedExceptions,
             BTreeSharedConstants
{
  //———————————-
  // fields
  //———————————-
  private PageFileHeader   header;
  private PageDatabaseFile dataFile;

  //———————————-
  // constructors
  //———————————-
  public BTreePageFile
    (
    String name
    )
    throws IOException, ClassNotFoundException
  {
    dataFile = new PageDatabaseFile(name);

    // read existing header
    dataFile.rewind();
    header = (PageFileHeader)dataFile.readObject();
  }

  public BTreePageFile
    (
    File file
    )
    throws IOException, ClassNotFoundException
  {
    dataFile = new PageDatabaseFile(file);

    // read existing header
    dataFile.rewind();
    header = (PageFileHeader)dataFile.readObject();
  }

  public BTreePageFile
    (
```

```
    String name,
    int order,
    int keyLen
    )
    throws IOException, ClassNotFoundException
{
  dataFile = new PageDatabaseFile(name);
  constructorHelper(order,keyLen);
}

public BTreePageFile
    (
    File file,
    int order,
    int keyLen
    )
    throws IOException, ClassNotFoundException
{
  dataFile = new PageDatabaseFile(file);
  constructorHelper(order,keyLen);
}

private void constructorHelper
    (
    int order,
    int keyLen
    )
    throws BTreeException, IOException, ClassNot-
        FoundException
{
  // verify parameters
  if (order < 3)
    throw err_inv_order;

  if (keyLen < 1)
    throw err_inv_keylen;

  // new file, new header
  header = new PageFileHeader();

  header.order   = order;
```

```
      header.keyLen   = keyLen;
      header.rootPtr = NULL_PTR;

      // write header to file
      dataFile.writeObject(header);

      // create a new root
      Page root = new Page(order,keyLen);

      // store root and update header
      root.header.filePtr = dataFile.getNextOpen();
      header.rootPtr   = dataFile.writeObject(root);

      // update header
      dataFile.rewind();
      dataFile.rewriteObject(header);
   }


   //——————————--
   // methods
   //——————————--
   public void write
      (
      Page pg,
      boolean root
      )
      throws BTreeException, IOException
   {
      // check page for compatability with this file
      if ((header.order   != pg.header.order)
      ||   (header.keyLen != pg.header.keyLen))
         throw err_inv_page;

      // if new page, find a place to write it
      if (pg.header.filePtr == NULL_PTR)
      {
         pg.header.filePtr = dataFile.getNextOpen();

         // write the new page
         dataFile.writeObject(pg);
      }
```

```
      else // write in old position
      {
        dataFile.seek(pg.header.filePtr);
        dataFile.rewriteObject(pg);
      }

      // if root, change root pointer
      if (root)
      {
        header.rootPtr = pg.header.filePtr;

        // update header
        dataFile.rewind();
        dataFile.rewriteObject(header);
      }
    }

    public Page read
      (
      long pos
      )
      throws BTreeException, IOException,
         ClassNotFoundException
    {
      // move to specified position in data file
      dataFile.seek(pos);

      // read and return a Page
      return (Page)dataFile.readObject();
    }

    public Page readRoot()
      throws BTreeException, IOException,
         ClassNotFoundException
    {
      return read(header.rootPtr);
    }

    public void delete
      (
      Page pg
```

```
    )
    throws BTreeException, IOException
{
    // move to specified position in data file
    dataFile.seek(pg.header.filePtr);

    // delete this record
    dataFile.delete();
}

public int getKeyLen()
{
    return header.keyLen;
}
}
```

Why don't I define `BTreePageFile` as a subclass `PageDatabase-File`? It's simply a matter of hiding unnecessary superclass methods; `PageDatabaseFile` implements a variety of methods that simply aren't required by the `BTreePageFile`. Java has no facility for hiding fields and methods inherited from a superclass.

`write` begins by comparing the order and key size stored in its header with the order and key size of the page being written. If these values don't match, the page is rejected and `write` throws an exception. This ensures that the `PageFile` will only contain pages with identical orders and key sizes.

If the `Page` being written has an assigned file pointer in its `header.FilePtr` member, `write` stores the `Page` in its original location. If `header.FilePtr` is empty (indicated by a `NULL_PTR` value), `write` checks to see if any "dead" records are available. If the deleted record list contains an entry, the new `Page` is written into the first deleted record. Otherwise, the new `Page` is appended to the file. If the `Page` has a `header.FilePtr` value of `NULL_PTR`, `header.FilePtr` is set to the location where the `Page` was written before it is stored. The `Page` `header` value is written first, followed by the pointer and link arrays, and then the keys written as a fixed-length block.

The `read` method performs the same actions to retrieve a stored `Page`. To read the root record, use the `readRoot` replace.

`delete` removes a `Page` from the `PageDatabaseFile`.

BTree Database Class

Now we get to the meat: the BTreeDatabase template class. A BTreeDatabase has a BTreePageFile object for storing Pages and an ObjectDatabaseFile object for storing Objects. When data is stored in a BTreeDatabase, it is associated with a key in the PageDatabaseFile. To find a record, a key is used to retrieve the long of its associated data from a Page in the PageFile.

I'll break up the description of BTreeDatabase, which contains more than 800 lines of Java code. Initially, the class defines fields and an inner class used to return information from the search method:

```
public class BTreeDatabase
  implements BTreeSharedConstants
{
  //——————————-
  // inner classes
  //——————————-
  private class SearchResult
  {
    public boolean found;
    public Page page;
    public int  pos;

    // constructor
    public SearchResult
      (
      boolean f,
      Page pg,
      int  n
      )
    {
      found = f;
      page = pg;
```

```
        pos   = n;
      }
   }

   //————————-
   // exceptions
   //————————-
   private static final BTreeException err_locked =
     new BTreeException("BTree file locked");

   //————————-
   // fields
   //————————-
   private ObjectDatabaseFile dataFile;
   private BTreePageFile    treeFile;

   private boolean locked = false;
   private Pageroot;
   private String   dataName;
   private String   treeName;

   private BTreeCallback recTravCallback;
```

In the **BTreeDatabase** class, root contains the current root **Page** of the **BTree**; keeping the root resident in memory speeds most operations. The **locked** field is set by the **setLocked** method; when **true**, the **write** and **delete** replaces will generate an exception, preventing changes in the files. Two files, **dataFile** and **treeFile**, respectively, contain data records and the BTree pages.

Constructors

A new **BTreeDatabase** is constructed by providing a base file name and an order. It begins by calling a helper method to assign values to the file names of the data and page files. Then, it creates file objects; if these files have a zero length, the constructor knows that it is creating a new database. The **BTreePageFile** will automatically create a root page or read an existing page file as required.

```java
// constructor to open existing files
public BTreeDatabase
  (
  String baseName
  )
  throws IOException, BTreeException,
      ClassNotFoundException
{
  setNames(baseName);

  // open files
  treeFile = new BTreePageFile(treeName);
  dataFile = new ObjectDatabaseFile(dataName);

  // read root page of index
  root = treeFile.readRoot();
}

// constructor to create new files
public BTreeDatabase
  (
  String baseName,
  int order,
  int keyLen
  )
  throws IOException, BTreeException,
      ClassNotFoundException
{
  setNames(baseName);

  // delete any existing files
  File f1 = new File(treeName);
  f1.delete();

  f1 = new File(dataName);
  f1.delete();

  // create file objects
  treeFile =
      new BTreePageFile(treeName,order,keyLen);
  dataFile = new ObjectDatabaseFile(dataName);
```

```
        // read root page of index
        root = treeFile.readRoot();
}

// helper method
private void setNames
    (
    String baseName
    )
{
    dataName = baseName + ".dat";
    treeName = baseName + ".idx";
}
```

Writing Records

To write a record in a **BTreeDatabase**, both a key and data must be provided. The **write** replace stores the data object in the **Data** file, which returns a **long** indicating the location of the **DataBlock** in the file. That pointer and the key are then passed to the **insertKey** replace, which updates the **BTree**.

```
public void writeObject
    (
    String key,
    Object obj
    )
    throws IOException, BTreeException,
        ClassNotFoundException
{
    // check locks
    if (locked)
        throw err_locked;

    // truncate the key
    if (key.length() > treeFile.getKeyLen())
        key = key.substring(0,treeFile.getKeyLen());
```

```
    // write the data record
    long pos = dataFile.writeObject(obj);

    // insert key into tree
    insertKey(key,pos);
}
```

The `Search` replace is a private member; it is called initially with the root page of the tree, and it moves down the tree, following links, by calling itself. If `Search` finds the search key, `keypage` is assigned the page in which the key was found and `pos` is set to the key's location within that page. If the key was not found, `Search` returns `false`, sets `keypage` to the leaf page where the search key should be inserted, and sets `pos` to the position in that page where the key belongs. The `read`, `write`, and `delete` replaces use `Search` to find keys or the leaf into which a key should be inserted.

```
    // find a node
    private SearchResult search
      (
      Page pg,
      String key
      )
      throws IOException, BTreeException, ClassNot-
          FoundException
    {
      int pos = 0;

      if (pg.header.numKeys == 0)
        return new SearchResult(false,pg,pos);

      while (true)
      {
        if (pos == pg.header.numKeys)
          break;

        int comp = pg.key[pos].compareTo(key);

        if (comp == 0)
          return new SearchResult(true,pg,pos);
        else
```

```
        {
          if (comp < 0)
            ++pos;
          else
            break;
        }
    }

    if (pg.lnk[pos] == NULL_PTR)
      return new SearchResult(false,pg,pos);
    else
      return search(treeFile.read(pg.lnk[pos]),key);
  }
```

insertKey is a private member; it is only called by the write. insertKey begins by calling search. If the key was found, insertKey deletes the data record associated with its entry in the Page, and then sets the Page to point to the new record referenced by dataptr. Thus, duplicate keys cause a new data record to replace the old data associated with a key.

```
    // insert node into leaf
    private void insertKey
      (
      String key,
      long   ptr
      )
      throws IOException, BTreeException,
         ClassNotFoundException
    {
      // search for the key
      SearchResult ins = search(root,key);

      if (ins.found)
      {
        // delete old data record
        dataFile.seek(ins.page.ptr[ins.pos]);
        dataFile.delete();

        // store new data record pointer
        ins.page.ptr[ins.pos] = ptr;
```

```
            // rewrite modified page
            treeFile.write(ins.page,false);
        }
        else
        {
            // check to see if page is full
            if (ins.page.header.numKeys ==
                ins.page.header.maxKeys)
            {
                // temporary arrays
                String [] tempKeys =
                    new String [ins.page.header.maxKeys + 1];
                long    [] tempPtrs =
                    new long    [ins.page.header.maxKeys + 1];

                // store new item
                tempKeys[ins.pos]       = key;
                tempPtrs[ins.pos]       = ptr;

                // copy entries from insertion page to temps
                int nt = 0; // index for temp arrays
                int ni = 0; // index for insertion page

                while (ni < ins.page.header.maxKeys)
                {
                    // skip over inserted data
                    if (ni == ins.pos)
                        ++nt;

                    // copy data
                    tempKeys[nt] = ins.page.key[ni];
                    tempPtrs[nt] = ins.page.ptr[ni];

                    // next one
                    ++ni;
                    ++nt;
                }

                // create a new leaf
                Page sibPage = new Page(ins.page.
                    header.order,ins.page.header.keyLen);
```

```
            sibPage.header.parentPtr =
                ins.page.header.parentPtr;
            treeFile.write(sibPage,false);

            // clear key counts
            ins.page.header.numKeys = 0;
            sibPage.header.numKeys  = 0;

            // copy keys from temp to pages
            for (ni = 0; ni < ins.page.header.minKeys; ++ni)
            {
               ins.page.key[ni] = tempKeys[ni];
               ins.page.ptr[ni] = tempPtrs[ni];

               ++ins.page.header.numKeys;
            }

            for (++ni ; ni <= ins.page.header.maxKeys; ++ni)
            {
               sibPage.key[ni - 1 - ins.page.header.minKeys]
                   = tempKeys[ni];
               sibPage.ptr[ni - 1 - ins.page.header.minKeys]
                   = tempPtrs[ni];

               ++sibPage.header.numKeys;
            }

            // replace remaining entries with null
            for (ni = ins.page.header.minKeys; ni <
                ins.page.header.maxKeys; ++ni)
            {
               ins.page.key[ni] = new String();
               ins.page.ptr[ni] = NULL_PTR;
            }

            // write pages
            treeFile.write(ins.page,false);
            treeFile.write(sibPage,false);

            // promote key and its pointer
            if (ins.page.header.parentPtr == NULL_PTR)
```

```
                    {
                      // creating a new root page
                      promoteRoot
                        (
                        tempKeys[ins.page.header.minKeys],
                        tempPtrs[ins.page.header.minKeys],
                        ins.page,
                        sibPage
                        );
                    }
                    else
                    {
                      // promote key into parent page
                      Page parPage =
                          treeFile.read(ins.page.header.parentPtr);

                      promoteInternal
                        (
                        parPage,
                        tempKeys[ins.page.header.minKeys],
                        tempPtrs[ins.page.header.minKeys],
                        sibPage.header.filePtr
                        );
                    }
                  }
                  else
                  {
                    // move keys to make room for new one
                    for (int n =
                        ins.page.header.numKeys; n > ins.pos; —n)
                    {
                      ins.page.key[n] = ins.page.key[n - 1];
                      ins.page.ptr[n] = ins.page.ptr[n - 1];
                    }

                    ins.page.key[ins.pos] = key;
                    ins.page.ptr[ins.pos] = ptr;

                    ++ins.page.header.numKeys;

                    // write updated page
```

```
        treeFile.write(ins.page,false);
    }
  }

  root = treeFile.readRoot();
}
```

If the key was not found, `search` returns the leaf page in `ins.page` where the key should be inserted at `ins.pos`. If `ins.page` is not full, the key is inserted by shifting keys to the left and placing the new key and its data record pointer in the opened position. When `ins.page` is full, it needs to be split and the median key is promoted. The split is accomplished by creating a temporary list of keys and data record pointers, in which the new key and its data pointer are located in their correct relationship to other keys. The first half of these keys is copied back into `ins.page`, and the second half are copied into the sibling page. The median key is then promoted. If `inspage` has a parent, `insertKey` promotes the median key into the parent page via `promoteInternal`; otherwise, `promoteRoot` is called to generate a new root page.

The private `promoteInternal` replace inserts a key promoted by splitting into a parent page.

```
    // promote key into parent
    private void promoteInternal
      (
      Page    insPage,
      String key,
      long    ptr,
      long    link
      )
      throws IOException, BTreeException,
         ClassNotFoundException
    {
      if (insPage.header.numKeys ==
         insPage.header.maxKeys)
      {
        // temporary array
```

```java
String [] tempKeys =
    new String [insPage.header.maxKeys + 1];
long []    tempPtrs = new long
    [insPage.header.maxKeys + 1];
long []    tempLnks = new long
    [insPage.header.order    + 1];

tempLnks[0] = insPage.lnk[0];

// copy entries from inapage to temps
int nt  = 0;
int ni  = 0;
int pos = 0;

// find insertion point
while ((pos < insPage.header.numKeys) &&
    (insPage.key[pos].compareTo(key) < 0))
  ++pos;

// store new info
tempKeys[pos] = key;
tempPtrs[pos] = ptr;
tempLnks[pos + 1] = link;

// copy existing keys
while (ni < insPage.header.maxKeys)
{
  if (ni == pos)
    ++nt;

  tempKeys[nt] = insPage.key[ni];
  tempPtrs[nt] = insPage.ptr[ni];
  tempLnks[nt + 1] = insPage.lnk[ni + 1];

  ++ni;
  ++nt;
}

// generate a new leaf node
Page sibPage = new Page(insPage.header.order,
    insPage.header.keyLen);
```

```
sibPage.header.parentPtr =
    insPage.header.parentPtr;

// clear key counts
insPage.header.numKeys = 0;
sibPage.header.numKeys = 0;

insPage.lnk[0] = tempLnks[0];

// copy keys from temp to pages
for (ni =
    0; ni < insPage.header.minKeys; ++ni)
{
  insPage.key[ni]  = tempKeys[ni];
  insPage.ptr[ni]  = tempPtrs[ni];
  insPage.lnk[ni + 1] = tempLnks[ni + 1];

  ++insPage.header.numKeys;
}

sibPage.lnk[0] =
    tempLnks[insPage.header.minKeys + 1];

for (ni = insPage.header.minKeys + 1; ni <=
    insPage.header.maxKeys; ++ni)
{
  sibPage.key[ni - 1 - insPage.header.minKeys] =
      tempKeys[ni];
  sibPage.ptr[ni - 1 - insPage.header.minKeys] =
      tempPtrs[ni];
  sibPage.lnk[ni - insPage.header.minKeys] =
      tempPtrs[ni + 1];

  ++sibPage.header.numKeys;
}

// replace remaining entries with null
for (ni = insPage.header.minKeys; ni <
    insPage.header.maxKeys; ++ni)
{
  insPage.key[ni]  = new String();
```

```
    insPage.ptr[ni]   = NULL_PTR;
    insPage.lnk[ni + 1] = NULL_PTR;
}


// write pages
treeFile.write(insPage,false);
treeFile.write(sibPage,false);

// update parent links in child nodes
for (ni = 0; ni <= sibPage.header.numKeys; ++ni)
{
  Page child = treeFile.read(sibPage.lnk[ni]);
  child.header.parentPtr = sibPage.header.filePtr;
  treeFile.write(child,false);
}

// promote key and pointer
if (insPage.header.parentPtr == NULL_PTR)
{
  // create a new root
  promoteRoot
    (
    tempKeys[insPage.header.minKeys],
    tempPtrs[insPage.header.minKeys],
    insPage,
    sibPage
    );
}
else
{
  // read parent and promote key
  Page parPage =
      treeFile.read(insPage.header.parentPtr);

  promoteInternal
    (
    parPage,
    tempKeys[insPage.header.minKeys],
    tempPtrs[insPage.header.minKeys],
    sibPage.header.filePtr
    );
```

```
      }
    }
    else
    {
      int pos = 0;

      // find insertion point
      while ((pos < insPage.header.numKeys) &&
          (insPage.key[pos].compareTo(key) < 0))
        ++pos;

      // shift keys right
      for (int n = insPage.header.numKeys; n > pos; —n)
      {
        insPage.key[n] = insPage.key[n - 1];
        insPage.ptr[n] = insPage.ptr[n - 1];
        insPage.lnk[n + 1] = insPage.lnk[n];
      }

      insPage.key[pos]= key;
      insPage.ptr[pos]= ptr;
      insPage.lnk[pos+ 1] = link;

      ++insPage.header.numKeys;

      // write updated page
      treeFile.write(insPage,false);
    }
  }
```

When the root node is split by insertKey or PromoteKey, they call the promoteRoot replace to generate a new root that contains a single key.

```
  // promote key by creating new root
  private void promoteRoot
    (
    String key,
    long ptr,
    Page lessPage,
    Page grtrPage
```

```
        )
        throws IOException, BTreeException,
            ClassNotFoundException
    {
        // create a new root page
        Page newRoot = new Page
            (root.header.order,root.header.keyLen);

        // add key and links to root
        newRoot.key[0] = key;
        newRoot.ptr[0] = ptr;
        newRoot.lnk[0] = lessPage.header.filePtr;
        newRoot.lnk[1] = grtrPage.header.filePtr;

        newRoot.header.numKeys = 1;

        // write new root to tree
        treeFile.write(newRoot,true);

        // update children
        lessPage.header.parentPtr = newRoot.header.filePtr;
        grtrPage.header.parentPtr = newRoot.header.filePtr;

        treeFile.write(lessPage,false);
        treeFile.write(grtrPage,false);
    }
```

Reading Records

Reading a record from the file is very simple: search for the key in the BTree page files, and if it is found, read the DataFile record identified by that key's Ptr value. If the record isn't found, read returns null.

```
    public Object readObject
        (
        String key
        )
        throws IOException, BTreeException,
            ClassNotFoundException
```

```
          {
            // check locks
            if (locked)
              throw err_locked;

            // truncate the key
            if (key.length() > treeFile.getKeyLen())
              key = key.substring(0,treeFile.getKeyLen());

            // search for key
            SearchResult result = search(root,key);

            if (result.found)
            {
              dataFile.seek(result.page.ptr[result.pos]);

              return dataFile.readObject();
            }
            else
              return null;
          }
```

Deleting Records

And now we come to deletion. The `delete` replace performs the first stage of deletion, which involves removing a key from a leaf page. The `delete` replace begins by calling `search` to find the key in the tree. If the key was not found, the `replace` simply returns, since it can't delete a key that isn't there!

```
      public void deleteObject
        (
        String key
        )
        throws IOException, BTreeException,
          ClassNotFoundException
      {
        // check locks
        if (locked)
          throw err_locked;
```

```
                    // truncate the key
                    if (key.length() > treeFile.getKeyLen())
                      key = key.substring(0,treeFile.getKeyLen());

                    // find record to be deleted
                    SearchResult del = search(root,key);

                    if (del == null)
                      return;

                    // delete data record
                    dataFile.seek(del.page.ptr[del.pos]);
                    dataFile.delete();

                    // is this a leaf node?
                    if (del.page.lnk[0] == NULL_PTR)
                    {
                      // remove key from leaf
                      —del.page.header.numKeys;

                      // slide keys left over deleted one
                      for (int n = del.pos; n <
                          del.page.header.numKeys; ++n)
                      {
                        del.page.key[n] = del.page.key[n + 1];
                        del.page.ptr[n] = del.page.ptr[n + 1];
                      }

                      del.page.key[del.page.header.numKeys] =
                          new String();
                      del.page.ptr[del.page.header.numKeys] =
                          NULL_PTR;

                      // write changed record
                      treeFile.write(del.page,false);

                      // adjust the tree, if needed
                      if (del.page.header.numKeys <
                          del.page.header.minKeys)
                        adjustTree(del.page);
                    }
```

```
        else // deleting an internal page
        {
            // get the successor page
            Page sucPage =
                treeFile.read(del.page.lnk[del.pos + 1]);

          while (sucPage.lnk[0] != NULL_PTR)
            sucPage = treeFile.read(sucPage.lnk[0]);

            // first key is the "swappee"
            del.page.key[del.pos] = sucPage.key[0];
            del.page.ptr[del.pos] = sucPage.ptr[0];

            // delete swapped key from successor page
            — sucPage.header.numKeys;

            for (int n = 0; n < sucPage.header.numKeys; ++n)
            {
              sucPage.key[n] = sucPage.key[n + 1];
              sucPage.ptr[n] = sucPage.ptr[n + 1];
              sucPage.lnk[n + 1] = sucPage.lnk[n + 2];
            }

            sucPage.key[sucPage.header.numKeys]  =
                new String();
            sucPage.ptr[sucPage.header.numKeys] = NULL_PTR;
            sucPage.lnk[sucPage.header.numKeys + 1] =
                NULL_PTR;

            // write modified records
            treeFile.write(del.page,false);
            treeFile.write(sucPage,false);

            // adjust tree for leaf node
            if (sucPage.header.numKeys <
                sucPage.header.minKeys)
              adjustTree(sucPage);
        }
    }
```

`delete` checks the page where the key was found; if the page is a leaf, it simply removes the key. If the page has children, it is an internal (possibly root) page. For an internal node, `delete` searches through the tree, finding the key which immediately succeeds the deleted key. The successor key is found by looking at the subtree containing keys greater than the deleted key, travelling down the tree until a leaf is found. The first key in that leaf is the successor, and its values replace those of the deleted key. Then the successor key is deleted from the leaf. If the leaf contains less than `Hdr.MinKeys` keys, `delete` calls the `adjustTree replace`.

```
// adjust tree if leaf is too small
private void adjustTree
  (
  Page pg
  )
  throws IOException, BTreeException,
     ClassNotFoundException
{
  // check for root
  if (pg.header.parentPtr == NULL_PTR)
    return;

  // get parent page
  Page parPage = treeFile.read(pg.header.parentPtr);

  // find pointer to pg
  int n = 0;

  while (parPage.lnk[n] != pg.header.filePtr)
    ++n;

  // read sibling pages
  Page sibMore = null;
  Page sibLess = null;

  if (n < parPage.header.numKeys)
    sibMore = treeFile.read(parPage.lnk[n+1]);

  if (n > 0)
    sibLess = treeFile.read(parPage.lnk[n-1]);
```

```
    if ((sibLess == null) || (sibMore == null))
      return;

    // choose to redistribute or concatenate nodes
    if (sibLess.header.numKeys >
        sibMore.header.numKeys)
    {
      —n;

      if (sibLess.header.numKeys >
          sibLess.header.maxKeys)
          redistribute(n,sibLess,parPage,pg);
      else
        concatenate(n,sibLess,parPage,pg);
    }
    else
    {
      if (sibMore.header.numKeys >
          sibMore.header.maxKeys)
          redistribute(n,pg,parPage,sibMore);
      else
        concatenate(n,pg,parPage,sibMore);
    }
  }
```

The parameter `pg` references a page which contains `order / 2 - 1` keys; when `adjustTree` is called by `delete`, `pg` will reference the leaf page from which a key was deleted. `adjustTree` finds the sibling nodes of `pg`. Note that `pg` will have at least one sibling, and it may have two. If a `pg` has only one sibling, the other (non-existent) sibling is assumed to contain zero keys for comparison purposes. `adjustTree` also reads `pg`'s parent page.

`adjustTree` calls the `concatenate` replace to combine `pg` with a sibling, or the `redistribute` replace to redistribute keys between `pg`, its parent page, and a sibling page. `redistribute` is called if one of `pg`'s siblings has more than `MinKeys` keys; otherwise, `concatenate` is called. A comparison is made to redistribute or concatenate with the sibling that has the most keys; thus, `pg` may be the page to the right of the parent's separation key, or it may be to the left, depending on the number of keys in the sibling with which it is processed. Calls to both `concatenate` and `redistribute` include the index of the key in the parent page that separates `pg` and its sibling; this key is hereafter called the *separation key*.

```
// redistribute keys among siblings and parent
private void redistribute
  (
  int pos,
  Page lessPage,
  Page parPage,
  Page morePage
  )
  throws IOException, BTreeException,
     ClassNotFoundException
{
  // check for leaf page
  if (lessPage.lnk[0] == NULL_PTR)
  {
    if (lessPage.header.numKeys >
      morePage.header.numKeys)
    {
      // move a key from lessPage to morePage
      for (int n = morePage.header.numKeys;
         n > 0; —n)
      {
        morePage.key[n] = morePage.key[n - 1];
        morePage.ptr[n] = morePage.ptr[n - 1];
      }

      // store parent separator in morePage
      morePage.key[0] = parPage.key[pos];
      morePage.lnk[0] = parPage.ptr[pos];

      // increment morePage key count
      ++morePage.header.numKeys;

      // decrement lessPage key count
      —lessPage.header.numKeys;
```

```
                          //move last key in lessPage to parPage
                              as separator
                          parPage.key[pos] =
                              lessPage.key[lessPage.header.numKeys];
                          parPage.ptr[pos] =
                              lessPage.ptr[lessPage.header.numKeys];


                          // clear last key in lessPage
                          lessPage.key[lessPage.header.numKeys] =
                              new String();
                          lessPage.ptr[lessPage.header.numKeys] =
                              NULL_PTR;
                      }
                      else
                      {
                        // move a key from morePage to lessPage
                        for (int n = lessPage.header.numKeys;
                            n > 0; —n)
                        {
                          lessPage.key[n] = lessPage.key[n - 1];
                          lessPage.ptr[n] = lessPage.ptr[n - 1];
                        }


                        // store parent separator in morePage
                        lessPage.key[0] = parPage.key[pos];
                        lessPage.lnk[0] = parPage.ptr[pos];


                        // increment morePage key count
                        ++lessPage.header.numKeys;


                        // decrement lessPage key count
                        —morePage.header.numKeys;


                        // move last key in lessPage to
                            parPage as separator
                        parPage.key[pos] =
                              morePage.key[morePage.header.numKeys];
                        parPage.ptr[pos] =
                              morePage.ptr[morePage.header.numKeys];
```

```
                    // clear last key in morePage
                    morePage.key[morePage.header.numKeys] =
                        new String();
                    morePage.ptr[morePage.header.numKeys] =
                        NULL_PTR;
                }
            }
            else
            {
                if (lessPage.header.numKeys >
                    morePage.header.numKeys)
                {
                    // move a key from lessPage to morePage
                    for (int n = morePage.header.numKeys;
                        n > 0; --n)
                    {
                        morePage.key[n] = morePage.key[n - 1];
                        morePage.ptr[n] = morePage.ptr[n - 1];
                        morePage.lnk[n + 1] = morePage.lnk[n];
                    }

                    morePage.lnk[1] = morePage.lnk[0];


                    // store parPage separator key in morePage
                    morePage.key[0] = parPage.key[pos];
                    morePage.ptr[0] = parPage.ptr[pos];
                    morePage.lnk[0] =
                        lessPage.lnk[lessPage.header.numKeys];


                    // update child link
                    Page child = treeFile.read(morePage.lnk[0]);

                    child.header.parentPtr =
                        morePage.header.filePtr;

                    treeFile.write(child,false);


                    // increment morePage key count
                    ++morePage.header.numKeys;
```

```
                    // decrement lessPage key count
                    —lessPage.header.numKeys;

                    // move last key in lessPage to
                         parPage as separator
                    parPage.key[pos] =
                        lessPage.key[lessPage.header.numKeys];
                    parPage.ptr[pos] =
                        lessPage.ptr[lessPage.header.numKeys];

                    // clear last key in lessPage
                    lessPage.key[lessPage.header.numKeys] =
                        new String();
                    lessPage.ptr[lessPage.header.numKeys] =
                        NULL_PTR;
                    lessPage.ptr[lessPage.header.numKeys + 1] =
                        NULL_PTR;
                }
                else
                {
                    // store parPage separator key in lessPage
                    lessPage.key[lessPage.header.numKeys] =
                        parPage.key[pos];
                    lessPage.ptr[lessPage.header.numKeys] =
                        parPage.ptr[pos];
                    lessPage.lnk[lessPage.header.numKeys + 1] =
                        morePage.lnk[0];

                    // update child link
                    Page child = treeFile.read(lessPage.lnk[0]);

                    child.header.parentPtr =
                        lessPage.header.filePtr;

                    treeFile.write(child,false);

                    // increment lessPage key count
                    ++lessPage.header.numKeys;

                    // move last key in morePage to
                         parPage as separator
```

```
                parPage.key[pos] = morePage.key[0];
                parPage.ptr[pos] = morePage.ptr[0];

                // decrement morePage key count
                —morePage.header.numKeys;

                // move a key from morePage to lessPage
                int n;

                for (n = 0; n > morePage.header.numKeys; ++n)
                {
                  morePage.key[n] = morePage.key[n + 1];
                  morePage.ptr[n] = morePage.ptr[n + 1];
                  morePage.lnk[n] = morePage.lnk[n + 1];
                }

                morePage.lnk[n] = morePage.lnk[n + 1];

                // clear last key in morePage
                morePage.key[n]   = new String();
                morePage.ptr[n]   = NULL_PTR;
                morePage.ptr[n + 1] = NULL_PTR;
              }
            }

            // write updated pages
            treeFile.write(lessPage,false);
            treeFile.write(parPage,false);
            treeFile.write(morePage,false);

            // update cached root if necessary
            if (parPage.header.parentPtr == NULL_PTR)
              root = parPage;
          }
```

redistribute looks long and complicated, but it is actually one process implemented for special cases. Redistribution will either occur from lessPage to morePage or from morePage to lessPage; when redistributing keys among internal nodes, links will have to be changed as well, while leaf nodes can have their keys redistributed without worrying about links. This gives us four cases. In each case, the separator key is moved from the parent into the page which is short a key. The page that has extra keys provides a new separator key. No further adjustments in the tree are required, since no page is reduced below `MinKeys` keys.

`concatenate` begins by appending the separation key to `lessPage`; the separation key is then removed from the parent page. The keys from `morePage` are sequentially added to `lessPage`, and `morePage` is deleted. `concatenate` updates the parent links in all moved nodes so that they point back to `lessPage`. If the parent page now contains zero keys, it is deleted and `lessPage` becomes the new root. And, if the parent page has been reduced to fewer than `MinKeys`, `concatenate` calls `adjustTree`. This is, of course, recursive, since `adjustTree` calls `concatenate`.

```
// concatenate sibling pages
private void concatenate
  (
  int pos,
  Page lessPage,
  Page parPage,
  Page morePage
  )
  throws IOException, BTreeException,
      ClassNotFoundException
{
  // move separator key from parPage into lessPage
  lessPage.key[lessPage.header.numKeys] =
      parPage.key[pos];
  lessPage.ptr[lessPage.header.numKeys] =
      parPage.ptr[pos];

  lessPage.lnk[lessPage.header.numKeys + 1] =
      morePage.lnk[0];

  // increment lessPage key count
  ++lessPage.header.numKeys;

  // delete separator from parPage
  —parPage.header.numKeys;
```

```
int n;

for (n = pos; n < parPage.header.numKeys; ++n)
{
  parPage.key[n] = parPage.key[n + 1];
  parPage.ptr[n] = parPage.ptr[n + 1];
  parPage.lnk[n + 1] = parPage.lnk[n + 2];
}

// clear unsused key from parent
parPage.key[n] = new String();
parPage.ptr[n] = NULL_PTR;
parPage.lnk[n + 1] = NULL_PTR;

// copy keys from morePage to lessPage
int ng = 0;
n = lessPage.header.numKeys;

while (ng < morePage.header.numKeys)
{
  ++lessPage.header.numKeys;

  lessPage.key[n]   = morePage.key[ng];
  lessPage.ptr[n]   = morePage.ptr[ng];
  lessPage.lnk[n + 1] = morePage.lnk[ng + 1];

  ++ng;
  ++n;
}

// delete morePage
treeFile.delete(morePage);

// is this a leaf?
if (lessPage.lnk[0] == NULL_PTR)
{
  // adjust child pointers
  for (n = 0; n <= lessPage.header.numKeys; ++n)
  {
    Page child = treeFile.read(lessPage.lnk[n]);
```

```
                  child.header.parentPtr =
                    lessPage.header.filePtr;

                  treeFile.write(child,false);
              }
          }

          // write lessPage and parent
          if (parPage.header.numKeys == 0)
          {
            treeFile.delete(parPage);

            lessPage.header.parentPtr = NULL_PTR;

            treeFile.write(lessPage,true);

            root = lessPage;
          }
          else
          {
            treeFile.write(parPage,false);
            treeFile.write(lessPage,false);

            // reset cached root page if needed
            if (parPage.header.parentPtr == NULL_PTR)
              root = parPage;

            // if parent is too small, adjust
            if (parPage.header.numKeys <
                parPage.header.minKeys)
              adjustTree(parPage);
          }
      }
```

InOrder Traversal

BTrees allow sequential access to indexed data records. To examine all the records in a `BTreeDatabase`, in sorted order, call the `inOrder` member.

```
public void inOrder
    (
    BTreeCallback callback
    )
    throws BTreeException, IOException,
        ClassNotFoundException
{
    // verify
    if (callback == null)
      return;

    // lock the database
    locked = true;

    // store reference to callback
    recTravCallback = callback;

    // call recursive method
    recurseTraverse(root);

    // unlock database
    locked = false;
}
```

The **BTreeCallback** interface identifies an application that processes each record as it is encountered.

```
public interface BTreeCallback
{
  void processBTreeRecord
    (
    String key,
    Object obj
    );
}
```

In-order processing of a BTree is recursive, as described earlier in the chapter. The **inOrder** method "locks" the database to prevent changes, saves the callback object, and then calls **recurseTraverse** to examine the index and return sorted records.

```java
void recurseTraverse
  (
  Page pg
  )
  throws BTreeException, IOException,
     ClassNotFoundException
{
  // verify
  if (pg == null)
    return;

  int n;

  // recursively sequence thru keys in page
  for (n = 0; n < pg.header.numKeys; ++n)
  {
    // follow the link...
    if (pg.lnk[n] != NULL_PTR)
      recurseTraverse(treeFile.read(pg.lnk[n]));

    // read record and pass to callback
    if (pg.ptr[n] != NULL_PTR)
    {
      dataFile.seek(pg.ptr[n]);
      recTravCallback.processBTreeRecord(pg.key[n],
            dataFile.readObject());
    }
  }

  // handle "greatest" link
  if (pg.lnk[n] != NULL_PTR)
    recurseTraverse(treeFile.read(pg.lnk[n]));
}
```

An Example

The following application exercises the BTree classes, building a database and retrieving records according to key and in order.

```java
import java.applet.*;
import java.awt.*;
import java.io.*;

import Chapter12Frame;
import coyote.io.*;

public class Chapter12
  extends Applet
  implements BTreeCallback
{

  public String getAppletInfo()
  {
    return "Java Algorithms and Components:
        Chapter Twelve" +
         "Copyright 1997 Scott Robert Ladd" +
         "All rights reserved";
  }

  public void init()
  {
    // define applet area
    setSize(320, 240);
    setLayout(new BorderLayout());
    setBackground(Color.lightGray);

    // create output list
    TextArea output = new TextArea();
    add(output,BorderLayout.CENTER);

    try
    {
      exercise1(output);
      exercise2(output);
      exercise3(output);
    }
    catch (Exception ex)
    {
      output.append("-> " + ex.getClass().getName()
        + ": " + ex.getMessage());
```

```
      }
   }


   private final static String [] names =
   {
     "alpha",
     "beta",
     "gamma",
     "delta",
     "epsilon",
     "zeta",
     "eta",
     "theta",
     "iota",
     "kappa",
     "lambda",
     "mu",
     "nu",
     "xi",
     "omicron",
     "pi",
     "rho",
     "sigma",
     "tau",
     "upsilon",
     "phi",
     "chi",
     "psi",
     "omega"
   };


   private void exercise1
      (
      TextArea output
      )
      throws IOException, BTreeException,
         ClassNotFoundException
   {
      String rec;
```

```
BTreeDatabase db =
    new BTreeDatabase("Chapter12",7,10);

int toDo = names.length;

// write records
for (int n = 0; n < toDo; ++n)
{
  db.writeObject(names[n],names[n]);
  output.append("writing record
      #" + n + ": " + names[n] + "\n");
}

// read records
output.append("\n");
for (int n = toDo - 1; n >= 0; —n)
{
  rec = (String)db.readObject(names[n]);
  output.append("key '" + names[n]
      + "' returned: " + rec + "\n");
}

// replace records
output.append("\n");
rec = new String("NEW" + names[10]);
db.writeObject(names[10],rec);
output.append("Replaced '" + names[10]
    + " with: " + rec + "\n");
rec = (String)db.readObject(names[10]);
output.append("Read back: " + rec + "\n");

rec = new String("NEW" + names[21]);
db.writeObject(names[21],rec);
output.append("Replaced '" + names[21]
    + " with: " + rec + "\n");
rec = (String)db.readObject(names[21]);
output.append("Read back: " + rec + "\n");

// delete records
output.append("\n");
```

```
    db.deleteObject(names[0]);
    output.append("deleted: " + names[0] + "\n");

    db.deleteObject(names[10]);
    output.append("deleted: " + names[10] + "\n");

    db.deleteObject(names[13]);
    output.append("deleted: " + names[13] + "\n");
}

private void exercise2
  (
  TextArea output
  )
  throws IOException, BTreeException,
      ClassNotFoundException
{
  String rec;

  BTreeDatabase db = new BTreeDatabase("Chapter12");

  // read records
  output.append("\n");
  for (int n = names.length - 1; n >= 0; —n)
  {
    rec = (String)db.readObject(names[n]);
    output.append("key '" + names[n]
        + "' returned: " + rec + "\n");
  }
}


TextArea globalOutput;

private void exercise3
  (
  TextArea output
  )
  throws IOException, BTreeException,
      ClassNotFoundException
{
  String rec;
```

```
                BTreeDatabase db = new BTreeDatabase("Chapter12");

                globalOutput = output;

                output.append("\n");

                db.inOrder(this);
            }

        public void processBTreeRecord
            (
            String key,
            Object obj
            )
        {
            globalOutput.append("Key = " + key
                + ", rec = " + (String)obj + "\n");
        }
    }
```

Onward

I've always liked including something "different" in my books — code
that is, perhaps, less general purpose and more interesting than
the average algorithm. A recent project caused me to write code
for an embedded navigation and astronomy system. Some of that
code follows.

Chapter

Where and When

**Heaven signifies night and day,
cold and heat, times and seasons.**

— Sun Tzu, *On The Art of War*

Time measures motion, and we base our clocks and
calendars on the apparent movements of celestial
bodies. We ask when the sun will rise tomorrow, or
how high Arcturus will rise tonight, or when the next
full moon will be. Questions of place invariably
involve time, and vice versa — for, as Einstein
showed us, time and space are mutually relative. And
so, to understand the movements in the heavens, we
need to know where we are and what time it is. While
these algorithms may not be the stuff of everyday
business applications, I think these final three chapters show how Java trancends its Internet roots to act
as a powerful application development tool.

While working on this book, I was developing
Java software for navigation and astronomy. NASA
uses Java applets in controlling some of its space
probes; I've found Java useful in working with Global

Positioning System (GPS) units and my telescope. What follows are classes I developed in pursuit of a GPS-based automated tracking system; in the future, Java will become an even more important tool as it moves into the realm of embedded systems like the one I worked on.

And besides, this stuff is *fun*.

Utility Classes

All of my "where and when" code is contained in the package **coyote.kepler**. I named the package for Johannes Kepler (1571-1630), an astronomer and natural philosopher in Germany. He developed the first universal laws of gravitation, compiled one of the first star catalogs, and was instrumental in moving the human perspective from one of superstition to one of science.

Java provides several classes for working with dates and times; for the most part, I'll be working with dates in terms of the **java.util.GregorianCalendar** class, which is based on the most common western calendar.

First, I created an exception type, **KeplerException**, to identify run-time errors that occur within this library.

```
package coyote.kepler;

public class KeplerException
  extends RuntimeException
{
  public KeplerException()
  {
    super();
  }

  public KeplerException
    (
    String s
    )
  {
```

```
        super(s);
    }
}
```

For angular measurements, I needed a tool to encapsulate degrees, minutes, and seconds. The `DegMinSec` class does just that, allowing a translation between decimal degrees and individual angular fields.

```
package coyote.kepler;

public class DegMinSec
{
    //————————————-
    // fields
    //————————————-
    private short   deg;
    private short   min;
    private double sec;

    //————————————-
    // exceptions
    //————————————-
    private static final KeplerException err_inv_min =
        new KeplerException("invalid minutes");

    private static final KeplerException err_inv_sec =
        new KeplerException("invalid seconds");

    //————————————-
    // constructors
    //————————————-
    public DegMinSec()
    {
        deg = 0;
        min = 0;
        sec = 0.0;
    }

    public DegMinSec
        (
```

```
  short   d,
  short   m,
  double  s
  )
{
  setDegrees(d);
  setMinutes(m);
  setSeconds(s);
}

public DegMinSec
  (
  double d
  )
{
  // get degrees
  double t = KMath.trunc(d);
  setDegrees((short)t);
  d -= t;

  // get minutes
  d *= 60.0;
  t = KMath.trunc(d);
  setMinutes((short)t);
  d -= t;

  // get seconds
  setSeconds(d * 60.0);
}

//————————--
// methods
//————————--
public double asDecimal()
{
  return (double)deg + min / 60.0 + sec / 3600.0;
}

public String toString()
{
  return new String
```

```
      (
      deg + "d " +
      min + "m " +
      sec + "s"
      );
}

//————————-
// properties
//————————-
public void setDegrees
   (
   short d
   )
{
   deg = d;
}

public short getDegrees()
{
   return deg;
}

public void setMinutes
   (
   short m
   )
{
   if ((m < 0) || (m >= 60))
      throw err_inv_min;

   min = m;
}

public short getMinutes()
{
   return min;
}

public void setSeconds
   (
```

```
      double s
      )
   {
     if ((s < 0.0) || (s >= 60.0))
       throw err_inv_sec;

     sec = s;
   }

   public double getSeconds()
   {
     return sec;
   }
}
```

The DegMinSec class provides an example of my design for other classes in **coyote.kepler**. The values of the fields are set via property methods, even from within the constructors. This allows me to perform range checking on values in a single place, encapsulating error control. One constructor extracts degrees, minutes, and seconds from a decimal angle, passing the extracted values to the property setting methods for verification and assignment to fields. The asDecimal method returns a decimal value calculated from the separate fields.

I also defined a number of constants for my "kepler" package; these I placed within the Constants class. I'll explain more about the meaning of these values at pertinent points within the following text.

```
   package coyote.kepler;

   public class Constants
   {
     //———————--
     // constants
     //———————--
     public final static double PI2        = Math.PI * 2.0;
```

```
public final static double RADperDEG = Math.PI / 180.0;
public final static double DEGperRAD = 1.0 / RADperDEG;

// epochs
public final static double J1900 =
    2415020.0;   // 31 Dec 1899 noon
public final static double B1950 =
    2433282.423; //  1 Jan 1950 22:09
public final static double J2000 =
    2451545.0;   //  1 Jan 2000 noon


public final static double JULIAN_YEAR   =
    365.25;
public final static double JULIAN_CENTURY =
    10.0 * JULIAN_YEAR;


// other values
public final static double SIDEREAL_RATIO =
    1.0027379092558;
public final static double EARTH_RAD      =
    6378140.0;
public final static double EARTH_RAD_P  = 6356755.0;


public final static double GEOCENTRIC_K    =
    (EARTH_RAD_P * EARTH_RAD_P)

                                         /

                    (EARTH_RAD * EARTH_RAD);
}
```

Finally, I created a KMath class to provide a set of useful set of static utility methods for numerical calculations. The trigonometric methods provided by the **java.util.Math** package all operate in terms of radians; most real-world work, however, involves angles expressed in terms of degrees. I defined a set of trigonometric methods for double values containing angles in terms of degrees. These methods convert the input or output of **java.util.Math** methods to and from radians.

```
package coyote.kepler;

public class KMath
{
  //————————————-
  // trig methods
  //————————————-
  public static double asinh(double x)
  {
    return Math.log(x + Math.sqrt(x * x + 1.0));
  }

  public static double acosh(double x)
  {
    return Math.log(x + Math.sqrt(x * x - 1.0));
  }

  public static double atanh(double x)
  {
    return Math.log((1.0 + x) / (1.0 - x)) / 2.0;
  }

  public static double sind(double x)
  {
    return Math.sin(x * Constants.RADperDEG);
  }

  public static double cosd(double x)
  {
    return Math.cos(x * Constants.RADperDEG);
  }

  public static double tand(double x)
  {
    return Math.tan(x * Constants.RADperDEG);
  }

  public static double asind(double x)
  {
    return Math.asin(x) * Constants.DEGperRAD;
  }
```

```
      public static double acosd(double x)
      {
        return Math.acos(x) * Constants.DEGperRAD;
      }

      public static double atand(double x)
      {
        return Math.atan(x) * Constants.DEGperRAD;
      }

      //————————————--
      // truncation and fraction extraction
      //————————————--

      public static double trunc
        (
        double x
        )
      {
        if (x < 0.0)
          return Math.ceil(x);
        else
          return Math.floor(x);
      }

      public static double frac
        (
        double x
        )
      {
        return x - trunc(x);
      }

    }
```

The `trunc` and `frac` methods provide sorely-needed facilities not implemented by **java.util.math**. To obtain the integer portion (i.e., the digits to the left of the decimal point) of a `double`, call `trunc`; to obtain the fractional part, call `frac`.

Latitude & Longitude

Our view of the sky is relative to our position on the spherical Earth. Identifying an Earth-based location begins at the equator, a plane that bisects the planet into northern and southern hemispheres. The equator is a *great circle*, meaning that its plane passes through the center of the Earth; the equator is also perpendicular to a line running through the north and south poles. Figure 13-1 shows the plane of the equator on a globe.

Figure 13-1

The Great Circle of the Equator

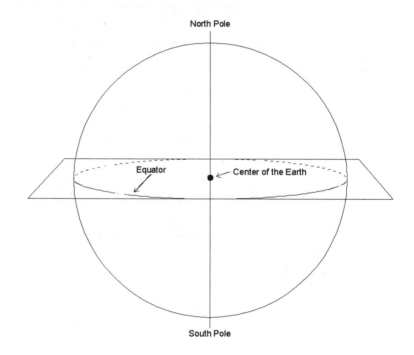

Just two angular values can specify any location on the Earth's surface. The *latitude* is a measure of distance north or south of the equator, figured as the angle between the plane of the equator and a line drawn from a point to the center of the Earth. The equator is defined as latitude 0°; at the North Pole, the latitude is +90°, while the South Pole is at latitude -90°. In Figure 13-2, the latitude of point P is the angle θ.

Figure 13-2

Spherical Coordinates

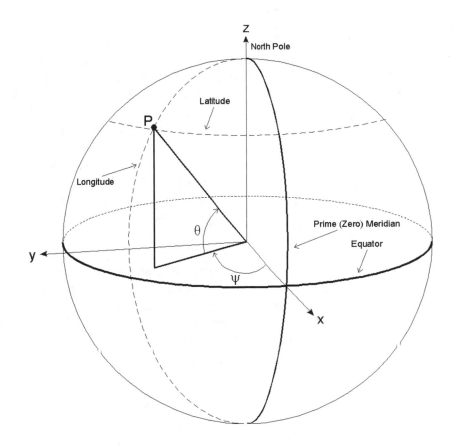

You'll notice a dotted line running through P from north to south. This second position angle, identified by the Greek letter ψ, is the *longitude*, a measurement of distance along the equator from the 0°, or *prime meridian*, line. For consistency's sake, the universal convention places the prime meridian on a line running from the north to south poles through Greenwich, England. In most calculations — including those in this book — a longitude west of Greenwich is positive and an east longitude is negative. Longitude is measured on half circles, with 180° in both the east and west directions; the common 180° line runs through the center of the Pacific Ocean, and is known as the International Date Line. It is one day earlier east of the date line than it is to the west — I'll explain that rule when I look at time in the next section.

The prime meridian could be any longitude, but consistency in navigation and maps requires an agreed-upon standard. But why is the zero mark set in Greenwich, and not, say, New York City or Tokyo? Beginning in the 17th century, England began a program to develop a system of navigation based on latitudes and longitudes; to that end, the English established a Royal Observatory at Greenwich for studying the positions of the moon and stars. When the final system of longitude was adopted in 1884, England's dominance at sea gave it the power to set the base meridian in Greenwich. I think it is quite remarkable that, in a world of varying cultures and political contentions, the system of latitude and longitude is universal.

Figure 13-3 shows a globe marked with longitude and latitude lines every 15°. To demonstrate the coordinate system, I've plotted the location of two cities: Buenos Aires, Argentina (at 58° 30'W, 34° 35'S) and Moscow, Russia (at 37° 35'E, 55° 45'N). You can see the reason why another name for latitude is *parallel* — all lines of latitude parallel each other in circles around the globe.

Figure 13-3

Latitude and Longitude

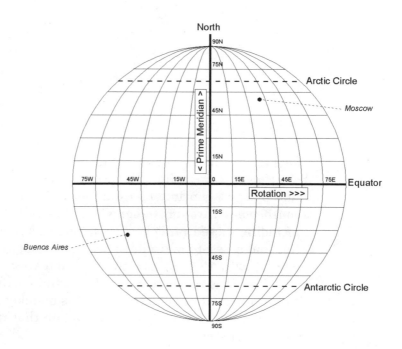

If you know the latitude and longitude of two places, you can find the distance between them. First, calculate the angle between the two points, using the following formula from spherical geometry:

$$\cos A=\cos(\psi_1-\psi_2)\cos\theta_1\cos\theta_2+\sin\theta_1\sin\theta_2 \qquad (13.1)$$

Using the example cities of Buenos Aires and Moscow, from Figure 13-3, we get:

$$\cos A=\cos(58.5°-(-37.58°))\cos(-34.58°)\cos(55.75°)+\sin(-34.58°)\sin(55.75°)$$
$$\cos A=-0.518$$
$$A=121.2°$$

Once you know the angle between two points, it's a simple matter to use the following formula to calculate the distance between them.

$$D=2\pi r \frac{A}{360°} \qquad (13.2)$$

The radius of the Earth, r, is approximately 6370 kilometers. Setting A to 121.2° gives the distance between Buenos Aires and Moscow as 13,476 kilometers.

The impetus for developing latitude and longitude came from mariners, who couldn't use landmarks for navigation on the open seas. By studying the movements of the stars, sailors could locate themselves and tell time. Now, we turn our attention to time.

The Flattened Earth

The Earth is not a sphere; the equator bulges outward due to the planet's rotation. You can see this effect clearly when looking at the gaseous planets Jupiter and Saturn; they have a distinctly "squashed" look to them. In geometric terms, the Earth is a *geoid*, not a sphere, and its polar and equatorial radii differ slightly. According to the International Astronomical Union (IAU):

```
      polar radius rp = 6,378,140 meters
   equatorial radius re = 6,356,755 meters
```

The difference isn't much, but it does affect our view of the stars by changing our latitude slightly. Most maps show *geodetic* latitudes, based on lines perpendicular to a tangent plane on the Earth's surface. Another type of type of latitude, *geographic*, is calculated as the angle of a plumb line with the equator; both geodetic and geographic latitudes measure similar angles. If the Earth were a sphere, a plumb line would point toward the center of the planet — but the flattening of the planet makes this true only at the equator and poles. So neither geodetic nor geographic latitude is accurate from the perspective of astronomy, which calculates coordinates from the center of the Earth. For tracking the stars, we need to calculate a *geocentric* latitude: a line drawn from the point of observation to the center of the Earth.

Figure 13-4 shows the relationship of geodetic (ϕ) and geocentric (ϕ') latitude. The difference is defined by the formula:

$$\tan\phi' = \frac{r_p^2}{r_e^2}\tan\phi$$

(13.3)

$$\frac{r_p^2}{r_e^2} = \frac{6,356,755^2}{6,378,140^2} = 0.9933055$$

Figure 13-4
Geodetic (ϕ) and
Geocentric (ϕ') Latitude

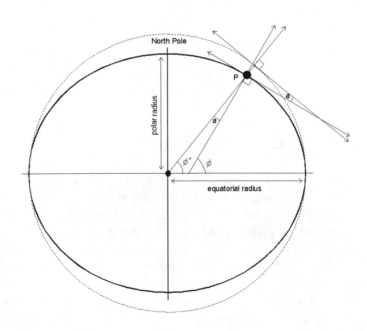

A geocentric latitude is slightly smaller then the equivalent geodetic latitude, except at the poles and equator. The greatest difference is about 11.55' at a geodetic latitude of 45° North or South.

Astronomical calculations give celestial coordinates in terms of the Earth's center; if we want to be truly accurate in plotting the stars, it is best to use the geocentric latitude of our observing position. My observing site is located at 37° 48' North latitude; I can calculate my geocentric latitude ϕ' from formula (13.3):

$$\theta' = \tan^{-1}(0.9933055 \tan(37°48'))$$
$$\theta' = 37°37'$$

Implementation

Taking the formulas above in hand, I created a `Location` class to define the longitude and latitude of a place.

```
package coyote.kepler;

public class Location
{
  //——————————--
  // fields
  //——————————--
  private double longitude;
  private double latitude;

  //——————————--
  // exceptions
  //——————————--
  private static final KeplerException err_inv_lat =
    new KeplerException("invalid latitude");

  private static final KeplerException err_inv_lon =
    new KeplerException("invalid longitude");

  //——————————--
  // constructors
  //——————————--
```

```
public Location()
{
  longitude = 0.0;
  latitude  = 0.0;
}


public Location
  (
  double lon,
  double lat
  )
{
  setLongitude(lon);
  setLatitude(lat);
}


public Location
  (
  DegMinSec dms
  )
{
  setLongitude(dms.asDecimal());
  setLatitude(dms.asDecimal());
}


//————————-
// methods
//————————-
public double angle
  (
  Location loc
  )
{
  return KMath.acosd(KMath.cosd(longitude -
      loc.longitude)
          * KMath.cosd(latitude) *
              KMath.cosd(loc.latitude)
          + KMath.sind(latitude) *
              KMath.sind(loc.latitude));
}
```

```
public double distance
   (
   Location loc,
   double radius
   )
{
   return ((radius + radius) * Math.PI *
      angle(loc) / 360.0);
}

public double distance
   (
   Location loc
   )
{
   return distance(loc, Constants.EARTH_RAD);
}

public Location toGeocentric()
{
   double newlat = KMath.atand(Constants.GEOCENTRIC_K
                 * KMath.tand(latitude));

   return new Location(longitude,newlat);
}

public String toString()
{
   return new String
      (
      longitude + "LON, " +
      latitude  + "LAT"
      );
}

//——————————-
// properties
//——————————-
public void setLongitude
   (
   double lon
```

```
    )
  {
    if ((lon < -180.0) || (lon > +180.0))
      throw err_inv_lon;

    longitude = lon;
  }

  public double getLongitude()
  {
    return longitude;
  }

  public DegMinSec getLongitudeDMS()
  {
    return new DegMinSec(longitude);
  }

  public void setLatitude
    (
    double lat
    )
  {
    if ((lat < -90.0) || (lat > +90.0))
      throw err_inv_lat;

    latitude = lat;
  }

  public double getLatitude()
  {
    return latitude;
  }

  public DegMinSec getLatitudeDMS()
  {
    return new DegMinSec(latitude);
  }
}
```

A `Location` object can be constructed from a pair of decimal values, a pair of `DegMinSec` objects, or with `longitude` and `latitude` set to zero with the default constructor. The fields can be retrieved either in decimal form or as `DegMinSec` objects. To convert a location to geocentric latitude, use `toGeocentric`. The `angle` method calculates the angle between two `Locations`; `distance` uses `angle` to determine the `distance` between two points. One version of distance requires a radius parameter, while the second verion "plugs in" the equitorial diameter of the earth.

Time

Time "begins" at 0° longitude in Greenwich; locations west of the prime meridian have earlier times on their clocks, and locations east have later times. It takes the earth 24 hours to rotate 360° on its axis, meaning that the sun traverses 15° of longitude for every hour of the day. Many calculations in this book refer to a longitudinal angle in terms of hours, with each 15° of longitude equal to one hour of angle.

Time steadily moves from day to night without much consideration for the requirements of human society. Consider, for example, an airplane leaving Lisbon, Portugal, at noon on a Monday. Lisbon is at about 39° north latitude; if the plane flies West at about 1300 km/hour, it will keep pace with the rotation of the Earth. Four and a half hours later, when the plane flies over Washington, DC, the sun will still be at noon — and noon it remains, from the aircraft's perspective, until the plane completely circles the globe and lands in Lisbon again. For the aircraft's passengers, it is still noon on Monday; to their friends and relatives in Lisbon, a night has passed and it is now Tuesday.

To accurately follow the apparent movement of the sun, your clock should be set based on your longitude west of Greenwich. If a clock in Greenwich reads noon, my watch should, according to strict solar time, read 4:50 AM, since my latitude of 107° 40' places me 7 hours and 10 minutes "behind" Greenwich. Someone in Moscow would see the sun rise two-and-a-half hours before dawn appears in Greenwich.

But setting time according to the movement of the sun is inconvenient and confusing; for example, if I traveled 65 kilometers east to Creede, Colorado, I would need to set my watch ahead three minutes to match the sun. In a world of deadlines and schedules, it simply isn't practical to depict precise solar time on our clocks — yet we need to account for differences in time between various places around the globe.

The compromise is to create time zones based on the average hourly position of the sun. Since the sun's position changes by 15° of longitude each hour, each time zone encompasses approximately 15° of longitude. Thus, my longitude of 107° 40' falls within the seventh time zone west of Greenwich; when it is noon in Greenwich, my watch reads 5:00 AM. But longitude alone cannot always determine your time zone, which has an irregular border based on political boundaries. And we can't forget the effects of Daylight Savings Time, Benjamin Franklin's invention that adjusts clock time to reflect the longer daylight hours of summer.

What does all of this mean? First and foremost, it means that clock time has little or no relationship to the motions of the stars or even the sun. A hallmark of science is its reliance on standard frames of reference; someone in Australia must use conventions held in common with a colleague in Arizona. So people concerned with coordinated time define their work in terms of Universal Time, or UT, which is the actual time in Greenwich of an event. The local clock time can be converted to UT through simple additions or subtracts for time zones and Daylight Savings Time. For example, when a clock in my time zone reads 2:00PM, the Universal Time is seven (six during Daylight Savings Time) hours later, or 9:00PM.

Several caveats apply when comparing our calendar to the planet's movements. Figure 13-5 schematically shows the movement of the Earth around the sun for the year 1996. You'll note that the year begins three days before the planet arrives at perihelion (its closest approach to the sun). And the solstices and equinoxes correspond only somewhat with the Earth's position in orbit; the winter solstice, for example, is ten days before January first and two weeks before perihelion.

Figure 13-5

The Earth's Orbit
in 1996

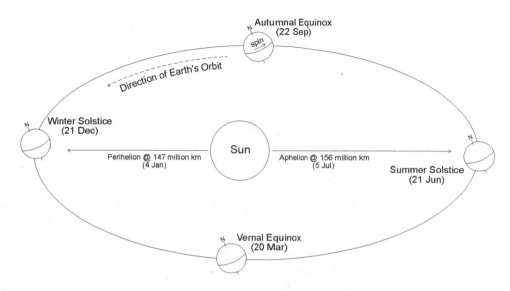

The Earth's axis is tilted, by about 23.5°, to the plane of its orbit, as our planet moves around the sun, the angle of the sun changes. At the summer solstice, the northern hemisphere is pointed toward the sun, receiving overhead sunlight, while the southern hemisphere views the sun low on the horizon during its winter. When the winter solstice arrives 6 months later, the northern hemisphere experiences winter while the southern hemisphere enjoys summer. The equinoxes fall midway between the solstices, and mark a time when the sun shines directly down at the equator.

The Gregorian Calendar

People based their calendars on lunar phases and seasons, but it became apparent that the number of days and months in a year were not integers. The anomalistic year, in which the Earth orbits from perihelion to perihelion, is 365.2596 days long. It takes the Earth 365.2422 days to move from one vernal equinox to the next, and that is called the *tropical year*. Finally, the *sidereal year* measures 365.2564 days, the time required for one complete revolution of the earth about the sun, relative to the fixed stars. The tropical year is the one we use for tracking the seasons, and it will be my definition of year from hereon, unless otherwise specified.

A calendar containing exactly 365 days will become out of step with the tropical year, falling behind about one day every four years. The first Roman calendars tried to reconcile the 29$\frac{1}{2}$ day lunar month with the year, creating a 354 day calendar that included periodic "leap months" to maintain consistency between dates and seasons. In 46 B.C, Julius Caesar mandated the use of a calendar that had twelve months totaling 365 days, with an extra "leap" day being added every four years. But the Julian calendar, while an improvement over its predecessor, slowly began falling out of synch with the seasons due to its 11 minute difference from the tropical year. Pope Gregorius XIII mandated calendar reform in 1582, when the Julian calendar had slipped more than ten days behind the tropical year. The Gregorian calendar, which we use today, adds a leap day every 4 years, except in years evenly divisible by 100 but not by 400. The year 1900 did not have a leap day, but 2000 will. Differing from the tropical year by only about a half-minute, the `Gregorian` calendar will be essentially accurate for three millennia. Java provides a generic `Calendar` class, a concrete example of which is the `GregorianCalendar` class. for the purpose of this book, I'll be defining most dates and times in terms of `GregorianCalendar` objects.

The Julian Calendar

Calendar dates do not lend themselves to calculations. Try finding, for example, the 1000th day after 12 July 1997; you'll need to keep track of leap years and varying numbers of days in different months. Astronomers (and others who manipulate dates) prefer the *Julian date*: a count of days since the beginning of the *Julian period*. French scholar Joseph Scaliger defined the Julian dating system in 1582, as part of his work on the Gregorian calendar; the period was named for his father Julius Caesar Scaliger, and not after the unrelated Roman calendar. Joseph Scaliger set the first Julian Day at noon on 1 January 4713 B.C., the most recent date on which three archaic chronological cycles coincided — a 15-year Roman taxation cycle, a 19-year lunar cycle, and a 28-year solar cycle.

So how do we calculate the Julian Date? Several formulas exist; I use the following procedure, which assumes that y_0 is the four-digit year, m_0 is the month, and d_0 is the day number. The functions $INT(x)$ and $FRAC(x)$ return, respectively, the integer and fractional parts of x.

$$y_1 = \begin{cases} y_0, & \text{if } m_0 \geq 3 \\ y_0 - 1, & \text{if } m_0 = 1 \text{ or } 2 \end{cases}$$

$$m_1 = \begin{cases} m_0, & \text{if } m_0 \geq 3 \\ m_0 + 12, & \text{if } m_0 = 1 \text{ or } 2 \end{cases} \qquad (13.4)$$

$$x = 2 - INT(y_1/100) + INT(y_1/400)$$

$$J = 1720994.5 + INT(365.35 y_1) + INT(30.6001(m_1+1)) + d_0 + x$$

The formulas in (13.4) compute the Julian Date, J, at midnight (0 hours UT) on the specified date. For example, to calculate the Julian Date for midnight, 16 January 1997:

$$d_0 = 16$$
$$m_0 = 1$$
$$y_0 = 1997$$

$$\text{since } m_0 = 1$$
$$m_1 = m_0 + 12 = 13$$
$$y_1 = y_0 - 1 = 1996$$

$$x = 2 - INT(y_1/100) + INT(y_1/400) = 2 - 19 + 4 = -13$$

$$J = 1720994.5 + INT(365.25 \cdot 1996) + INT(30.6001(13+1)) + 16 - 13$$
$$J = 1720994.5 + 729039 + 428 + 3$$
$$J = 2450464.5$$

To convert from a Julian Date to a calendar date, use the process shown in (13.5).

$$j_i = INT\ (J+0.5)$$
$$j_f = FRAC\ (J+0.5)$$

$$x = INT\left(\frac{j_f - 1867216.25}{36524.25}\right)$$

$$n_1 = j_i + 1 + x - INT\ (x/4)$$

$$n_2 = n_1 + 1524$$

$$n_3 = INT\left(\frac{n_2 - 122.1}{365.25}\right)$$

$$n_4 = INT\ (365.25n_3) \qquad (13.5)$$

$$n_5 = INT\left(\frac{n_2 - n_4}{30.6001}\right)$$

$$d = n_2 - n_4 - INT\ (30.6001n_5) + j_f$$

$$m = \begin{cases} n_5 - 1, & \text{if } n_5 \le 13.5 \\ n_5 - 13, & \text{if } n_5 > 13.5 \end{cases}$$

$$y = \begin{cases} n_3 - 4716, & \text{if } m > 2.5 \\ n_3 - 4715, & \text{if } m \ge 2.5 \end{cases}$$

The following example converts the Julian date 2450702.5 to a Gregorian calendar date:

$$j_i = INT\ (2450702.5 + 0.5) = 2450703$$
$$j_f = FRAC\ (2450702.5 + 0.5) = 0$$

$$x = INT \left(\frac{2450703 - 1867216.25}{36524.25} \right) = 15$$

$$n_1 = 2450703 + 1 + 15 - INT\ (15/4) = 2450716$$

$$n_2 = 2450716 + 1524 = 2452240$$

$$n_3 = INT \left(\frac{2452240 - 122.1}{365.25} \right) = 6713$$

$$n_4 = INT\ (365.25 \cdot 6713) = 2451923)$$

$$n_5 = INT \left(\frac{2452240 - 2451923}{30.6001} \right) = 10$$

$$d = 2452240 - 2451923 - INT\ (30.6001 \cdot 10) + j_f = 11$$
$$m = 10 - 1 = 9$$
$$y = 6713 - 4716 = 1997$$

A Julian date of 2450702.5 converts to the Gregorian calendar date of 11 September 1997.

Julian dates prove their utility in calculations. Looking back to the question of finding the thousandth day after 12 July 1997, we can find the answer by following these steps:

1. Find the Julian date for 12 July 1997, which is 2,450,642.5.

2. Add 1,000 to get the required destination date, giving a Julian date of 2,451,642.5.

3. Convert the destination Julian date to a calendar value, which results in the date 7 April 2000.

To find the number of days between dates, simply subtract their Julian equivalents. Also note that Julian dates begin at noon; the 17 July 1997 Julian date at midday is 2,450,642, while the Julian Date at midnight of that day is 2,450,641.5.

Sidereal Time

Because everything in the universe is moving, we must declare *when* a celestial coordinate is being given, and relative to *what*. For astronomers, the vernal (spring) equinox provides a consistent frame of reference for both time and place. At the moment of an equinox, an equatorial view parallel to the sun is also parallel to the plane of the Earth's orbit. In the astronomical coordinate system, the time Greenwich faces the vernal equinox is the zero point, just as the prime meridian defines the zero point of longitude.

Figure 13-6 illustrates the relationship of the Earth's orbit and the vernal equinox. At the time of the vernal equinox, the longitude of Greenwich also points to the center of the sun. As the year progresses, the positions of the Sun and vernal equinox diverge. The direction of the vernal equinox is fixed relative to the Earth, and the time between culminations of the vernal equinox is the *sidereal day*. The Sun, however, changes position relative to the Earth, by almost a full degree each *solar day*; thus the Earth must turn an extra degree between culminations of the sun. This means that the solar day is 3 minutes and 56.56 seconds longer than the sidereal day. For astronomers to use the vernal equinox as a reference point, they must determine the current *sidereal time* from the solar time. In essence, when you calculate the sidereal time, you determine the direction of the last vernal equinox.

Figure 13-6
Sidereal and Solar Time

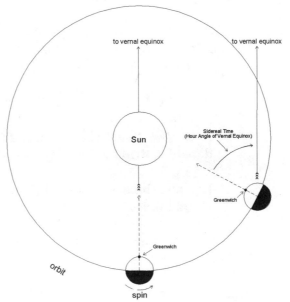

The formulas given in (13.6) show how a GMST (denoted by the Greek symbol Θ) is calculated from UT.

t = time UT

J = Julian Date at 0 hours UT

$$T = \frac{J - 2415020}{36525} \qquad (13.6)$$

$\Theta_{0UT} = 24 \cdot FRAC\,(0.27691398 + 100.00219359T + 0.000001075T^2)$

$\Theta = \Theta_{0UT} + 1.002737963t$

The last equation accounts for a fraction of a sidereal day that has passed in t hours.

For example, the GMST at 14:00 UT on 16 January 1997 (Julian date 2450464.5) is:

$$T = \frac{2450464.5 - 2415020}{36525} = 0.9704175$$

$\Theta_{0UT} = 24\ FRAC\,(97.320738) = 7.6977046 = 7{:}42$

$\Theta = 7.6977046 + 1.002737963 \cdot 14 = 21.7360361 = 21{:}44$

For values of Θ greater than or equal to 24 hours, subtract 24. In astronomical calculations, it can often be useful to add the sidereal time to Julian dates as a fraction of a day.

$$J_1 = J + \frac{\Theta}{24} \qquad (13.7)$$

So the Julian date for 14:00 UT on 16 January 1997 would be:

$$J_1 = 2450464.5 + \frac{21.7360361}{24}$$

$$J_1 = 2450465.4056682$$

Thus far, I've discussed the mean sidereal time at Greenwich (GMST), using universal time. Greenwich Mean Sidereal Time measures the angle between the zero meridian and the last vernal equinox, without accounting for short-term perturbations such as nutation. The Greenwich Apparent Sidereal Time (GAST) includes the "equation of the equinoxes," a calculation I'll discuss in Chapter 14.

It is your *local mean sidereal time* (LMST) that determines the position of the celestial sphere over your location. To calculate LMST, you must subtract the offset for your time zone from local clock time to obtain a UT for computing the GMST. Next, divide your longitude by 15 to calculate the number of actual hours your clock time differs from UT, and add that value to GMST to obtain your LMST.

At longitude L, the Local Mean Sidereal Time (denoted by Θ_L) can be computed from the GMST (Θ) by the formulas in 2.8.

$$\Theta_L = \Theta - \frac{L}{15} \text{ for West Longitudes}$$

$$\Theta_L = \Theta + \frac{L}{15} \text{ for East Longitudes}$$

My usual observing location is at 107° 40' West longitude. If I have my telescope out at 07:00 on 16 January 1997, the universal time would be seven hours later, or 14:00. The GMST would be 21.7361074, as calculated above. My LMST would be:

$$\Theta_L = 21.7361074 - \frac{107.66667}{15}$$

$$\Theta_L = 14.5583274 = 14:33$$

When I refer to sidereal time in later chapters, I'm talking about the LMST for the place of observation (unless specified otherwise).

Implementation

I wanted to encapsulate all the date calculations above into a single class of objects. I created the `AstroDate` class to contain a Julian date, a Julian date at 0 UT, a local mean sidereal time, and a separate time 0 UT value, irrespective of date.

```
package coyote.kepler;

import java.util.*;

public class AstroTime
{
  //——————————-
  // fields
  //——————————-
  private double jd;
  private double jd0;
  private double lmst;
  private double ut0;


  //——————————-
  // constructors
  //——————————-

  public AstroTime
    (
    GregorianCalendar date,
    double offset,
    double longitude
    )
  {
    double f, g, a, t, h;

    double dhour = Factors.angleToDec
             (
             date.get(Calendar.HOUR_OF_DAY),
             date.get(Calendar.MINUTE),
             date.get(Calendar.SECOND)
             );

    if (date.get(Calendar.MONTH) >= 3)
    {
      f = date.get(Calendar.YEAR);
      g = date.get(Calendar.MONTH);
    }
    else
    {
```

```
  f = date.get(Calendar.YEAR)   -  1;
  g = date.get(Calendar.MONTH) + 12;
}


// leap year determination
a = 2.0 - KMath.trunc(f / 100.0) +
    KMath.trunc(f / 400.0);


// calculate julian date at 0 UT
jd0 = KMath.trunc(365.25 * f)
    + KMath.trunc(30.6001 * (g + 1.0))
    + date.get(Calendar.DAY_OF_MONTH)
    + a + 1720994.5;


// account for timezone offset
h = dhour + offset;


if (h < 0.0)
{
  // previous day
  h += 24.0;
  jd0 -=  1.0;
}
else
  if (h >= 24.0)
  {
    // next day
    h  -= 24.0;
    jd0 +=  1.0;
  }


// compute Julian centuries
t = Factors.J2000Centuries(jd0);


// compute GMST at 0h UT
ut0 = 24110.54841
  + 8640184.812866 * t
  + 0.093104 * t * t
  - 0.0000062 * t * t * t;
```

```java
    // convert to hours
    ut0 /= 3600.0;

    while (ut0 <   0.0)
      ut0 += 24.0;

    while (ut0 >= 24.0)
      ut0 -= 24.0;

    // compute sidereal time
    lmst = ut0 + h * Constants.SIDEREAL_RATIO;

    // add UT sidereal time to julian date
    jd = jd0 + h / 24.0;

    // adjust for longitude
    lmst -= longitude / 15.0;

    if (lmst >= 24.0)
      lmst -= 24.0;
  }

public GregorianCalendar asDate
    (
    double offset
    )
{
  int year, month, day, hour, min, sec;
  double jd0;

  // separate date and time
  if (KMath.frac(jd) > 0.5)
    jd0 = KMath.trunc(jd) + 0.5;
  else
    jd0 = KMath.trunc(jd) - 0.5;

  // calculate time
  double t = (jd - jd0) * 24.0 - offset;

  if (t < 0.0)
  {
```

```
      t += 24.0;
      jd0 -= 1.0;
   }


hour = (int)t;
t = KMath.frac(t) * 60.0;
min  = (int)t;
sec  = (int)(KMath.frac(t) * 60.0 + 0.5);


// calculate date
double i = KMath.trunc(jd0) + 1.0;
double a;

if (i < 2299161.0)
   a = i;
else
   {
   double x =
       KMath.trunc((i - 1867216.25) / 36524.25);
   a = i + 1.0 + x - KMath.trunc(x / 4.0);
   }


double b = a + 1524.0;
double c = KMath.trunc((b - 122.1) / 365.25);
double d = KMath.trunc(365.25 * c);
double e = KMath.trunc((b - d) / 30.6001);


day = (int)(b - d - KMath.trunc(30.6001 * e));


double m;

if (e < 13.5)
   m = e - 1.0;
else
   m = e - 13.0;


month = (int)m;

if (m > 2.5)
   year = (int)(c - 4716.0);
```

```
        else
          year = (int)(c - 4715.0);

        return new GregorianCalendar
            (year,month,day,hour,min,sec);
    }

    public String toString()
    {
      return new String
        (
          "  jd = "   + jd
        + "\n jd0 = " + jd0
        + "\nlmst = " + lmst
        + "\n0 ut = " + ut0
        );
    }


    //——————————-
    // properties
    //——————————-
    public double GetJD()
    {
      return jd;
    }

    public double GetJD0()
    {
      return jd0;
    }

    public double GetLMST()
    {
      return lmst;
    }

    public double GetUT0()
    {
      return ut0;
    }
}
```

An `AstroDate` is constructed from a `GregorianDate` object, a time zone offset, and a latitude. The `asDate` method returns a `GregorianCalendar` value based on an `AstroDate`'s Julian Date. Property methods allow fields to be read; however, due to the necessity for coordination between field values (which are all mutually dependent), I don't allow these fields to be changed once an `AstroDate` has been created.

Onward

Now that we know how to locate ourselves in time and space, it's time to look at finding the apparent positions of objects on the celestial sphere. The next chapter delves into astronomical coordinate systems, a bit of spherical trigonometry, and some further understanding of the Earth's orbit.

Chapter

Stellar Cartography

**Astronomy... compels the soul
to look upwards,
and draws it from the things
of this world to the other.**

— Plato, *The Republic,* bk. 7, sec. 529.

In a recent science fiction movie (unnamed because the owning company is *very* jealous of its copyrights and trademarks), two men worked in a laboratory aboard an enterprising starship. The walls of the room presented interactive maps of celestial bodies — stars, planets, and nebulae, all arranged in a stunning graphic display that rotated and changed at the direction of the scientists. They aptly called this laboratory *stellar cartography.*

You can buy applications to display star maps on your computer's screen. But, for me, it isn't enough to have someone else's software present information; I've always been a mathematician at heart, wanting to know the numbers and formulas behind the wonders of nature. So when an opportunity arose to develop navigational software that involved the projection of star maps, I jumped at the opportunity. The end result was a package of Java classes that allowed a GPS unit to link with a computer, providing real-time star maps and terrain info. While I can't assume you have a GPS unit and associated hardware, I can show you how Java worked when plotting movements in the heavens.

Movement in the Heavens

Watch the stars for any length of time, and you'll notice that they seem to travel circular paths centered on a point above your horizon. In the northern hemisphere, one star appears motionless at the center of its circling companions. That star is Polaris, and it lies less than a degree from the actual celestial pole. The southern hemisphere lacks a pole star — and in a few thousand years, changes in the Earth's orbit will leave the northern hemisphere's pole pointing toward nothing.

It isn't the stars that are moving, it's you. Polaris just happens to be located in the direction pointed to by Earth's North pole, and the stars circle it every sidereal day due to the Earth's rotation. The stars closest to the pole turn on the tightest path, while stars far from the pole dip below the horizon. The height of the celestial pole is equal to the latitude of the observer. The celestial poles lie on the horizon when you stand at the equator, and Polaris will be directly overhead when you visit the North Pole.

While the stars may seem to turn from our perspective, they maintain their positions relative to each other. As Figure 14-1 shows, the stars all move the same distance during the same period of time — and the same stars will follow the same circular paths, no matter where you are on Earth. If we are going to track the stars, we need a system of reference that reflects the mutually-relative positions of stars while also being adaptable to observers at different locations.

Figure 14-1

Movement of
the Stars

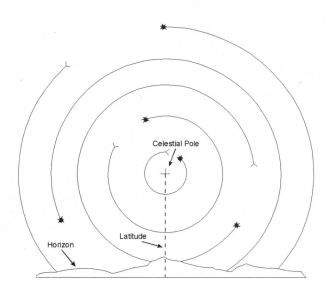

Geometry in the Round

Scientists developed just such a system, based on an obsolete view of the universe. Ancient astronomers believed that the stars and planets were attached to a rotating *celestial sphere*, which surrounded the Earth. While we know that the celestial sphere is a myth, it provides a useful model for determining the positions of heavenly bodies.

Astronomers use spherical coordinates for locating objects in the sky. In Chapter 2, I showed how any point P on the surface of a sphere can be located through two angular values: ψ measured counterclockwise around the xy-plane, and θ as an angular distance above or below the xy-plane. For locating something on the surface of the Earth, ψ and θ correspond respectively to longitude and latitude. Figure 14-2 shows a point P on a sphere; three equations define the xyz-frame coordinates of P:

$$x = \cos\psi\cos\theta$$
$$y = \sin\psi\cos\theta \qquad (14.1)$$
$$z = \sin\theta$$

Figure 14-2 also shows an alternative frame of reference for P, based on a rotation of the y and z axes around the x axis.

Figure 14-2
Rotating Spherical
Coordinates

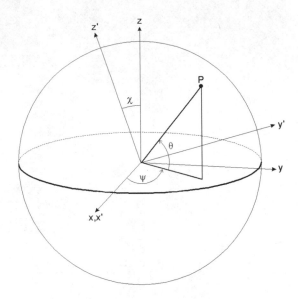

Look straight down the unchanged x axis, and evaluate the angular changes in z and y in a two-dimensional frame. Figure 14-3 shows how to construct a set of equations that calculate $x'y'z'$-frame coordinates from the original xyz-frame coordinates and the angle of rotation χ.

Figure 14-3
Rotated Frame,
Rectangular View

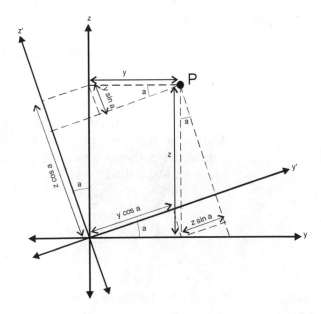

The $x'y'z'$-frame coordinates of P can be calculated using these formulas:

$$x'=x$$
$$y'=y\cos\chi+\sin\chi \quad (14.2)$$
$$z'=z\cos\chi-y\sin\chi$$

Since we know how to calculate x, y, and z from the angles ψ and θ, we can substitute the equations for the xyz-frame coordinates into the formulas for $x'y'z'$-frame coordinates, creating a set of equations in which the position of P is expressed entirely in terms of angles.

$$\cos\psi'\cos\theta'=\cos\psi\cos\theta$$
$$\sin\psi'\cos\theta'=\sin\psi\cos\theta\cos\chi+\sin\theta\sin\chi \quad (14.3)$$
$$\sin\theta'=\sin\theta\cos\chi-\sin\psi\cos\theta\cos\chi$$

Understanding a rotated frame of reference is important because our view of the heavens is, in fact, rotated. To locate an object in the celestial sphere, we must map coordinates defined in terms of the celestial sphere to the actual view we have of the horizon.

The *equatorial coordinate* system defines its xy-plane as extending from the Earth's equator, out to the abstract celestial sphere; the z axis is a line running through the terrestrial poles. You can view equatorial coordinates as another system of latitude and longitude: the prime meridian becomes the direction of the vernal equinox, longitude is replaced by an angle called *right ascension*, and latitude on the celestial sphere is termed *declination*. Figure 14-4 shows the celestial sphere surrounding the Earth, and the orientation of the poles, equator, and angles.

Figure 14-4

The Equatorial
Coordinate System

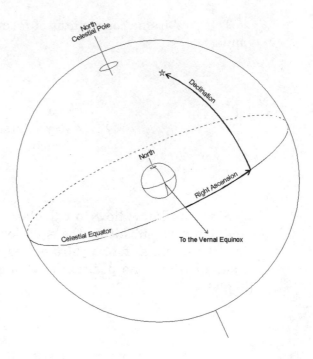

The celestial equator and lines of declination form great circles. As described in Chapter 13, a great circle passes through the center point of a sphere, defining two equal hemispheres. A *spherical triangle* is formed by the arcs of three intersecting great circles, as shown in Figure 14-5.

Figure 14-5

A Spherical Triangle

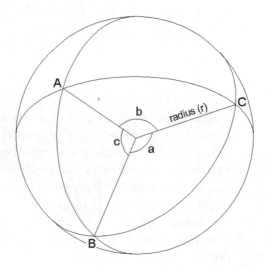

The length of arc *AB* equals the sphere's radius r multiplied by the angle c, the later being *AB*'s *central angle* expressed in radians. To further simplify the trigonometry, define a *unit* sphere by setting the radius of the sphere to one; thus the length of any arc in a spherical triangle equals the magnitude of its central angle.

So how do spherical triangles relate to equatorial coordinates? When you look at the night sky, you are looking at the celestial sphere from an angle equal to your latitude. Figure 14-6 shows how this affects your view of the stars; the equations of spherical triangles, plus the trigonometric equations developed earlier, allow you to convert an equatorial position in right ascension and declination to horizon coordinates of altitude and azimuth.

Figure 14-6

Relationship of Equatorial and Horizon Coordinates

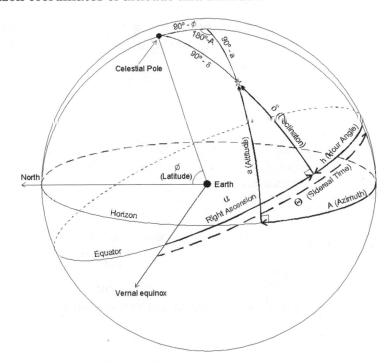

Equation (14.4) describes the simple relationship of the sidereal time, right ascension, and hour angle:

$$\Theta = h + a \qquad (14.4)$$

To calculate an object's hour angle, subtract the right ascension from the sidereal time. Note that you measure both azimuth and hour angle in a clockwise direction from the south meridian.

Your latitude defines the angle of rotation between the celestial equator and your horizon. Figure 14-6 shows how you can form a spherical triangle, at the top of the diagram, from the star's altitude, declination, and the celestial pole. That triangle is a tool for relating various quantities to angles in a rotated coordinate system. These relationships include:

$$\psi = 90° - A$$
$$\theta = a$$
$$\psi' = 90° - h \qquad (14.5)$$
$$\theta' = \delta$$
$$\chi = 90° - \phi$$

In cases where an angle is being subtracted from 90°, we can use these trigonometric relationships to simplify equations:

$$\sin(90° - x) = \cos x$$
$$\cos(90° - x) = \sin x \qquad (14.6)$$

Substituting identities in (14.5) into the equations derived in (14.3) gives us a set of expressions for converting equatorial to horizon coordinates.

$$\sin A \cos a = \sin h \cos \delta$$
$$\cos A \cos a = \cos h \cos \delta \sin \phi - \sin \delta \sin \phi \qquad (14.7)$$
$$\sin a = \cos h \cos \delta \cos \phi + \sin \delta \sin \phi$$

The inverse set of substitutions provides equations that convert horizon coordinates to the equatorial system.

$$\psi = 90° - h$$
$$\theta = \delta$$
$$\psi' = 90° - A$$
$$\theta' = a$$
$$\chi = -(90° - \phi) \quad (14.8)$$

$$\sin h \cos \delta = \sin A \cos a$$
$$\cos h \cos \delta = \cos A \cos a \sin \phi + \sin a \cos \phi$$
$$\sin \delta = \sin a \sin \phi - \cos A \cos a \cos \phi$$

Since the vernal equinox is specified in terms of time, angles of right ascension (RA) measure counterclockwise angles of between 0 to 24 hours. Each hour of right ascension equals 15 degrees. Declination, like latitude, has a value between +90° and -90°.

Adjustments

Thus far, I've described computations that should be more than adequate for the vast majority of observers. Given a sky atlas with coordinates, you should be able to plot a reasonably accurate map of any section of the sky. But "reasonably accurate" isn't always good enough for astrophotographers and others who require great precision from their observations. Obtaining great precision requires the understanding and application of several factors.

Epochs

The universe is an unstable place; the gravity that holds the universe together also causes periodic changes in the coordinates of celestial objects. Planets tug at each other, slightly altering orbits; stars move around the center of the galaxy and relative to each other. With universe in constant flux, we must reference coordinates to a specific point in time called an *epoch*. We can then adjust coordinates, from the base epoch, to a time of observation, by including the periodic effects of relative motion and perturbations in the Earth's orbit.

The IAU specified in 1984 that epochs would be calculated using the following formula, with the standard epoch being set at noon on 1 January 2000.

$$Julian\ Epoch = J[2000 + (JD - 2451545.0)/365.25] \qquad (14.9)$$

For instance, the epoch for 2 July 1996 at 4:00UT would be J1996.5 —the middle of the year, and $3\frac{1}{2}$ years prior to the standard epoch of J2000. Such differences between epochs provide measures for calculating coordinate changes in time. Modern references express coordinates in terms of J2000, expecting an astronomer to adjust coordinates for a specific time of observation. Most algorithms alter coordinates from J2000 to a specified destination epoch; a few calculations count years from B1900, which has a Julian date of 2415020.0.

Prior to 1984, many star catalogs based coordinates on the Besselian epoch of B1950. That system was named in honor of Friedrich Wilhelm Bessel, a nineteenth century Prussian astronomer with a penchant for precise calculations and observations. The Besselian epoch formulation accounted for the exact length of the year:

$$Besselian\ Epoch = B[1900+(JD-2514020.31352)/365.242198781] \qquad (14.10)$$

The Besselian epoch B1950 is the Julian date 2433282.423. Some algorithms require a number of Julian centuries between epochs, calculated by dividing the difference in Julian dates by 36525 days.

Precession

We owe much of our astronomical science to Hipparchus, a Greek scientist of the second century B.C. A meticulous researcher, his estimate of the tropical year differed from modern calculation by only $6\frac{1}{2}$ minutes. Hipparchus invented trigonometry and devised a system of latitude and longitude; he also created the first compilation of star positions, based on careful observation. And in creating his list of stars, Hipparchus discovered the precession of the equinoxes.

Precession is the steady change in the direction of the celestial pole. While the angle of the Earth's axis is kept steady by the gyroscope effect, the direction in which the axis points is changing due to the gravitational influence of other bodies in the solar system. Precession causes the celestial pole to circle 23.5° away from a point in the constellation Draco. While the north celestial pole is now located near Polaris, the pole will be close to Errai (g Cepheus) in twenty-five hundred years. Four thousand years ago, when the Egyptians built the pyramids, Thuban (a Draconis) marked the celestial pole. In 26,000 years, the pole will return to the vicinity of Polaris, completing its cycle.

Precession is a primary cause of horological changes in celestial coordinates; to accurately locate an object, its coordinates must be adjusted from the epoch of calculation to the epoch of observation. Such a conversion is accomplished via a rotation matrix that adjusts the rectangular coordinates of an object from one epoch to another. Three angles, ζ_A, z_A, and θ_A, reflect the movement of the pole, providing values for the matrix when converting to and from the epoch J2000.

$$\zeta_A = 0.6406161°T + 0.0000839°T^2 + 0.0000050T^3$$
$$z_A = 0.6406161°T + 0.0003041°T^2 + 0.0000051T^3 \qquad (14.11)$$
$$\theta_A = 0.5567530°T - 0.0001185°T^2 + 0.0000116T^3$$

Use the equations in (14.1) to calculate an *xyz*-frame coordinate for an object on a unit sphere, storing the result in a three element vector *r*. To convert coordinates from J2000 to a new epoch, multiply the coordinate vector *r* by a matrix *P* containing these values:

$$\cos\delta_A\cos\theta_A\cos z_A - \sin\delta_A\sin z_A, -\sin\zeta_A\cos\theta_A\cos z_A - \cos\zeta_A\sin z_A, -\sin\theta_A\cos z_A$$
$$\cos\delta_A\cos\theta_A\sin z_A + \sin\delta_A\cos z_A, -\sin\zeta_A\cos\theta_A\sin z_A + \cos\zeta_A\cos z_A, -\sin\theta_A\sin z_A$$
$$\cos\delta_A\sin\theta_A, \qquad\qquad -\sin\zeta_A\sin\theta_A, \qquad\qquad \cos\theta_A$$

To convert the coordinate vector to J2000 from another epoch, transpose the matrix before performing the multiplication. In terms of matrix math, the formulas are:

$$\mathbf{r_j} = \mathbf{rP}$$
$$\mathbf{r} = \mathbf{r_j P'} \qquad (14.12)$$

The final step is to convert the adjusted *xyz*-frame coordinates back to right ascension and declination values:

$$\delta = \sin^{-1}\mathbf{r}_{j(2)}$$
$$a = \cos^{-1}(\mathbf{r}_{j(0)}/\cos(\delta))$$

If the sine of the right ascension is negative, subtract *a* from 360°. Finally, divide the right ascension, which is in degrees, by 15°, converting it to hours.

Changes in the Earth's axis aren't alone in altering the coordinates of objects in time. We also need to account for proper motion, the movement of stars relative to our solar system.

Proper Motion

Everything in the universe is in motion, changing the relative positions of celestial objects. Proper motion measures changes in right ascension and declination, usually providing yearly values. In calculating the future coordinates of objects, we must note both changes in the Earth's orbit and movements in objects themselves.

Figure 14-7 shows the changes wrought by proper motion on the stars of the constellation Auriga, over the next 100,000 years. While several stars move only slightly, Menkalinan and η travel about two degrees — and Capella sweeps completely across the constellation! Capella is one of the "fastest" stars in the heavens; Arcturus and Sirius also have larger proper motions. Barnard's Star, a red dwarf less than 6 light years away, moves an astonishing 10.3 arc seconds annually.

Figure 14-7
Proper Motion in Auriga

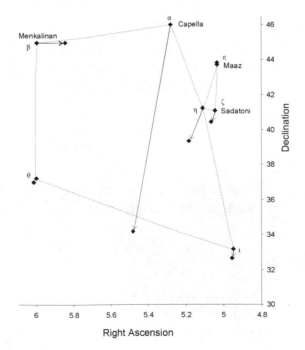

Proper motion, μ, has two components for movement in right ascension and declination, μ_α and μ_δ. Star catalogs usually define these values in arc seconds per century; for example, in the FK5, Capella has a μ_α of 0.728 and a μ_δ of -42.47. These equations calculate the change in position during a given period of time:

$$\Delta a = (t-t_0)\,\mu_\alpha/100$$
$$\Delta \delta = (t-t_0)\,\mu_\delta/100$$
(14.13)

In general, before plotting the position of a star, you'll want to adjust its coordinates to the epoch (Julian date) of the time of observation.

Aberration

Since the speed of light is finite, motion toward or away from an object changes its apparent position. Known as *aberration*, this phenomenon occurs in astronomical observations due to the orbit of the Earth around the sun. Hurtling through space at 30 km/sec, our view of the cosmos is skewed by up to 21 seconds of arc. To include the consequences of aberration in right ascension and declination, use these formulas.

$$\Delta a = (-X\,\sin a + Y\,\cos a)\,/\,(173.14\,\cos\delta)$$
$$\Delta \delta = (-X\,\cos a\,\sin\delta - Y\,\sin a\,\sin\delta + Z\,\cos\delta)/173.14$$
(14.14)

X, Y, and Z are derivatives of the Earth's rectangular coordinates in reference to the sun. The value l is the apparent longitude of the sun for Julian date JD. Their values can be approximated by these formulas:

$$\lambda = 280.461° + 0.9856474° \,(JD - 2451545.0)$$
$$X = + 0.0172 \sin\lambda$$
$$Y = -0.0158 \cos\lambda$$
$$Z = -0.0068 \cos\lambda$$
(14.15)

Aberration changes with the position of the Earth in its orbit, and it does not alter the positions of stars relative to each other or to the epoch. Apply aberration to the RA and declination coordinates before computing an azimuth and altitude for a time of observation, and after including changes due to precession and proper motion.

The formulas above calculate *annual aberration*, which stems from the Earth's movement around the sun. Another form of aberration is *diurnal*, caused by the rotation of the Earth on its axis. At most, diurnal aberration only changes our perspective by a third of an arc second — and it can be practically ignored.

Refraction

The Earth's atmosphere causes significant changes in horizon coordinates by refracting the light of celestial objects. Directly overhead, refraction is virtually nonexistent — but at the horizon, the atmosphere bends light by as much as a half-degree; the sun has physically traveled below the horizon when we see it starting to "set." In essence, refraction raises the altitude of an object with respect to the horizon, and we need to account for it in our observations.

The precise amount of refraction depends on temperature, atmospheric turbulence, and barometric pressure. By nature, these factors are inconstant, making it nearly impossible to determine the precise amount of refraction. For practical purposes, an approximation is adequate. In formula (14.16), a is an object's non-refracted altitude, P is the barometric pressure in millibars and T is the temperature (°C).

$$\Delta a = P(0.1594 + 0.0196a + 0.00002a^2)/((273 + T)(1 + 0.505a + 0.0845a^2)) \quad (14.16)$$

Apply refraction after computing horizon coordinates and before displaying or plotting an object's position.

In adjusting coordinates for precession and proper motion, the program differs by no more than a few tenths of an arc second from the values given in the FK5. Such accuracy is more than sufficient, since variations in refraction and other factors would obscure further precision.

Implementation

In developing this code, I encapsulated several static utility methods methods in a class named `Factor`.

```java
public class Factors
{
  // calculate Julian Centuries since J2000
  public static double J2000Centuries(double jd)
  {
    return (jd - Constants.J2000) /
        Constants.JULIAN_CENTURY;
  }

  // calculate Julian Centuries since J1900
  public static double J1900Centuries(double jd)
  {
    return (jd - Constants.J1900) /
        Constants.JULIAN_CENTURY;
  }

  // epsilon value in degrees
  public static double obliquityOfEcliptic
    (
    double jd
    )
  {
    double t = J2000Centuries(jd) / 10.0;

    return (((((((((( 2.45e-10
        * t + 5.79e-9)
        * t + 2.787e-7)
        * t + 7.12e-7)
        * t - 3.905e-5)
        * t - 2.4967e-3)
        * t - 5.138e-3)
        * t + 1.9989)
        * t - 0.0152)
        * t - 468.0927)
        * t + 84381.412)
```

```
            / 3600.0;
  }

  // solar mean longitude
  public static double solarLongitude(double jd)
  {
    double lng = 280.461 + 0.9856474 *
        (jd - Constants.J2000);

    while (lng <   0.0)
      lng += 360.0;

    while (lng > 360.0)
      lng -= 360.0;

    return lng;
  }
}
```

Horizon coordinates include an altitude (height above the horizon) and azimuth (the direction as a compass point). I've encapsulated this data type in the HorizonCoordinates class.

```
package coyote.kepler;

public class HorizonCoordinates
{
  //——————————-
  // fields
  //——————————-
  protected double altitude;
  protected double azimuth;


  //——————————-
  // exceptions
  //——————————-
  private static final KeplerException err_inv_alt =
    new KeplerException("invalid altitude");

  private static final KeplerException err_inv_azi =
    new KeplerException("invalid azimuth");
```

```
//————————-
// constructors
//————————-
public HorizonCoordinates()
{
  altitude = 0.0;
  azimuth  = 0.0;
}

// construct from specific values
public HorizonCoordinates
  (
  double alt,
  double azi
  )
{
  setAltitude(alt);
  setAzimuth(azi);
}

// construct from coordinates
public HorizonCoordinates
  (
  EquatorialCoordinates rd,
  double lmst,
  double lat
  )
{
  // compute hour angle
  double ha  = 15.0 * (lmst - rd.getRA());
  double dec = rd.getDec();

  // compute altitude
  altitude = KMath.asind(KMath.sind(lat) *
      KMath.sind(dec)
          + KMath.cosd(lat) * KMath.cosd(dec) *
              KMath.cosd(ha));

  // compute azimuth
  double q = KMath.cosd(ha) * KMath.sind(lat)
      - KMath.tand(dec) * KMath.cosd(lat);
```

```
    azimuth  = KMath.atan2d(KMath.sind(ha),q) + 180.0;
}


//————————-
// methods
//————————-

// apply refraction
public void applyRefraction
  (
  double pres,
  double temp
  )
{
  if (altitude < 0.0)
    return;

  double alt2 = altitude * altitude;

  altitude += pres
        * ( 0.1594 + 0.0196 * altitude +
            0.00002 * alt2)
        / ((273.0 + temp)
          * (1.0 + 0.505 * altitude +
            0.0845 * alt2));
}

public String toString()
{
  return new String
    (
    "Alt "   + (new DegMinSec(altitude)) +
    ", Azi " + (new DegMinSec(azimuth))
    );
}


//————————-
// properties
//————————-
public void setAltitude
  (
```

```
      double alt
      )
{
  if ((alt < -90.0) || (alt > 90.0))
    throw err_inv_alt;

  altitude = alt;
}

public double getAltitude()
{
  return altitude;
}

public void setAzimuth
  (
  double azi
  )
{
  if ((azi < 0.0) || (azi >= 360.0))
    throw err_inv_azi;

  azimuth = azi;
}

public double getAzimuth()
{
  return azimuth;
}
}
```

Horizon coordinates is a data structure class, much like Latitude from the previous chapter. You can construct HorizonCoordinates from explicit values or from an EquatorialCoordinates object, a local mean standard time, and a latitude.

Ecliptic coordinates, which locate a position on the celetial sphere, can be considered identical to Latitude. Equatorial coordinates, however, are much more complex, and are defined by the EquatorialCoordinates class:

```java
package coyote.kepler;

public class EquatorialCoordinates
{
  //——————————-
  // fields
  //——————————-
  protected double ra;
  protected double dec;


  //——————————-
  // exceptions
  //——————————-
  private static final KeplerException err_inv_ra =
    new KeplerException("invalid right ascension");

  private static final KeplerException err_inv_dec =
    new KeplerException("invalid declination");


  //——————————-
  // constructors
  //——————————-
  public EquatorialCoordinates()
  {
    ra  = 0.0;
    dec = 0.0;
  }

  // construct from specific values
  public EquatorialCoordinates
    (
    double r,
    double d
    )
  {
    setRA(r);
    setDec(d);
  }

  // construct from HorizonCoord and location
  public EquatorialCoordinates
```

```
        (
        HorizonCoordinates altaz,
        double st,
        double lat
        )
    {
        double ha;
        double alt = altaz.getAltitude();
        double azi = altaz.getAzimuth();

        // compute declination
        dec = KMath.asind(KMath.sind(lat) *
            KMath.sind(alt)
          + KMath.cosd(lat) * KMath.cosd(alt) *
                KMath.cosd(azi));

        // compute hour angle
        double q = KMath.cosd(azi) * KMath.sind(lat)
                - KMath.tand(alt) * KMath.cosd(lat);

        ha = KMath.atan2d(KMath.sind(azi),q) / 15.0;

        // compute RA from hour angle
        if (ha < 0.0)
          ha += 24.0;

        ra = st - ha;

        if (ra < 0.0)
          ra += 12.0;
    }

    // construct from EclipticCoord and location
    public EquatorialCoordinates
        (
        Location ec,
        double jd
        )
    {
        // compute sidereal time and obliquity
        double eps = Factors.obliquityOfEcliptic(jd);
```

```
    double lat = ec.getLatitude();
    double lng = ec.getLongitude();

    // compute declination
    dec = KMath.asind(KMath.sind(lat) *
        KMath.cosd(eps)
      + KMath.cosd(lat) * KMath.sind(eps) *
          KMath.sind(lng));

    // compute hour angle
    double q = KMath.cosd(lng);

    ra = KMath.atand( (KMath.sind(lng) *
        KMath.cosd(eps)
      - KMath.tand(lat) * KMath.sind(eps)) / q);

    // compute RA from hour angle
    if (q < 0.0)
      ra += 12.0;

    if (ra < 0.0)
      ra += 24.0;
}


//————————--
// methods
//————————--

// reduce for precession & other factors
public void applyPrecession
  (
  double  jd,
  boolean toJ2000
  )
{
    // get RA in degrees
    double tra = ra * 15.0;

    // compute times
    double t1 = Factors.J2000Centuries(jd);
    double t2 = t1 * t1;
```

```
        double t3 = t2 * t1;

        // compute angles fo mean equinox and equator
        double zeta  = 0.6406161 * t1
             + 0.0000839 * t2
             + 0.0000050 * t3;

        double z = 0.6406161 * t1
             + 0.0003041 * t2
             + 0.0000051 * t3;

        double theta = 0.5567530 * t1
             - 0.0001185 * t2
             - 0.0000116 * t3;

        // precalc trig functions of angles
        double c_zeta  = KMath.cosd(zeta);
        double s_zeta  = KMath.sind(zeta);
        double c_z = KMath.cosd(z);
        double s_z = KMath.sind(z);
        double c_theta = KMath.cosd(theta);
        double s_theta = KMath.sind(theta);

        double []   xyz0 = new double [3];
        double []   xyz  = new double [3];
        double [][] prec = new double [3][3];

        // get rectangular coordinates
        xyz0[0] = KMath.cosd(tra) * KMath.cosd(dec);
        xyz0[1] = KMath.sind(tra) * KMath.cosd(dec);
        xyz0[2] = KMath.sind(dec);

        xyz[0] = 0.0;
        xyz[1] = 0.0;
        xyz[2] = 0.0;

        // load precession/rotation matrix
        if (toJ2000)
        {
          prec[0][0] =
              c_zeta  * c_theta * c_z - s_zeta * s_z;
```

```
      prec[0][1] =
          c_zeta   * c_theta * s_z + s_zeta * c_z;
      prec[0][2] =
          c_zeta   * s_theta;
      prec[1][0] =
          -s_zeta   * c_theta * c_z - c_zeta * s_z;
      prec[1][1] =
          -s_zeta   * c_theta * s_z + c_zeta * c_z;
      prec[1][2] =
          -s_zeta   * s_theta;
      prec[2][0] =
          -s_theta * c_z;
      prec[2][1] =
          -s_theta * s_z;
      prec[2][2] =
          c_theta;
  }
  else
  {
    prec[0][0] =
        c_zeta   * c_theta * c_z - s_zeta * s_z;
    prec[0][1] =
        -s_zeta   * c_theta * c_z - c_zeta * s_z;
    prec[0][2] =
        -s_theta * c_z;
    prec[1][0] =
        c_zeta   * c_theta * s_z + s_zeta * c_z;
    prec[1][1] =
        -s_zeta   * c_theta * s_z + c_zeta * c_z;
    prec[1][2] = -s_theta * s_z;
    prec[2][0] =   c_zeta   * s_theta;
    prec[2][1] = -s_zeta   * s_theta;
    prec[2][2] =   c_theta;
  }

  // multiply matrices
  for (int k = 0; k < 3; ++k)
    for (int j = 0; j < 3; ++j)
      xyz[k] += xyz0[j] * prec[k][j];

  // get angles from coordinates
```

```
        double pdec = KMath.asind(xyz[2]);
        double pra  = KMath.acosd(xyz[0] /
            KMath.cosd(pdec)) / 15.0;

      if (KMath.sind(tra) < 0.0)
        pra = 24.0 - pra;

      // store precessed value
      ra  = pra;
      dec = pdec;
    }

  // include proper motion
  public void applyProperMotion
      (
      double  jd,
      double  pmr, // in arc seconds / year
      double  pmd, // in arc seconds / year
      boolean up
      )
  {
      double t = (jd - Constants.J2000) /
          Constants.JULIAN_YEAR;

      if (up)
        t = -t;

      ra  += t * pmr / 3600.0;
      dec += t * pmd / 3600.0;
    }

  // include annual aberration
  public void applyAnnualAberration
      (
      double jd
      )
  {
      double L = Factors.solarLongitude(jd);

      // derivatives of Earth's rectangular coordinates
      double dX =  0.0172 * KMath.sind(L);
```

```
      double dY = -0.0158 * KMath.cosd(L);
      double dZ = -0.0068 * KMath.cosd(L);

      // RA in degrees
      double tra = ra * 15;

      // adjust RA
      double dra  = (- dX * KMath.sind(tra) + dY *
         KMath.cosd(tra))
               / (173.14 * KMath.cosd(dec));

      // adjust Dec
      double ddec = (- dX * KMath.cosd(tra) *
         KMath.sind(dec)
            - dY * KMath.sind(tra) * KMath.sind(dec)
            + dZ * KMath.cosd(dec)) / 173.14;

      // include changes
      ra  += dra;
      dec += ddec;
   }

   // calculate culmination
   public double culmination
      (
      double lat,
      double alt
      )
   {
      double x = - KMath.tand(lat) * KMath.tand(dec);

      if (Math.abs(x) > 1.0)
         return -1.0;

      x += KMath.sind(alt) / (KMath.cosd(dec) *
         KMath.cosd(lat));

      return KMath.acosd(x) / 15.0;
   }

   // calculate rising time
```

```
public double timeOfRising
  (
  double ut0,
  Location loc
  )
{
  double t;
  double ha  = culmination(loc.getLatitude(),-
      0.833333333333333);
  double lon = loc.getLongitude();

  if (ha < 0.0)
    return ha;

  t = (ra - (lon > 0.0 ? 360.0 - lon : -lon)
      - ha - ut0)
            / Constants.SIDEREAL_RATIO;

  while (t < 0.0)
    t += 24.0;

  return t;
}

// calculate setting time
public double timeOfSetting
  (
  double ut0,
  Location loc
  )
{
  double t;
  double ha  = culmination(loc.getLatitude(),-
      0.833333333333333);
  double lon = loc.getLongitude();

  if (ha < 0.0)
    return ha;

  t = (ra - (lon > 0.0 ? 360.0 -
      lon : -lon) + ha - ut0)
```

```
                       / Constants.SIDEREAL_RATIO;

  while (t < 0.0)
    t += 24.0;

  return t;
}

public String toString()
{
  return new String
    (
    "RA " + (new HourMinSec(ra)) +
    ", Dec " + (new DegMinSec(dec))
    );
}

//———————-
// properties
//———————-
public void setRA
  (
  double r
  )
{
  if ((r < 0.0) || (r >= 24.0))
    throw err_inv_ra;

  ra = r;
}

public double getRA()
{
  return ra;
}

public void setDec
  (
  double d
  )
{
```

```
    if ((d < -90.0) || (d > 90.0))
      throw err_inv_dec;

    dec = d;
  }

  public double getDec()
  {
    return dec;
  }
}
```

An `EquatorialCoordinate` contains double values for right ascension (`ra`) and declination (`dec`). Property methods ensure that any assignments made to these values are within acceptable ranges. You can construct an `EquatorialCoordinate` object from explicit values or from `HorizonCoordinates` and `Location` objects. I'll describe the algorithms and purposes of other methods, such as `applyPrecession`, at the end of this chapter.

Examples

Were I going out on 8 February 1998 for an observing session at 20:00 Mountain Standard Time (MST), I could calculate the locations of objects from their right ascensions and declinations. For this example, I'll use Castor — a lovely and bright binary star — and M101, a face-on spiral galaxy in Ursa Major. The coordinates for M101 are RA 14^h 03^m, Dec 54° 27'; Castor will be found at RA 7^h 33^m, Dec 31° 58'. My observing location is near Silverton, Colorado, at 37° 48' North latitude and 107° 40' West longitude.

From the formulas in Chapter 2, we can calculate the Julian Date as 2450853.5 (at 0UT) and the Local Mean Sidereal Time as 05:05. Also in Chapter 2, I calculated my geocentric latitude as 37° 37'. Here's how I plug the coordinates for M101 into the equations that calculate its location. First, I compute the hour angle from the LMST and sidereal time, according to equation 3.4:

h=5:05–14:03=5.08333–14.05=-8.96667
h=-8.96667^h·15°=-134.5°

Then, I calculate the altitude a using the third equation in (14.7):

$\sin a = \cos(-134.5°)\cos(54°27')\cos(37°37') + \sin(54°27')\sin(37°37')$
$\sin a = 0.173807$
$a = 10.009237° = 10°00'$

I rearrange the last equation in (14.8) to determine M101's azimuth:

$$\cos A = \frac{\sin(54°27') - \sin(37°37')\sin(10°)}{\cos(10°)\cos(37°37')}$$

$\cos A = 0.907013$
$A = 24.904213° = 24°54'$

And now for Castor:

$h = 5{:}05 - 7{:}33 = 5.08333 - 7.55 = -2.466667$
$h = -2.466667^h \cdot 15° = -37.0°$

$\sin a = \cos(-37.0°)\cos(31°58')\cos(37°37') + \sin(31°58')\sin(37°37')$
$\sin a = 0.0859666$
$a = 59.279139° = 59°17'$

$$\cos A = \frac{\sin(31°58') - \sin(37°37')\sin(59°17')}{\cos(59°17')\cos(37°37')}$$

$\cos A = 0.009801$
$A = 89.438450° = 89°26'$

So, M101 will be at altitude 10°, azimuth 24° 54', while Castor can be found at altitude 59° 17', azimuth 89° 26'. This tells me that M101 will be a bit too close to the horizon for viewing, but Castor will be nicely located, nearly 60° high to the east.

In terms of Java, the following segment of code accomplishes the above calculations:

```
GregorianCalendar dtWhen =
  new GregorianCalendar(1998,2,8,20,0,0);

AstroTime jsWhen =
  new AstroTime(dtWhen,myTimeZone,myLocGeo.
    getLongitude());

EquatorialCoordinates eqM101 =
  new EquatorialCoordinates(14.05,54.45);

EquatorialCoordinates eqCastor =
  new EquatorialCoordinates(7.55,31.917);

HorizonCoordinates aaM101 =
  new HorizonCoordinates(eqM101,jsWhen.GetLMST()
    ,myLocGeo.getLatitude());

HorizonCoordinates aaCastor =
  new HorizonCoordinates(eqCastor,jsWhen.GetLMST()
    ,myLocGeo.getLatitude());

output.append("At times:\n" + jsWhen + "\n");
output.append("  M101 will be at " + aaM101   + "\n");
output.append("Castor will be at " + aaCastor + "\n");

// date and time of observation
GregorianCalendar  dtObs =
  new GregorianCalendar(1996,2,8,22,0,0);

AstroTime jsObs =
  new AstroTime(dtObs,myTimeZone,myLocGeo.
    getLatitude());

EquatorialCoordinates eqSirius =
  new EquatorialCoordinates(6.75,-16.717);

HorizonCoordinatesaaSirius =
  new HorizonCoordinates(eqSirius,jsWhen.GetLMST()
```

```
      ,myLocGeo.getLatitude());

output.append("Sirius will be at " + aaSirius + "\n");

HorizonCoordinatesaaUnknown =
  new HorizonCoordinates(35.5,185.5);

EquatorialCoordinates eqUnknown =
  new EquatorialCoordinates(aaUnk,jsObs.GetLMST()
      ,myLocGeo.getLatitude());

output.append("\n  Unknown object has " +
    eqUnknown + "\n");
```

Notes

In calculating the azimuth, be aware that you'll sometimes need to "adjust" your result so that the answer lies within the correct quadrant. If sin(h) is negative, then subtract the azimuth you've calculated from 360° to obtain a correct value.

You can use this chapter's formulas to identify objects from their horizon coordinates. If, during the same observing session, I see a very bright star with an altitude of 30° 50' and an azimuth of 152°, I could solve for the star's right ascension and declination using the equations above. In this case, the unknown star has an RA of 6° 45' and a declination of -16° 43'. Looking in a star catalog, I find that the observed star was Sirius, the Dog Star in Canis Major.

Onward

To finish out the book, I'll put together some of the material from these chapters, building a Java application to display maps of the stars.

15

A Star Map Plotter

The material in the last few chapters has led up to the Java application described in this chapter: a tool for plotting star charts. Perhaps this isn't the most common application in the world of business — but then, I wanted to provide something a bit out-of-the-ordinary for finishing up this book. For many programmers I know, learning a programming language begins by selecting a "fun" development project. It's easier to learn when we enjoy what we're doing.

Design

Open a monthly astronomy magazine, and you'll usually find a circular star chart in the center pages. These maps depict an overhead view of the night sky from some pre-defined location at a set time — say, midnight on the fifteenth of the month in San Francisco. In all likelihood, even if you do live in San Francisco, you'll be observing the heavens at some other time. And these maps usually don't apply to people living in the Southern Hemisphere, either. What I wanted was a small application for displaying the celestial sphere for any location and time. With the tools developed in the preceding chapters, such an application is relatively easy to create.

The program required a database of star locations, movements, and magnitudes (brightnesses). I extract raw numbers for the 1061 brightest stars (all those with a visual magnitude greater than 5.1) from a database known as the Fifth Fundamental Catalogue, a standard stellar reference produced by W. Fricke, H. Schwan, T. Lederle, and others for the Rechen-Institut, Heidelberg, Germany, in 1988. The database application, **Ch15Make**, looks like this:

```java
import java.applet.*;
import java.awt.*;
import java.io.*;

import Ch15MakeFrame;

import coyote.kepler.*;
import coyote.io.*;

public class Ch15Make extends Applet
{
  public String getAppletInfo()
  {
    return "Java Algorithms and Components: Chapter 15
       Make\n" +
          "Copyright 1997 Scott Robert Ladd\n" +
          "All rights reserved\n";
  }

  // raw data from FK5 catalog (1061 items)
  private final static double [][] FK5Data =
  {
    {0.026571944,-76.93428889,-1.877,-17.69,4.78},
    {0.032675278,-5.985916667,0.342,-4.11,4.41},
    {0.062330833,-16.66400278,0.184,-0.91,4.55},
    {0.088928889,-4.292386111,-0.058,8.87,4.61},
    {0.139795833,29.09043889,1.039,-16.33,2.06},
    {0.152970833,59.14977222,6.827,-18.09,2.27},
    {0.156849722,-44.25255833,1.186,-18.11,3.88},
    {0.172015833,46.07228056,0.074,0.03,5.03},
    {0.220598333,15.18355556,0.019,-1.2,2.83},
    {0.243380278,20.20668333,0.66,0,4.8},
```

```
          .
          .
          .
    {23.77320139,3.486802778,-0.199,-2.47,5.06},
    {23.78429306,58.651975,0.787,5.72,4.87},
    {23.79854417,67.80682222,0.255,-0.13,5.04},
    {23.81543389,-27.86970278,0.792,-10.64,4.57},
    {23.86843778,-81.98116389,-2.629,-1.88,5.1},
    {23.87480333,19.12026667,-0.037,-3.63,5.08},
    {23.90640056,57.49941111,-0.031,-0.2,4.1},
    {23.96264861,25.14138333,-0.247,-3.32,4.66},
    {23.97788722,-2.444005556,-0.341,-7.21,4.86},
    {23.98852833,6.863283333,1.028,-11.51,4.01},
    {23.99860389,-64.42285556,0.766,-2.42,4.5}
};

public void init()
{
  // define applet area
  setSize(320, 240);
  setLayout(new BorderLayout());
  setBackground(Color.lightGray);

  // create output list
  TextArea output = new TextArea();
  add(output,BorderLayout.CENTER);

  // delete old file
  File f = new File("FK5Data.dat");
  f.delete();

  // create database
  try
  {
    ObjectDatabaseFile starData =
        new ObjectDatabaseFile(f);

    for (int n = 0; n < FK5Data.length; ++n)
    {
      FK5RawData data = new FK5RawData();
```

```
            data.RA   = FK5Data[n][0];
            data.Dec  = FK5Data[n][1];
            data.pmRA = FK5Data[n][2];
            data.pmDec = FK5Data[n][3];
            data.VMag = FK5Data[n][4];

            starData.writeObject(data);

            output.append("wrote rec " + n + "\n");
        }
    }
    catch (Exception ex)
    {
        // do nothing
    }

    output.append("DONE");
}


private boolean m_fStandAlone = false;

public static void main(String args[])
{
    Ch15MakeFrame frame =
        new Ch15MakeFrame("Ch15Make");

    frame.setVisible(true);
    frame.setVisible(false);
    frame.setSize(frame.insets().left +
        frame.insets().right  + 320,
        frame.insets().top + frame.insets().bottom + 240);

    Ch15Make applet_Ch15Make = new Ch15Make();

    frame.add("Center", applet_Ch15Make);
    applet_Ch15Make.m_fStandAlone = true;
    applet_Ch15Make.init();
    applet_Ch15Make.start();
    frame.setVisible(true);
}
}
```

I've removed most of the elements in the `starData` array for the sake of brevity; you'll find the complete application on the enclosed CD-ROM.

The `FK5RawData` class defines a simple serializable structure for the database.

```java
package coyote.kepler;

import java.io.*;

//
//
// FK5RawData
//
//
public class FK5RawData
  implements Serializable
{
  // serialization constant
  static final long serialVersionUID =
      4029471186592464045L;

  // public data fields
  public double RA;
  public double Dec;
  public double pmRA;
  public double pmDec;
  public double VMag;
}
```

With the database in hand, my next task was to determine how the star data would be presented by the application. I decided on an overhead spherical projection, similar to those used in most astronomy magazines. Each star will be plotted at a time, date, and location specified by a set of application input controls. Brighter stars will be plotted in white, with succesive shades of gray depicting fainter stars.

Implementation

The source code for the star map application is as follows:

```java
import java.applet.*;
import java.awt.*;
import java.awt.event.*;
import java.util.*;

import Chapter15Frame;

import coyote.io.*;
import coyote.kepler.*;

public class Chapter15
  extends Applet
  implements ActionListener
{
  //——————————-
  // fields
  //——————————-
  private static final int NUM_STARS = 1061;
  private FK5RawData [] starData;

  private Panel     controls;
  private Panel     statBar;
  private FieldCanvas view;

  private Button btnReset;
  private Button btnPlot;

  private TextField fldYear;
  private TextField fldMon;
  private TextField fldDay;

  private TextField fldHour;
  private TextField fldMin;
  private TextField fldZone;
```

```
        private ButtonbtnIncr;
        private Checkbox  chkDST;

        private TextField fldLon;
        private TextField fldLat;

        private Label  status;

        private static final Color [] MAG =
        {
          new Color(255,255,255),
          new Color(252,252,252),
          new Color(232,232,232),
          new Color(200,200,200),
          new Color(136,136,136),
          new Color( 72, 72, 72)
        };

        //———————————-
        // methods
        //———————————-
        public String getAppletInfo()
        {
          return "Java Algorithms and Components:
              Chapter Fifteen" +
              "Copyright 1997 Scott Robert Ladd" +
              "All rights reserved";
        }

        public void init()
        {
          // define applet area
          setSize(480,573);
          setLayout(new BorderLayout());
          setBackground(Color.lightGray);

          // load the database
          try
          {
            // allocate in-memory database
            starData = new FK5RawData [NUM_STARS];
```

```
      // open database
      ObjectDatabaseFile db =
          new ObjectDatabaseFile("FK5Data.dat");

      // load record
      for (int n = 0; n < NUM_STARS; ++n)
        starData[n] = (FK5RawData)db.readObject();
    }
    catch (Exception ex)
    {
      // do nothing
    }

    // create controls
    fldYear  = new TextField(4);
    fldMon   = new TextField(2);
    fldDay   = new TextField(2);

    Panel datePanel = new Panel();
    datePanel.setLayout(new FlowLayout(1));

    datePanel.add(new Label("Date:"));
    datePanel.add(fldYear);
    datePanel.add(new Label("/"));
    datePanel.add(fldMon);
    datePanel.add(new Label("/"));
    datePanel.add(fldDay);
    // datePanel.add(new Label("yy/mm/dd"));

    fldHour  = new TextField(2);
    fldMin   = new TextField(2);
    fldZone  = new TextField(2);

    Panel timePanel = new Panel();
    timePanel.setLayout(new FlowLayout(1));

    timePanel.add(new Label("Time:"));
    timePanel.add(fldHour);
    timePanel.add(new Label(":"));
    timePanel.add(fldMin);
    timePanel.add(new Label("Zone:"));
```

```
timePanel.add(fldZone);

fldLon = new TextField(6);
fldLat = new TextField(6);

Panel lonPanel = new Panel();
lonPanel.setLayout(new FlowLayout(1));
lonPanel.add(new Label("Lon:"));
lonPanel.add(fldLon);

Panel latPanel = new Panel();
latPanel.setLayout(new FlowLayout(1));
latPanel.add(new Label("Lat:"));
latPanel.add(fldLat);

chkDST  = new Checkbox("DST");

btnIncr = new Button("Incr");
btnIncr.addActionListener(this);

btnReset = new Button("Reset");
btnReset.addActionListener(this);

btnPlot  = new Button("Plot!");
btnPlot.addActionListener(this);

// create control panel
controls = new Panel();

// create grid bag layout
GridBagLayout lay = new GridBagLayout();
GridBagConstraints gbc = new GridBagConstraints();
controls.setLayout(lay);

// add GUI elements
gbc.fill= GridBagConstraints.BOTH;
gbc.weightx = 1.0;
gbc.weighty = 1.0;
gbc.anchor  = GridBagConstraints.EAST;

controls.add(datePanel,gbc);
```

```
      controls.add(latPanel,gbc);
      controls.add(btnIncr);
      controls.add(new Label());
      gbc.gridwidth =
          GridBagConstraints.REMAINDER; // reset
      controls.add(btnReset,gbc);

      gbc.gridwidth = 1; // reset
      controls.add(timePanel,gbc);
      controls.add(lonPanel,gbc);
      controls.add(chkDST);
      controls.add(new Label());
      gbc.gridwidth =
          GridBagConstraints.REMAINDER; // reset
      controls.add(btnPlot,gbc);

      // create center panel
      view = new FieldCanvas();

      // create status panel
      statBar = new Panel();
      statBar.setLayout(new FlowLayout());

      status = new Label("Java Algorithms,
          Chapter 15 - Star Plotter");
      statBar.add(status);

      // add panels to main display
      add(controls,BorderLayout.NORTH);
      add(view,BorderLayout.CENTER);
      add(statBar,BorderLayout.SOUTH);

      // set initial values
      reset();
   }

   public void actionPerformed
     (
     ActionEvent event
     )
   {
```

```
        if (event.getSource() == btnReset)
          reset();
        else
        {
          if (event.getSource() == btnIncr)
            increment();
          else
            plot();
        }
    }

    private void reset()
    {
      GregorianCalendar now = new GregorianCalendar();

      now.setTimeZone(TimeZone.getTimeZone("MST"));

      fldYear.setText(String.valueOf
          (now.get(Calendar.YEAR)));
      fldMon.setText(String.valueOf
          (now.get(Calendar.MONTH) + 1));
      fldDay.setText(String.valueOf
          (now.get(Calendar.DAY_OF_MONTH)));
      fldHour.setText(String.valueOf
          (now.get(Calendar.HOUR_OF_DAY)));
      fldMin.setText(String.valueOf
          (now.get(Calendar.MINUTE)));
      fldZone.setText(String.valueOf
          (now.get(Calendar.ZONE_OFFSET) / 3600000.0));

      fldLon.setText("107.67");
      fldLat.setText("37.8");

      controls.repaint();
    }

    private void increment()
    {
      // get astro date
      GregorianCalendar cal = new GregorianCalendar
        (
```

```
        Integer.parseInt(fldYear.getText()),
        Integer.parseInt(fldMon.getText()),
        Integer.parseInt(fldDay.getText()),
        Integer.parseInt(fldHour.getText()),
        Integer.parseInt(fldMin.getText())
        );

    Date now = cal.getTime();

    long millis = now.getTime();
    now.setTime(millis + 600000);

    cal.setTime(now);

    // increment time (doesn't work!)
    // cal.add(Calendar.MINUTE,10);

    // now display the date and time
    fldYear.setText(String.valueOf
        (cal.get(Calendar.YEAR)));
    fldMon.setText(String.valueOf
        (cal.get(Calendar.MONTH)));
    fldDay.setText(String.valueOf
        (cal.get(Calendar.DAY_OF_MONTH)));
    fldHour.setText(String.valueOf
        (cal.get(Calendar.HOUR_OF_DAY)));
    fldMin.setText(String.valueOf
        (cal.get(Calendar.MINUTE)));

    // plot new image
    plot();
}

private void plot()
{
    // assume plot button pressed
    Graphicsg = view.getImageGraphics();
    Dimension dim = view.getSize();

    int w = dim.width  / 2;
    int h = dim.height / 2;
```

```
    int radius = h;

    // clear viewport
    g.setColor(Color.black);
    g.fillRect(0,0,dim.width,dim.height);

    // get location
    Location where = new Location
        (
        (Double.valueOf(fldLon.getText())).doubleValue(),
        (Double.valueOf(fldLat.getText())).doubleValue()
        );

    where = where.toGeocentric();

    // get time zone
    double tz = (Double.valueOf
        (fldZone.getText())).doubleValue();

    if (chkDST.getState())
        tz += 1.0;

    // get astro date
    GregorianCalendar cal = new GregorianCalendar
        (
        Integer.parseInt(fldYear.getText()),
        Integer.parseInt(fldMon.getText()),
        Integer.parseInt(fldDay.getText()),
        Integer.parseInt(fldHour.getText()),
        Integer.parseInt(fldMin.getText())
        );

    AstroTime when =
        new AstroTime(cal,tz,where.getLongitude());

    // plot stars
    for (int n = 0; n < NUM_STARS; ++n)
    {
        // compute equatorial components
        EquatorialCoordinates eq = new Equatorial
            Coordinates(starData[n].RA,starData[n].Dec);
```

```
eq.applyPrecession(when.getJD(),false);
eq.applyProperMotion(when.getJD(),
    starData[n].pmRA,starData[n].pmDec,false);


// compute horizon coordinates
HorizonCoordinates aa = new HorizonCoordinates
    (eq,when.getLMST(),where.getLatitude());
aa.applyRefraction(1000.0,10.0);


if (aa.getAltitude() <= 0.0)
  continue;


double azi = aa.getAzimuth();
double alt = (90.0 - aa.getAltitude()) / 90.0;


// projection onto plane
int posX = radius + (int)(radius * alt *
    KMath.sind(azi));
int posY = radius - (int)(radius * alt *
    KMath.sind(90.0 - azi));


// assign star a color
int color =
    (int)(KMath.trunc(starData[n].VMag));


if (color < 0)
  color = 0;
else
{
  if (color > 5)
    color = 5;
}


g.setColor(MAG[color]);
g.drawRect(posX,posY,1,1);
}
```

```
    view.repaint();
    repaint();
  }

  private boolean m_fStandAlone = false;

  public static void main(String args[])
  {
    Chapter15Frame frame =
        new Chapter15Frame("Chapter15");

    frame.setVisible(true);
    frame.setVisible(false);
    frame.setSize(frame.getInsets().left +
        frame.getInsets().right  + 480,
          frame.getInsets().top  +
              frame.getInsets().bottom + 573);

    Chapter15 applet_Chapter15 = new Chapter15();

    frame.add("Center", applet_Chapter15);
    applet_Chapter15.m_fStandAlone = true;
    applet_Chapter15.init();
    applet_Chapter15.start();
    frame.setVisible(true);
  }
}
```

I've implemented this program as both an application and an applet; you'll find a version of it running at my web site.

Operation

Figure 15-1 shows the application in operation, with a star map displayed. At its top, the application provides a set of controls initialized to the current date and time; for latitude and longitude, the default values are those for my home town of Silverton, Colorado. Below these controls is the main display area containing the star map; at the bottom, I've included a line of text identifying the application.

Figure 15-1

A Star Map
Application

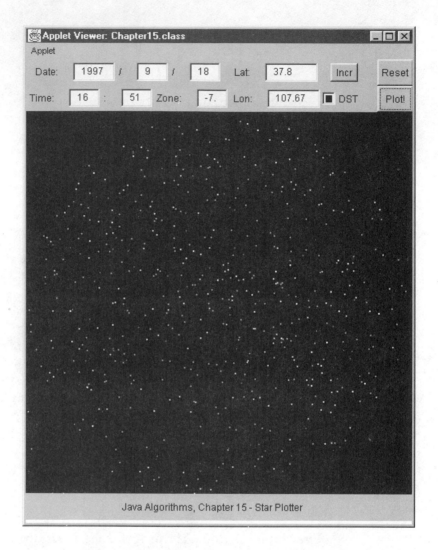

Initially, the program presents a blank map; click on the **Plot** button to display a map for the current time and date. North is in its traditional location at the top of the map. You can edit any of the text fields; to keep things simple, this version of the application doesn't do any range checking on arguments. Enter the date in year-month-day order; the time must be in 24-hour format. Check the **DST** box if Daylight Saving Time is in effect. The default latitude and longitude can be changed by editing two lines in the application. A more sophisticated application would probably maintain some sort of configuration database, perhaps within the same data file that holds the star data.

Three buttons control the actions of the program:

- **Incr** increments the time by ten minutes, and then replots the star map.

- **Plot!** plots the star map for the current date, time, and location.

- **Reset** sets the values of the fields to the current time and the default location.

I encountered an interesting problem while implementing this application: the `GregorianCalendar` class didn't perform time computations correctly in its add method. Adding ten minutes to a `GregorianCalendar` object resulted in a date of 1 January 1970, at ten minutes after midnight! This is no simple problem in a specific implementation of the Java packages; I tried compilers on several platforms, and found the problem in every one of them. So I converted the `GregorianCalendar` to a `Date`, and then incremented that intermediate object by ten minutes before constructing a new `GregorianCalendar`.

Final Thoughts

Java makes the job of object-oriented programming easier, but it doesn't promise that you'll use the tool right. I've begun moving many of my projects to Java, even though most of my work for the last decade has been in C++. While C++ has some advantages over Java in terms of flexibility and performance, I find that my code in Java is 20% shorter and far less buggy. In producing this book, I found several bugs in older algorithms, `ArrayIndexOutOfBoundsException` pointers being the most common problem. Java code comes out cleaner than C++; the former supports built-in dynamic memory management and a standard exception hierarchy. I won't be abandoning C++ anytime soon — but Java has found a permanent home in my suite of development tools.

I hope you've enjoyed this book, and that it's shown you some useful tools and techniques for Java development. As always, I wish you the best.

Index

About the Author

Scott Robert Ladd has been a full-time professional author for more than a decade. His articles appear in national magazines and newspapers, covering topics ranging from object-oriented programming to social issues and wildlife management.

Java Algorithms is Scott's 16th book about software development; his past books include *C++ Templates and Tools*, *C++ Simulations and Cellular Automata*, and *Genetic Algorithms in C++*. He is working on books about "Pure Java" and Dynamic HTML.

When Scott isn't typing on the computer, he enjoys travelling the American Southwest with his wife, Maria, and three daughters. Scott's hobbies include astronomy, reading and history; he enjoys hiking in the San Juan Mountains around his Colorado home. You can see his web site at http://www.frontier.net/~srladd.

Java(Development Kit
Version 1.1.4
Binary Code License

This binary code license ("License") contains rights and restrictions associated with use of the accompanying software and documentation ("Software"). Read the License carefully before installing the Software. By installing the Software you agree to the terms and conditions of this License.

1. Limited License Grant. Sun grants to you ("Licensee") a non-exclusive, non-transferable limited license to use the Software without fee for evaluation of the Software and for development of Java(compatible applets and applications. Licensee may make one archival copy of the Software. Licensee may not re-distribute the Software in whole or in part, either separately or included with a product. Refer to the Java Runtime Environment Version 1.1.4 binary code license (http://www.javasoft.com/ products/JDK/1.1.4/index.html) for the availability of runtime code which may be distributed with Java compatible applets and applications.

2. Java Platform Interface. Licensee may not modify the Java Platform Interface ("JPI", identified as classes contained within the "java" package or any subpackages of the "java" package), by creating additional classes within the JPI or otherwise causing the addition to or modification of the classes in the JPI. In the event that Licensee creates any Java-related API and distributes such API to others for applet or application development, Licensee must promptly publish an accurate specification for such API for free use by all developers of Java-based software.

3. Restrictions. Software is confidential copyrighted information of Sun and title to all copies is retained by Sun and/or its licensors. Licensee shall not modify, decompile, disassemble, decrypt, extract, or otherwise reverse engineer Software. Software may not be leased, assigned, or sublicensed, in whole or in part. Software is not designed or intended for use in on-line control of aircraft, air traffic, aircraft navigation or aircraft communications; or in the design, construction, operation or maintenance of any nuclear facility. Licensee warrants that it will not use or redistribute the Software for such purposes.

4. Trademarks and Logos. This License does not authorize Licensee to use any Sun name, trademark or logo. Licensee acknowledges that Sun owns the Java trademark and all Java-related trademarks, logos and icons including the Coffee Cup and Duke ("Java Marks") and agrees to: (i) to comply with the Java Trademark Guidelines at http://java.com/trademarks.html; (ii) not do anything harmful to or inconsistent with Sun's rights in the Java Marks; and (iii) assist Sun in protecting those rights, including assigning to Sun any rights acquired by Licensee in any Java Mark.

5. Disclaimer of Warranty. Software is provided "AS IS," without a warranty of any kind. ALL EXPRESS OR IMPLIED REPRESENTATIONS AND WARRANTIES, INCLUDING ANY IMPLIED WARRANTY OF MERCHANTABILITY, FITNESS FOR A PARTICULAR PURPOSE OR NON-INFRINGEMENT, ARE HEREBY EXCLUDED.

6. Limitation of Liability. SUN AND ITS LICENSORS SHALL NOT BE LIABLE FOR ANY DAMAGES SUFFERED BY LICENSEE OR ANY THIRD PARTY AS A RESULT OF USING OR DISTRIBUTING SOFTWARE. IN NO EVENT WILL SUN OR ITS LICENSORS BE LIABLE FOR ANY LOST REVENUE, PROFIT OR DATA, OR FOR DIRECT, INDIRECT, SPECIAL, CONSEQUENTIAL, INCIDENTAL OR PUNITIVE DAMAGES, HOWEVER CAUSED AND REGARDLESS OF THE THEORY OF LIABILITY, ARISING OUT OF THE USE OF OR INABILITY TO USE SOFTWARE, EVEN IF SUN HAS BEEN ADVISED OF THE POSSIBILITY OF SUCH DAMAGES.

7. Termination. Licensee may terminate this License at any time by destroying all copies of Software. This License will terminate immediately without notice from Sun if Licensee fails to comply with any provision of this License. Upon such termination, Licensee must destroy all copies of Software.

8. Export Regulation. Software, including technical data, is subject to U.S. export control laws, including the U.S. Export Administration Act and its associated regulations, and may be subject to export or import regulations in other countries. Licensee agrees to comply strictly with all such regulations and acknowledges that it has the responsibility to obtain licenses to export, re-export, or import Software. Software may not be downloaded, or otherwise exported or re-exported (i) into, or to a national or resident of, Cuba, Iraq, Iran, North Korea, Libya, Sudan, Syria or any country to which the U.S. has embargoed goods; or (ii) to anyone on the U.S. Treasury Department's list of Specially Designated Nations or the U.S. Commerce Department's Table of Denial Orders.

9. Restricted Rights. Use, duplication or disclosure by the United States government is subject to the restrictions as set forth in the Rights in Technical Data and Computer Software Clauses in DFARS 252.227-7013(c)(1)(ii) and FAR 52.227-19(c)(2) as applicable.

10. Governing Law. Any action related to this License will be governed by California law and controlling U.S. federal law. No choice of law rules of any jurisdiction will apply.

11. Severability. If any of the above provisions are held to be in violation of applicable law, void, or unenforceable in any jurisdiction, then such provisions are herewith waived to the extent necessary for the License to be otherwise enforceable in such jurisdiction. However, if in Sun's opinion deletion of any provisions of the License by operation of this paragraph unreasonably compromises the rights or increase the liabilities of Sun or its licensors, Sun reserves the right to terminate the License and refund the fee paid by Licensee, if any, as Licensee's sole and exclusive remedy.